IRRESISTIBLE
Overnights
in
Florida

IRRESISTIBLE
Overnights
in
Florida

by
Bob Rafferty
and
Loys Reynolds

Rutledge Hill Press®
Nashville, Tennessee

A Thomas Nelson Company

Published by Rutledge Hill Press, a Thomas Nelson Company, P.O. Box 141000, Nashville, Tennessee 37214.

Library of Congress Cataloging-in-Publication Data

Rafferty, Robert
    Irresistible overnights in Florida / by Bob Rafferty and Loys Reynolds.
      p. cm.
    ISBN 1-55853-818-6 (pbk.)
      1. Hotels—Florida—Guidebooks. 2. Bed-and-breakfast accommodations—Florida—Guidebooks. I. Reynolds, Loys. II. Title.
    TX907.3.F6 R34 2000
    647.94759'01—dc21

                                                 00-055258
                                                    CIP

Printed in the United States of America

1 2 3 4 5 6 7 8 9—05 04 03 02 01 00

To the wonderful people in Florida's hospitality industry who tirelessly serve the ever-increasing numbers of leisure and business travelers. In our research trips throughout the state, we were most favorably impressed by the warmth, creativity, and nurturing qualities they display in taking care of their guests.

Florida's Eight Vacation Regions

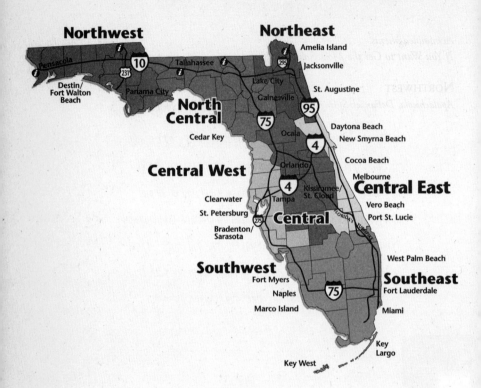

Northwest

Pensacola

Destin/
Fort Walton
Beach

Panama City

Tallahassee

Northeast

Amelia Island

Jacksonville

Lake City

Gainesville

St. Augustine

**North
Central**

Cedar Key

Ocala

Daytona Beach

New Smyrna Beach

Central West

Orlando

Cocoa Beach

Melbourne

Central East

Clearwater

Kissimmee/
St. Cloud

Tampa

Central

Vero Beach

Port St. Lucie

St. Petersburg

Bradenton/
Sarasota

Southwest

Fort Myers

Naples

Marco Island

West Palm Beach

Southeast

Fort Lauderdale

Miami

Key
Largo

Key West

CONTENTS

Acknowledgments   ix

If You Want to Get the Most from This Guide, Read This First   xi

NORTHWEST   1
*Apalachicola, DeFuniak Springs, Destin, Milton, Pensacola, Port St. Joe,
Santa Rosa Beach, Seaside*

NORTH CENTRAL   25
*Cedar Key, Gainesville, High Springs, Micanopy, Monticello, Quincy,
Steinhatchee, Tallahassee, Wakulla Springs*

NORTHEAST   43
*Amelia Island & Fernandina Beach, Crescent City, Flagler Beach,
Jacksonville, Orange Park, Ponte Vedra Beach, St. Augustine, Welaka*

CENTRAL WEST   81
*Crystal River, Sarasota Area, Bradenton Beach, Holmes Beach, Longboat
Key, Siesta Key, Brandon, Clearwater, Palm Harbor, Safety Harbor, St.
Petersburg, St. Pete Beach, Tampa, Land O'Lakes, Wesley Chapel*

CENTRAL   115
*Howey-in-the Hills, Mount Dora, Bartow, Haines City, Lakeland, Lake
Wales Area, Ocala, Ocklawaha, Weirsdale, Celebration, Kissimmee, Lake
Buena Vista, Maitland, Orlando, Sanford, Winter Park*

CENTRAL EAST   153
*Cassadaga & Lake Helen, DeLand, Cocoa Beach, Indialantic, Daytona
Beach, Daytona Beach Shores, New Smyrna Beach, Sebastian, Vero Beach*

SOUTHWEST   173
*Bokeelia, Cape Haze, Captiva Island, Clewiston, Engelwood, Fort Myers,
Matlacha, Naples, Pineland*

SOUTHEAST 191

*Port Salerno, Stuart, Boca Raton, Palm Beach, West Palm Beach, Lake
Worth, Palm Beach Gardens, Manalapan, Greater Fort Lauderdale,
Coconut Grove, Coral Gables, Key Biscayne, Miami, Miami Beach,
Flamingo (Everglades National Park), Big Pine Key, Duck Key, Key Largo,
Key West, Little Torch Key, Marathon*

Category Index 269
Index 281

ACKNOWLEDGMENTS

The whole thing started with several months of research choosing over 200 hotels, motels, and inns. (They call them "properties" in the travel trade). This was a monumental task that we couldn't have accomplished without the wholehearted cooperation of hundreds and hundreds of people in state agencies, convention and visitor bureaus (CVB), chambers of commerce (COC), public relations firms (PR), and finally, at the properties themselves. And cooperation we got!

Properly thanking everyone would be a book in itself, so we narrowed the list to those who went far beyond the call of duty:

- Our statewide guiding angel, Brandy Henley of Visit Florida, who provided us with detailed lists of the people to contact in every one of the eight regions, sometimes right down to the name of the best contact at a specific property.
- Katerine Morrison of the Governor's Office of Tourism.
- Mary Foley Billingsley of Historic Hotels of America, and Michelle Orlando of the Florida Chamber of Commerce Executives.

Also, we want to thank the following people in each region who were a tremendous help in setting up the actual visits:

Northwest Region: Anita Gregory, Apalachicola Bay COC; Julie Root, Beaches of South Walton; Lorraine Moore, Geiger & Associates (PR for Citrus County); Sherry Rushing, Destin/Fort Walton Beach CVB; and Leslie Isert, Pensacola Area COC.
North Central Region: John Pircher, Alachua County CVB; Judy Johnson, Cedar Key Area COC, and Shelly Knox, Moore Consulting Group (PR for Tallahassee area).
Northeast Region: Jay Humphreys, St. John's County CVB; Kim Prozzi, Jacksonville & the Beaches CVB; and Barbara Golden, Putnam County COC.
Central West Region: Alexandra Owen, Bradenton Area CVB; Wit Tuttell, St. Petersburg/Clearwater CVB; Alisa Bennett, Sarasota CVB; and Kelly Earnest, Tampa/Hillsborough CVB.
Central Region: Wayne Vaughan, Central Florida CVB; Dave Warren,

Lake County CVB and Jackie MacKay, Cramer Krasselt Public Relations (PR for Lake County); Loretta Shaffer, Kissimmee/St. Cloud CVB; Katie Mulhearn, Ocala/Marion County COC; Danielle Saba Courtenay and Carl Grunwald, Orlando/Orange County CVB; Jack West, Seminole County CVB; and Mary C. Kenny, PR for Grand Theme Hotels.

Central East Region: Susan McLain, Daytona Beach Area CVB; Renee Wente, Deland/West Volusia Visitors Bureau and Tricia Savard, Jiloty Communications (PR for West Volusia); Lori Burns, Indian River County COC; Abbie McClintock, Lanier Associates (PR for Southeast Volusia County); and Tom Bartosek, Space Coast Office of Tourism.

Southwest Region: Cheryl Lauzon, Charlotte County Visitors Bureau; Lee Rose, Lee Island Coast CVB; and Beth Preddy, Beth Preddy Public Relations (PR for Naples area).

Southeast Region: Joe Catrambone, Stuart/Martin County COC; Enid Atwater, Palm Beach County CVB; Cindy Malin, Greater Fort Lauderdale CVB; Michelle Abram, Greater Miami CVB; Melissa Olin, Goldman Properties; and Didi Bushnell, Stuart Newman Associates (PR for the Florida Keys).

We'd also like to thank all the brilliant people who turned run-of-the-mill lodgings into *irresistible overnights*. Without you there would be no book. In this group, we especially want to recognize three men and one woman for carrying out their delightfully different visions of what lodgings can be: Christ Blackwell, who developed the iconoclastic Island Outpost hotels (see The Marlin in Miami Beach), Tony Goldman, of Goldman Properties, whom *National Geographic* referred to as a one-man urban renewal company for his restoration of historic hotels in both New York and Miami Beach (see The Hotel in Miami Beach), Richard Kessler, of Kessler Enterprises, for his Grand Theme Hotels (see Doubletree Castle Hotel in Orlando), and Terry Whaples, one of the principal developers of the Holiday Inn Kidsuites concept (see Kidsuites sidebar in the Central Region).

Finally, we'd like to thank Larry Stone, publisher of Rutledge Hill Press, for offering us the opportunity to do this delightfully different guidebook; Geoff Stone, our editor, for his patience while working hand in hand with us to make it as complete and useful as possible, Brian Curtis, vice president of marketing, and Libby Beeson, our publicist, who are going to put this book on the travel book best-seller list.

IF YOU WANT TO GET THE MOST FROM THIS GUIDE, READ THIS FIRST

If you are looking for places to stay in Florida that are delightfully different, this book is for you. We are not talking about places just to spend the night, but ones that are so imaginatively special they are irresistible and, in many cases, an experience in themselves. These lodgings are not easy to find, which is why this book details only 203 hotels, motels, and inns out of more than five thousand in Florida.

Our selection is a widely diverse lot offering something for every taste and budget. Here you'll find the truly unique, such as the Jules' Undersea Lodge in the Keys, as well as cabins in state parks, bed-and-breakfast inns that often make you feel like you're staying in the home of a well-to-do friend, and Mobil Five-star and AAA Five-diamond hotels and resorts that make the words *luxurious* and *expensive* seem inadequate.

And this is our personal selection. There are undoubtedly other irresistible overnights we missed, but this selection is based on more than a year of research and more than twenty-five thousand miles on the road personally visiting many more than the 203 places that made the book. We found all 203 places to be delightfully irresistible and, although we have some personal favorites, recommend each and every one of them to you.

WHY WE LOVE FLORIDA

We are unashamedly biased, positive, and enthusiastic when we think, speak, or write about Florida. Ponce de Leon must have felt the same way when he named the peninsula because he saw it abundant in flowers. We love the sunshine, the surrounding ocean and gulf waters, the profusion of lakes, the lush tropical vegetation, the charming combination of Old Florida tin-roofed buildings and modern skyscrapers, and above all, the genuine warmth of the people. We have come to think of Florida as a flowering plant cultivated for its blossoms; a most unique plant because it has so many unusual and different blooms.

HOW TO READ THE LISTINGS

We had no intention of including all the minutia in the write-up on each lodging. All we're trying to do is let you know why we found each place irresistible and round it out with a few pertinent details. Anything more and we'd have to write an encyclopedia. If you want to know more, check the contact information for each listing. There you'll find the mailing address, website address, phone number with any toll free numbers first, fax number, high season rates, and total number of units.

UNDERSTANDING ROOM RATES

Naturally, room rates are tied in with seasonal supply and demand. High season demand means the supply gets tight and rates are high. (The same is true everywhere over major holidays.) As demand falls off, rates go down, which means the best rates are in low season when the weather is more temperamental. But between high and low seasons are what the trade refers to as the value or shoulder seasons. If you can travel during those times, chances are good you'll have the best combination of everything from weather to rates. Beginning in January south Florida has the best conditions, but when summer comes, the north part of Florida is prime.

In addition to seasonal rate changes, room rates depend on whether you want to be on the water, have a view, prefer a suite or a cottage, or a dozen other factors. Since it would take a catalog to list all the rates for all our delightfully different lodgings, we chose to simplify the process by only listing the high season rates for your full range of room options from the most basic room to (if they have one) a presidential suite. *These should be the top rates you run into in high season.* You can use these as a guide to determine if your high season choice fits your budget, or if it would be better to plan your visit in one of the value seasons or even the off-season.

But don't forget, these are the published rates. There are discounts, Discounts, and DISCOUNTS. If you belong to just about any national or local organization, like AAA or AARP, or a discount travel club, or even if you think the registration clerk resembles a relative of yours, ask for a discount. On a daily basis, a room is a perishable item. If it isn't sold that day, it's a loss to the management. Also ask about package deals. These can be a real bargain if the elements of the package suit you.

Another thing to check when making reservations is whether there's a minimum stay requirement. We've found some places have a two-night or three-night minimum over weekends or major holidays.

On the other hand, when you get a rate quote it probably will not include some extras that will show up on your bill. One of these is the local tax. Everyone adds on the sales tax, which is usually 6 or 7 percent depending on where you are in the state. In addition, most communities add several percent to that for what's called a bed tax, usually devoted to support the local tourist industry. Added together the sales/bed tax can add a substantial amount to your bill. To forewarn you of this usually unannounced addition, we have included a sales/bed tax listing under the heading of each community.

If you want to get a more accurate picture of what you'll really be paying for your room before you sign on, ask about specifics. Find out whether parking is free. Ask about extra fees to use athletic or other facilities.

SOME FINAL SUGGESTIONS

Unless there's a convention, downtown hotels that cater to business travelers during the week normally offer the best rates to leisure travelers on weekends. The opposite is true of resorts and bed-and-breakfasts. Their busiest times are weekends, so you might get the best deal on weekdays.

A number of major hotels have what's known as the Club Floor or the Concierge Floor. No matter what the name, they are usually open to reservations by anyone, and rooms on these floors come with a number of extra amenities. The extras may range from an extensive breakfast buffet and a tempting selection of between-meal snacks to free drinks. Rooms on these floors always cost more, sometimes substantially more. But we've found that occasionally the price difference is relatively small and well worth the extra amenities. Check it out.

If you have children, ask about them staying free. Others may offer free meals to children. Some Holiday Inns also offer Kidsuites, which we think is a brilliant idea. And check for children's programs that will give the adults some free time when vacationing with the family.

If you need a high-tech room, most of the major hotels have data ports, although they are not always conveniently located. And we were pleasantly surprised that many of the smaller hotels and even bed-and-breakfast inns had these, too.

Finally, try the Key Lime Pie—a true Florida treat. But to make sure you're getting the right stuff, check the color. It should be the light color of the lime juice (pale yellow), not dyed the color of the lime skin.

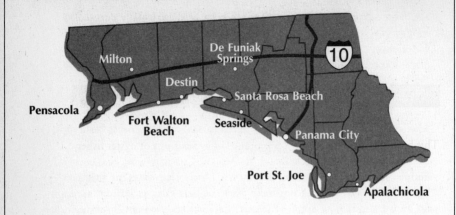

High Season: Late spring to early fall

(Note: With the exception of listings in Apalachicola and Port St. Joe, all listings in this region are in the central time zone. All lodging rates are for high season. Off-season rates can be significantly lower.)

APALACHICOLA

Sales tax 6 percent

This beautiful old seaside town is proud of its generations of oyster fishermen. Its citizens honor and applaud the Apalachicola Bay oyster that provides ninety percent of Florida's oyster crop, earning the town the title of the Oyster Capital of Florida. *Sports & Field* magazine has named this area one of the best places to fish in the United States. Fishing party boats and charters are available as are river tours for nature lovers.

Apalachicola River Inn

How would you like a room with a private balcony offering panoramic views of the Apalachicola River, the oyster fleet in the harbor, and both sunrises and sunsets? Its location on the harbor near the Gorrie Bridge gives this inn lots of rooms with a view, but the best of these are on the second floor where all have private balconies with perfect water views. Room twenty-four is a real prize with both more space and a larger balcony.

All rooms are individually decorated with wicker furniture, comforters, lots of pillows, and unique lamps. The twenty-three overnights range from the standard room with two double beds to the Hyacinth Suite that includes a whirlpool tub. The Inn also offers one apartment for families or guests who like more space and their own kitchen. The inn's marina provides slips for guest boats.

There are two highly regarded restaurants at the inn. Diners from as far away as Tallahassee and Georgia come to enjoy Caroline's. It is a full-service restaurant that is open for all meals, including fine dining in the evening. Across the parking lot the Boss Oyster Bar claims they shuck and serve more than fifty thousand oysters every year.

APALACHICOLA RIVER INN

Address:	123 Water Street, Apalachicola 32320
	www.apalachicolariverinn.com
Phone:	850/653-8139
Fax:	850/653-2018
Rates:	$70 – $130
Units:	23

Brigitte's Romantic Retreat

Brigitte is a romantic who is living her dream of being the proprietor of her own European-style bed-and-breakfast retreat.

German-born, she met her husband, Ken, when he was in the U.S. Air Force stationed in Germany. After her husband left the service and they settled in Tallahassee, she started looking for the right setting for her dream retreat. She found it here in a Victorian-style home built in 1915 by Billy Bryant, who is famous in the area for building fine homes and boats.

The old house needed major renovations. By 1995 it had been faithfully restored and furnished with antiques. All rooms throughout the house are furnished to create an ambiance that is unmistakably and romantically authentic Old World. The three guest rooms carry out this theme and are individually color-themed: one in gold, one in red, and one in blue.

Comfortable wicker rockers on the front porch invite guests to sit 'n' rock a spell. The porch is also the home of Einstein, a blue-and-gold macaw that enjoys greeting and chatting with guests. Brigitte's dream has been fulfilled even more since her retreat has become a favorite spot for weddings and honeymoons.

BRIGITTE'S ROMANTIC RETREAT

Address:	101 Sixth Street, Apalachicola, 32320
	www.romantic-retreat.com
Phone:	888/554-4376; 850/653-3270
Fax:	850/514-4386
Rates:	$75 – $130
Units:	3

The Consulate

In the early 1900s when Apalachicola was the third largest seaport on the Gulf, the French government established a consulate to oversee the commercial interests of its citizens who shipped timber and other goods from here. The consulate was located on the second floor of the Grady Building. Recently restored, the building is now on the National Register of Historic Places.

Located within easy walking distance of downtown, there are shops downstairs, and upstairs are four spacious and splendidly decorated river view suites that carry on the historic name of The Consulate.

The décor of each suite is themed to reflect the personality of its historical namesake. The Ambassador, Consul, and Attaché are named to reflect the French positions at the Consulate, while the Port Captain suite is named for the American official who shared space in the building.

All the suites have heart-of-pine floors, tin-plated eleven-foot ceilings, handcrafted walnut dressers, original artwork (most from local artists and artisans), and all the modern conveniences. All have a full designer kitchen, one or two bedrooms, dining and living areas, balconies with river or garden views, and laundry facilities.

Although the Ambassador Suite is the most expensive, it is also the most *expansive*. With two bedrooms, two baths, and a front and rear

balcony, it can be a bargain as a home away from home for a small family. The spacious master bedroom has its own bath and four-poster bed. The second bedroom has twin beds and a bath. From the large living room there's an entrance to the river view balcony. An added bonus is a dining room that's not only pleasantly suitable for your own daily meals, but for romantic dinners or entertaining.

THE CONSULATE

Address:	**76 Water Street, Apalachicola 32320**
	www.fla-beach.com
Phone:	**850/425-5487**
Fax:	**850/222-7952**
Reservations:	**Anchor Vacation Properties**
	82 Sixth Street, Apalachicola 32320
Phone:	**800/624-3964; 850/653-3333**
Rates:	**$105 – $200**
Units:	**4**

Coombs House Inn

Once a derelict, this 1905 three-story Victorian mansion was brought back to life in 1994 by Lynn Wilson, a highly regarded Fortune 500 interior designer, and her husband, Bill Spohrer, an airline executive. They restored it and named it after the original owner, lumber baron James Coombs. He was a Union army veteran from Maine who decided the Florida climate was more desirable. So he moved south, married a southern lady, and built this mansion. At that time, it was considered to be the most elegant home in Apalachicola, and it still vies for that title today.

You arrive through the forty-seven-inch-wide front door into a grand entryway with floors of tiger oak and walls of black cypress. It has beamed ceilings, an original hand-carved stairway, and beautiful leaded glass windows on the landing. Throughout the mansion you are surrounded by antiques, oriental rugs, and oil paintings from all over the world, all of which were selected by Lynn.

The ambiance of authentic elegance is reinforced by the fireplaces in each of the nine rooms. All of the rooms are different, but all have some combination of Victorian-era settees, poster or sleigh beds, English chintz curtains, and Asian area rugs on highly polished floors. All rooms have a private bath and, in deference to our modern age, a television and a phone.

An additional eight rooms are located in another restored Victorian half a block away. Built in 1911, it offers eight equally elegant bedrooms, a carriage house apartment, and Camellia Hall, a meeting room that opens to a deck overlooking a shaded back lawn with a charming gazebo, making it a popular spot for weddings. And, appropriately, this house also offers a honeymoon suite named Heaven (Room 11).

Bikes are available for guests and for those who want to go to the nearby island beaches so are beach chairs, towels, and umbrellas. For those who just want to sit 'n' rock, there are rocking chairs and a porch swing on the verandah.

COOMBS HOUSE INN

Address:	80 Sixth Street, Apalachicola 32320
	www.coombshouseinn.com
Phone:	850/653-9199
Fax:	850/653-2785
Rates:	$80 – $175
Units:	18 in two houses

The Gibson Inn

What started out as a seaman's hotel in a prosperous river port, the Gibson has become an elegant landmark. It was the first steam-heated hotel between Pensacola and Jacksonville and went through several ups and downs with the economy, but since the Koun brothers restored it in 1985, the Gibson has become an outstanding example of how to live Old Florida style. It has all the modern conveniences like full baths and television. Today, it's one of the few active inns in the nation listed in the National Register of Historic Places.

The floor, paneling, and stairwell of the Gibson's lobby are the original heart-of-pine and black cypress with precisely matched tongue-and-groove wainscoting rarely seen today. All thirty-one guest rooms are uniquely decorated with furnishings such as four-poster beds, antique armoires, ceiling fans, and wide basin pedestal sinks with brass or porcelain fixtures. Doors to vacant rooms are left open, and before registering, you can walk around and choose the one you like. Take a look at the spacious Bridal Room (Number 313), if it's available. Room 309 is reputed to have a friendly ghost.

If you enjoy sitting and rocking with a view of the downtown activities of a small town, the double-decked wraparound porches of this restored 1907 Victorian is the place to do it. The Governor's Suite offers a bonus of direct access to the porch.

If you are a mystery buff, the inn hosts more than half a dozen Murder Mystery Weekends each year. There is also a full-service restaurant with an excellent reputation, especially for its fresh seafood.

THE GIBSON INN

Address:	**P.O. Box 221, Apalachicola 32329**
	www.gibsoninn.com
Phone:	**850/653-2191**
Fax:	**850/653-3521**
Rates:	**$75 – $120**
Units:	**31**

DEFUNIAK SPRINGS

Sales tax 7 percent

Established as a railroad stop in the 1880s, the town was named by its developer for Frederick DeFuniak (pronounced duh-FEW-NEE-ack) who was chief engineer of the L&N Railroad and reputedly a French count. The "Springs" refers to the almost perfectly round, spring-fed lake located in the center of town. Florida State University and the Florida Teachers Association both got their start here during the the Victorian movement Chautauqua, which promoted self improvement through learning. In 1996 the Florida Chautaugua Winter Assembly was reborn here and now meets annually early in the year.

Hotel DeFuniak.

Originally built as a Masonic Lodge in 1920, the two-story building later became a residential hotel and went steadily downhill. When it came up for sale in 1995, Ann Robinson, who grew up in DeFuniak Springs but spent most of her life in Clearwater, got together a group of local relatives and friends (none with hotel experience) to buy it. It took two and a half years to restore the building to its Old Florida beginnings and convert it into the hotel she always thought it should be.

Entering the hotel is like stepping back into the 1920s. There is an old-fashioned wooden registration desk with a high counter and a line of mail slots behind it. Each of the four suites and eight guest rooms, all with baths, are charmingly decorated with warm, rich colors and tasteful furnishings in the style and ambiance of the '20s. Herb Hiller, author of the *Guide to Small and Historic Lodgings in Florida,* calls it "one of the finest small hotels in Florida." We agree.

The hotel restaurant, which has earned a large following of local residents,—always a good sign—offers lunch and dinner on weekdays and a Sunday buffet. The Tea Room offers tea every afternoon but Sunday.

HOTEL DEFUNIAK

Address:	400 E. Nelson Street, DeFuniak Springs 32433
	www.hoteldefuniak.com
Phone:	877/DEFUNIAK (333-8642); 850/892-4383
Fax:	850/892-5346
Rates:	$65 – $115
Units:	12

DESTIN

Bed tax 10 percent

The neighboring fishing villages and southern sea towns of Destin, Fort Walton Beach, and Okaloosa Island comprise the Emerald Coast with twenty-four miles of sugar white beaches. Destin, boasting to be the world's luckiest fishing village, has the saltwater world records and the largest charter boat fleet in Florida, and Fort Walton Beach has the largest air force base in the free world: Elgin Air Force Base.

Henderson Park Inn

Although it looks old, it was actually built in 1992 by Bill Abbott. He wanted to recreate a traditional New England hotel like the one where he and his father once worked. With its green mansard roof, shingled walls, white trim, and widow's walk, this inn could easily be at home on the coast of Maine; it fits well in Destin, too, surrounded by white sand and sea oats. It is located at the end of the road and borders the mile and a half of unspoiled beach of Henderson State Recreation Area, thus insuring that further development won't impair its prime location.

Henderson Park Inn is an adults only inn, with thirty-six executive suites and efficiency apartments in the two buildings. They are all furnished with a Victorian theme featuring antiques and reproductions of Queen Anne furnishings. The art throughout both buildings is from the French Impressionist period. Many of the rooms are named for painters from this period and each is appropriately decorated with prints of that artist's work.

All the rooms except one have sweeping views of the gulf. All have private baths and a number have balconies or private patios. Most rooms have four-poster beds, and some have whirlpools and fireplaces. Two of the more popular rooms are 203 and 303 in the main building.

These are corner rooms with fireplaces and balconies offering views of both the gulf and the beach.

The main building is more European in style while the newer one is more American. One difference, especially if you want a top floor room, is that the new building has an elevator while the main building does not. Both buildings are three stories with the main building housing the inn's locally popular full-service restaurant.

HENDERSON PARK INN

Address:	2700 Scenic Hwy 98, Destin 32541
	www.hendersonparkinn.com
Phone:	800/336-4853; 850/654-0400
Fax:	850/650-4233
Rates:	$95 – $290
Units:	36

Sandestin Golf and Beach Resort

This twenty-four hundred-acre resort is located on land bordering the Gulf of Mexico and Choctawhatchee Bay, which was once home to Creek Indians who used it as their ceremonial center and hunting grounds. Today, the only hunting that goes on here is for lost golf balls on the resort's courses.

They aren't kidding when they call it a Golf and Beach Resort. Being on the gulf, the sun, sea, and white sands are a given. As for the *golf*, there are four courses, including the Raven Golf Club designed by Robert Trent Jones, Jr. Added up they offer seventy-three holes. There's also the Golf Learning Center, which uses the latest hi-tech computer and video equipment to help the staff pros analyze and improve your game. And for would-be golfers seventeen or younger, they have a Junior Golf Program.

This is definitely a sports oriented resort. In addition to golf there are fourteen tennis courts of either natural grass, hydrogrid clay, or hard surfaces, and every guest gets one hour of complimentary court time daily. In addition to swimming in the gulf, there are four swimming pools; a health and fitness club; complimentary canoes and bikes; a variety of small watercraft for rent ranging from crabbing skiffs to waverunners; catch-and-release

lake and dock fishing; plus fishing, cruising, and sailing charters. If you come by boat, there's a ninety-eight-slip marina where you can dock. There is also an Ocean Sailing School Program, and the kids can enroll in the Kidsail Sailing Academy.

As for places to stay, the resort is made up of three communities whose name tells its primary location—Beachside, Dockside, and Linkside. Each community is then divided into charming neighborhoods. Although most of the twenty-five hundred units that make up the fifteen neighborhoods in these three areas are privately owned, about seven hundred units are in the rental pool. These include hundreds of one- to four-bedroom villas and townhouses as well as high-rise condo towers on the gulf.

In addition to the Kidsail and Junior Golf, there's plenty to keep the younger set happily involved. They will enjoy climbing up into Captain Joe Lee's two-story Tree House at the Baytowne Marina or playing in a pirate ship-shaped playground in a five-acre nature park. The resort also has Sand Pals and other supervised activities for children.

SANDESTIN GOLF AND BEACH RESORT

Address:	**9300 Hwy 98 West, Destin 32541**
	www.sandestin.com
Phone:	**800/622-1623; 850/267-8000**
Rates:	**$195 – $676**
Units:	**Approx. 700**

MILTON

Bed tax 9.5 percent

Milton is the major city in Santa Rosa County with many streams, creeks, and many springs winding through the isolated and peaceful Blackwater River State Forest. Providing more than a hundred miles of uninterrupted paddling, the Florida state legislature designated Santa Rosa County as the "Canoe Capital of Florida."

Adventures Unlimited

Adventures Unlimited Outdoor Center is an eighty-eight acre wilderness resort. They are an outfitter, providing gear and storage for those getting onto the waters, as well as a hotel, providing a place to stay between paddling trips. Bring your own or rent one of the four hundred canoes, four hundred tubes, or thirty kayaks.

There is a choice of accommodations from the Old Schoolhouse Inn to a number of cottages and cabins. Our favorite is the Old Schoolhouse Inn, which is not as "rough" as some of the other outdoorsy accommodations. Far from it. Cozy and homey are the words that come to mind. Originally built in 1926 as a four-room schoolhouse, it has been reborn as an eight-room bed-and-breakfast inn. Each spacious room has a private bath, gas fireplace, pecan and oak hardwood floors, and twelve-foot ceilings. All have heat and air-conditioning and are furnished with antiques, paintings, and books. Each room is themed around authors ranging from Hemingway to Marjorie Kinnan Rawlings to Dr. Seuss. The wide porches on both sides of the building have rocking chairs and swings.

A continental breakfast basket is delivered to inn guests each morning, and you can do some moderate food preparation since each inn room has a microwave, a small refrigerator, and a coffeemaker. But it is what the rooms don't have that might appeal to some guests—no phone, no television or radio, and no clock.

For families or small groups, there are several homey one- and two-bedroom, one-bath cottages that sleep four to six. These are set up much the same as the rooms at the inn. For those willing to take a short walk to a restroom, there are also a few inexpensive rustic camping cottages, each with a screened porch and air-conditioning. There are also accommodations for groups of twenty to sixty.

ADVENTURES UNLIMITED

Address:	**Route 6, Box 283, Milton 32570**
	www.adventuresunlimited.com
Phone:	**800/239-6864; 850/623-6197**
Fax:	**850/626-3124**
Rates:	**$39 – $109**
Units:	**14**

PENSACOLA

Bed tax 10.5 percent

This three hundred-year-old gulf coast community is called the "City of Five Flags" because at various times it was ruled by Spain, France, England, the Confederacy, and the United States. Each year the city celebrates the "Fiesta of Five Flags" for two weeks in June. Pensacola also proudly calls itself "America's First Place City" based on the Spanish colony established on its shores in 1559. Unfortunately, that colony failed, so Pensacola lost the title of "America's Oldest City" to St. Augustine.

Its deep water port ensured the area a long naval presence that started in 1825 and evolved into the present Naval Air Station, home of the Blue Angels and the National Museum of Naval Aviation. And being in the heart of Gulf Island National Seashore Pensacola provides fifty-two miles of unspoiled beaches.

Crowne Plaza, Pensacola Grand Hotel

When you enter this hotel, you enter through what was once a two-story Louisville & Nashville Railway depot that dates back to 1912. Now, through imaginative architectural design, it serves as part of the attractive lobby entrance to the hotel's fifteen-story tower. Because of the historic depot, the whole hotel complex is listed in the National Register of Historic Places. Many of the depot's original building materials, like its tile floors and wood paneling, have been restored. Adding to the historical ambiance are the opulent early twentieth-century furnishings and antiques.

The depot and tower are connected by a two-story solarium-style galleria and exhibition area. In this depot/lobby are the registration desk, restaurant, lounge, a surprisingly well-stocked guest library, and retail shops.

The hotel has 202 guest rooms and ten suites all decorated and furnished with custom-made contemporary furnishings. Eight of the ten suites have two levels connected by an interior spiral staircase. President George Bush stayed in the Presidential Suite (where else?) when he came to Pensacola. The hotel is the tallest building downtown, and since all rooms face south, you'll have a good view of Excambia Bay and the Gulf of Mexico. Other facilities include a heated pool on top of the depot structure and a fitness room.

The appropriately named 1912 Restaurant, which is popular locally as well as with guests, features an extensive menu in an elegant setting. One of the highlights of its décor is a piece of scalloped grillwork on one wall that is from Lloyd's of London. Near the lounge is a collection of Blue Angel memorabilia.

CROWNE PLAZA, PENSACOLA GRAND HOTEL

Address:	200 E. Gregory Street, Pensacola 32501
	www.pensacolagrandhotel.com
Phone:	800/348-3336; 850/433-3336
Fax:	850/432-7572
Rates:	$95 – $400
Units:	212

New World Inn

Its downtown waterfront location enhances this small hotel's status as a symbol of Pensacola's history. Even the property has an interesting history. It is land recovered from the bay in the 1880s by the dumping of thousands of tons of ballast from sailing vessels that came to the port from around the world. This included red granite from Sweden, broken tile from France, bluestone from Italy, dredgings from the Thames River, granite from South America, and lava rock from Mount Pelée.

Originally a box factory, the building was converted into an inn in the 1980s with some facets of the factory imaginatively retained and blended into the Victorian opulence of the hotel. In the lobby, for example, the red brick ceiling and supports from the factory add character. Here and there throughout the hotel, the walls are decorated with nineteenth-century etchings, prints, and photographs. A more modern touch is a photo gallery behind the registration desk that displays pictures of dozens of famous guests including Lucille Ball, Larry King, Ella Fitzgerald, and Charles Kuralt.

The fourteen rooms and one suite are elegantly furnished in styles loyal to Pensacola's history with some genuine antiques and excellent reproductions. Each room is named for a prominent person in the city's past and the room is decorated to depict the rich history of Pensacola during that person's time.

NEW WORLD INN

Address:	600 Palafox Street, Pensacola 32501
	www.newworldlanding.com
Phone:	850/432-4111
Fax:	850/432-6836
Rates:	$75 – $125
Units:	15

Pensacola Victorian Bed & Breakfast

Within walking distance of the downtown historic district, this restored Queen Anne Victorian is a piece of local history. It was built in 1892 by Capt. William Northrup, who wanted his dream home to be close to his land-based business interests and still let him smell the salt air. One of his businesses was shipping pine to Italy. For ballast on the return voyage the ships carried Italian granite, which Captain Northrup used as part of the foundation and a wall of his new home. His land-based accomplishments included being mayor and bank president. His home was a favorite gathering place for city leaders, and it was here that he persuaded them to found the city's Philharmonic Orchestra. This legacy of hospitality is carried on by innkeepers Chuck and Barbee Major, who have more than fifty years of experience in the restaurant and hospitality business between them.

The four guest rooms in the three-story home all have private baths, although one is across the hall. All are furnished with authentic Victorian furnishings. The Captain's Room has a fireplace and a charming cupola, while the Big White Room lives up to its name by being truly big. If you want to sit 'n' rock, there are rocking chairs and swings on the porch. English tea is available on Sunday afternoons by reservation.

PENSACOLA VICTORIAN BED & BREAKFAST

Address:	203 W. Gregory Street, Pensacola 32501
	www.pensacolavictorian.com
Phone:	800/370-8354; 850/434-2818
Fax:	850/429-0675
Rates:	$85 – $125
Units:	4

Yacht House Bed & Breakfast Inn

Owner Teresa Allen describes her life as eclectic and says her bed-and-breakfast seems to have brought it all together. After getting a master's degree in Europe and studying Spanish in Latin America, she taught English in universities in China, Thailand, and Kuwait. During her travels she was always a collector, and her collection is now the décor of the bed-and-breakfast's theme rooms. The Shanghai Suite has authentic Chinese décor; the Nairobi Suite is African with batiks and wood carvings; the Sahara Suite is where you'll encounter items from Egypt, Morocco, and the Sahara; the Bengal Room contains tapestries from India, Nepal, and Sri Lanka; and in the Amazon Room hangs art from the Aztecs, Mayas, and Incas of Central and South America. And for those who want a theme closer to home, there's the Mariner Room, with seafaring décor.

Pensacola's longest running bed-and-breakfast, the Yacht House rests on a wooded, grassy acre across from the historic Pensacola Yacht Club. The inn has six rooms and suites, two in the main house and four in the cottages, each with a private bath. All have second doors leading to verandahs or private sundecks, and three of the rooms have private garden decks with hot tubs. In addition to a scattering of travel, yachting, and other books in the rooms, guests can use the library, which has a large collection of books on a wide variety of subjects, as well a collection of 1940s to 1960s *Life* magazines, plus videos, and DVDs. (A VCR is available.) Teresa also offers tarot readings, by appointment.

YACHT HOUSE BED & BREAKFAST INN

Address:	**1820 Cypress Street, Pensacola 32501**
	www.yachthouse.com
Phone:	**850/433-3634**
Fax:	**850/433-3264**
Rates:	**$85 – $125**
Units:	**6**

PORT ST. JOE

Bed tax 8.5 percent

Florida's first constitution was signed here on January 11, 1839. The railroad arrived in 1909, helping make this a center for a timber empire. Much of the empire was developed by the Duponts, who moved in and virtually bought the town and established paper mills here. Legend has it that when drawing up the time zone lines, the Duponts lobbied to bend the line off the Apalachicola River to include Port St. Joe in the eastern time zone so their major plant would be on the same time as their headquarters in Tallahassee.

Château Nemours Seaport Inn

This is one of the few remaining historic homes that validates Port St. Joe as the center of the Dupont's early timber empire. It was built in 1937 for the exclusive use of Mrs. Jessie Ball Dupont, her guests, and her staff. The house, just a few hundred feet from St. Joseph Bay, is primarily constructed of locally harvested cypress, heart-of-pine, and cedar. The richness of these woods is still evident throughout the building.

In recent years the house was used as the St. Joe Paper Company's executive guesthouse until 1998 when Jeanette Palmer bought it. Jeanette is a business management consultant whose family had a beach house in nearby Mexico Beach. She wanted to settle in the area and loved the château, but it wasn't for sale. When she offered to buy it, the Dupont family's Nemours Foundation agreed to sell.

Although not in bad shape, it had been neglected. "I started to update the old wiring," she says, "and one thing led to another," which included removing the carpets to expose the richness of the original oak floors, stripping doors and trim, and returning the magnificent walnut staircase to its

previous splendor. In the restoration process she retained many of the original light fixtures, furniture, and collectibles, including many original art deco features and oil paintings, which give the place an authentic 1930s ambiance.

The inn has five guest rooms and a suite, each with a private bath, cable television, phone, and view of St. Joseph Bay. And there are porches on both floors. The three first-floor rooms have each been named for one of the Dupont family residences and the family yacht.

CHÂTEAU NEMOURS SEAPORT INN

Address:	**P.O. Box 122, Port St. Joe 32457**
	www.seaportchateau.com
Phone:	**850/229-6775**
Fax:	**850/229-6535**
Rates:	**$85 - $175**
Units:	**6**

Old Saltworks Cabins

Florida Trend magazine says the Old Saltworks Cabins are one of the best hidden getaway places in Florida. And as soon as you drive in through the lush tropical vegetation, you'll have to agree that it is both hidden and a getaway.

The name comes from an old Confederate saltworks that was attacked by the Union during the Civil War. Only a few bricks from the old saltworks remain, but you can see the history of the Union attack in the dioramas at the minimuseum at the office.

The location alone makes it a desirable destination. It is nestled between beautiful Cape San Blas and St. Joseph Bay where you can catch the sunrise on one side and the sunset on the other. Birders and nature photographers can have a field day here with more than 209 species of birds spotted, including migrating hawks, eagles, and peregrine falcons. Shore and wading birds can be seen throughout the year. It's also a delightful place for fishermen with redfish, trout, and scallops in the Bay and game fishing in the gulf. For the kids there is Fort Crooked Tree to play in.

The seven cabins are in harmony with their natural surroundings. There are cabins in the bush, with water views, and one that is on the beach. Despite their rustic exteriors all of the cabins are clean and comfortable. Basically furnished, they all have heat and air-conditioning and screened porches with picnic tables.

The largest lodging on the property is the Toth House, which has two bedrooms, two baths, a hot tub, a fireplace, a well-equipped kitchen, and a washer and dryer. This has a five-day minimum rental.

OLD SALTWORKS CABINS

Address:	**P.O. Box 526, Port St. Joe 32457**
	www.capesanblas.com/saltworks
Phone:	**850/229-6097**
Fax:	**770/739-9758 Attn: Blair**
Rates:	**$69 - $79**
Units:	**7; 1 house/5 day minimum ($600)**

Turtle Beach Inn

North Carolina native Trish Petrie is not only living her dream, she is also sharing it with her guests. Trish had a landscaping business in Tennessee and for many years dreamed of having a bed-and-breakfast located on a beautiful, unspoiled, uncrowded beach where she could swim. Her search for the perfect spot took her from the North Carolina coast to Florida. When she finally found this spot, she ran into trouble getting permission to build because the property is in a designated turtle hatching area. While she waited, she spent time at the beach and often saw the loggerhead sea turtles, and she knew she had to call it the Turtle Beach Inn. In keeping with this theme, she designed and ordered custom-made furnishings to carry out the ocean and sea turtle motif.

The two-story inn is built on stilts and is nestled among needled pines and cabbage palms on three sides. In the main house there are four gulf view rooms, sundecks, and several large covered porches on which to sit 'n' rock. The rooms are large, but if you want more room, there are two cottages: a one-bedroom and a two-bedroom.

Although, the favorite activity of most of the guests is peaceful relaxation, there are other choices such as canoeing, kayaking, horseback riding, fishing, swimming, boating, biking, and even golf. Ecotour packages to explore St. Vincent Island, a wildlife preserve, and other ecological areas are also available but need to be booked when you make your room reservation.

TURTLE BEACH INN

Address:	**140 Painted Pony Road, Port St. Joe 32456**
	www.indianpass.com/turtlebeach
Phone:	**850/229-9366**
Fax:	**850/229-9367**
Rates:	**$95 – $250**
Units:	**7**

SEA TURTLES

Sea turtles are large, air-breathing reptiles that spend their lives at sea. The exception is the female sea turtle who comes ashore during the warmest months, on a predetermined beach, to lay her eggs. Crawling up the beach, she digs a nest-hole, lays up to 150 eggs, covers them with sand, and goes back to the sea. About two months later the eggs all hatch at the same time, usually at night, and the tiny turtles make a dash for the sea, usually through a gauntlet of birds and other predators.

Sea turtles are protected by both federal and state laws that make it illegal to harass or harm them. To help the babies survive many communities have set up nest and hatching protection programs. A number of irresistible overnight lodgings (more than are listed here) participate in these programs.

SANTA ROSA BEACH

Bed tax 10 percent

A Highlands House

Joan and Ray Robins both had a great deal of hotel experience when, in 1996, they bought a three-bedroom beach cottage and added a second story with four bedrooms. In the process they redesigned the whole house in an antebellum style to resemble a summer home of an eighteenth century planter and to take advantage of the cooling breezes from the gulf.

The rooms are named after flowers and are attractively decorated in keeping with the antebellum ambiance. They have four-poster rice beds, wingback chairs, and private baths. The four front rooms have balconies with gulf views. The Hibiscus Room does not have a gulf view, but as compensation it does have a two-person whirlpool tub. The second story porch is furnished with oversized wicker rockers, so you can sit 'n' rock while enjoying the beautiful view of the gulf waters.

There is a stairway and a boardwalk at the front of the house that leads to the beach a short distance away. This is one of the few bed-and-breakfasts where children are not only accepted, but welcome.

A HIGHLANDS HOUSE

Address:	**P.O. Box 1189, Santa Rosa Beach 32459**
	www.ahighlandshousebbinn.com
Phone:	**850/267-0110**
Fax:	**850/267-3602**
Rates:	**under $96 – $160**
Units:	**8**

SEASIDE

Bed tax 8 percent

Seaside was built to resemble a quaint Old Florida town that is picket-fence perfect. The community layout, which has recieved worldwide acclaim, is designed to invite walking and neighborly interaction so as to end urban sprawl and help restore the sense of community. By strict design code the pastel-colored buildings are all raised on piles a few feet off the ground, the sides are clapboard, and the roofs are tin—all characteristic of Old Florida—and they are all behind white picket fences.

If you want to fully enjoy the ambiance of this extraordinary community, we strongly suggest you stay in the off-season, as throngs of visitors want to visit this "Hollywood" town that gained fame as the set of *The Truman Show*.

Josephine's French Country Inn

With its white pillars, porches on both floors, and a widow's walk, this inn looks like a transplanted southern plantation. It was built in 1990 to fit in with the Seaside design and is the town's only bed-and-breakfast.

Voted one of the top twelve inns in America by *Country Inns* magazine, it is for adults only. It offers seven rooms in the main house and two suites in the guest house, all of which exude southern charm with their furnishings, pine floors, brass light fixtures, and in most rooms, working fireplaces.

Innkeepers Bruce and Judy Albert were both in the hospitality business before moving here and count the inn's romantic gourmet restaurant as one of their most rewarding accomplishments. Bruce is the chef and enjoys cooking French cuisine. He grows his own organic herbs and vegetables, which he uses in the restaurant. The ten-table restaurant is usually only open Wednesday through Sunday.

JOSEPHINE'S FRENCH ·COUNTRY INN

Address:	**101 Seaside Avenue, Seaside 32459**
	www.josephinesfl.com
Phone:	**800/848-1840; 850/231-1940**
Fax:	**850/231-2446**
Rates:	**$165 – $240**
Units:	**9**

Seaside Cottages

While the majority of accommodations in the rental pool are one- and two-bedroom cottages, there are some six-bedroom houses that could easily hold a large family or a small group. All the cottages have porches, widow's walks, cupolas, icecream-colored clapboard siding, and crimped tin roofs. Latticework and gingerbread trim are everywhere.

Since the cottages are furnished by the owners, the interior of each one is different. All are well planned, with fully equipped kitchens, comfortable beds, and washers and dryers. Usually you'll find antiques or good reproductions. Many of the cottages also have personal touches like rocking chairs and handmade quilts.

The Honeymoon Cottages are smaller than most of those in the main section of town, but they are right on the beach, have hot tubs, and are a little closer to the shops and restaurants in the town center than the other cottage rentals. If you don't want a cottage, you can rent a townhouse, a suite or penthouse, or even an old-fashioned motel room. The town has several swimming pools, tennis courts, bike rentals, a playground, shuffleboard courts, and even croquet.

SEASIDE COTTAGES

Address:	**P.O. Box 4730, Seaside 32479**
	www.seasidefl.com
Phone:	**800/277-8696; 850/231-2228**
Fax:	**850/231-2293**
Rates:	**$185 – $700**
Units:	**270**

For Additional Information
on the Northwest Region:

ALACHUA COUNTY CVB
30 East University Avenue
Gainesville, FL 32601
352/374-5231
Fax: 352/338-3213
www.co.alachua.fl.us/acvacb

APALACHICOLA BAY COC
99 Market Street, Suite 100
Apalachicola, FL 32320
850/653-9419
Fax: 850/653-8219
www.apalachicola.com/chamber
www.baynavigator.com

BEACHES OF SOUTH WALTON
P.O. Box 1248
Santa Rosa Beach, FL 32459
800/822-6877; 850/267-1216
Fax: 850//267-3943
www.beachesofsouthwalton.com

DEFUNIAK SPRINGS VISITORS BUREAU
1162 Circle Dr.
DeFuniak Springs, FL 32433
850/892-5150

CITRUS COUNTY TOURIST DEVELOPMENT COUNCIL
801 S.E. Hwy 19
Crystal River, FL 34429
352/527-5223
Fax: 352/527-5317

DESTIN/FORT WALTON BEACH CVB
P.O. Box 609
Fort Walton Beach, FL 32549
800/322-3319; 850/651-7131
Fax: 850/651-7149
www.destin-fwb.com

PENSACOLA AREA COC
1401 E. Gregory Street
Pensacola, FL 32501
800/874-1234; 850/434-1234
Fax: 850/432-8211
www.pensacolachamber.com

SANTA ROSA COUNTY VISITOR INFORMATION CENTER
P.O. Box 5337
Navarre, FL 32566
800/480-7263; 850/939-2691
www.navarrefl.com

Quincy Monticello

Tallahassee
Wakulia Springs
High Springs
St. Marks
Gainsville
Micanopy
Steinhatchee
Cedar Key

High Season: Spring

(Note: All lodging rates are for high season. Off-season rates can be
significantly lower.)

CEDAR KEY

Sales tax 7 percent

The Cedar Keys are made up of about one hundred islands, including twelve restricted islands of the Cedar Keys National Wildlife Refuge, which is home to more than two hundred thousand nesting birds. The town of Cedar Key had its heyday in the late nineteenth century when it was an important fishing port and a source of wood for the pencil industry. A hurricane in 1896 destroyed much of this business, and the town never regained its former greatness.

Today Cedar Key is a charming little town known mostly for its excellent seafood, beautiful beaches, and laid-back lifestyle—they don't even have a stoplight. Fishing is still a major industry and is now joined by aquafarming. Two thirds of the state's clam farmers are in Cedar Key.

Cedar Key Bed & Breakfast

The Eagle Pencil Company, one of the major manufacturers of pencils from local cedar, built this house in 1880 to house its employees and guests. When the cedar ran out and the company left, it became a boarding house for a time, then a family home, and finally, in 1993 it was restored and began a new life as a bed-and-breakfast.

The couple who restored it loved doing restoration work, but found they really weren't interested in running a bed-and-breakfast. This proved fortunate for Bob Davenport and Lois Benninghoff, who were able to buy it in 1994 shortly after it opened.

Bob and Lois were high school sweethearts in Ohio but went their separate ways until they met again at their thirtieth high school reunion. The romance rekindled, and when they both decided their work in the corporate world still kept them apart too much, they decided to go into business together. Running a bed-and-breakfast seemed perfect. This decision brought them to Florida where they are now happy innkeepers.

There are six guest rooms in the main house, each furnished with antiques, a private bath, and porch access. A Honeymoon Cottage, decorated in bridal white, is attached to the rear of the verandah. We especially liked two adjoining rooms upstairs: Jack's Room, the largest in the house, and the Girl's Room, which has exclusive use of the upstairs balcony. Seclusion and escape are the priorities here, so there are no phones or televisions.

The lovely garden—a favorite spot for weddings—is shaded by a huge oak tree that is estimated to be at least 350 years old. You can tour the key on bicycles that are provided. For the more adventurous, they also have a one-person sea kayak.

CEDAR KEY BED & BREAKFAST

Address:	**P.O. Box 700, Cedar Key 32625**
	www.cedarkeybedbreakfast.com
Phone:	**877/543-5051; 352/543-9000**
Fax:	**352/543-8070**
Rates:	**$75 - $120**
Units:	**7**

GAINESVILLE AREA

(Gainsville, High Springs, Micanopy)

If you hear Floridians talking about the "Gators," odds are they are not talking about the swamp creatures that are well-known residents of the state, but about sports tams of the University of Florida in Gainesville. It is the state's oldest (1853), biggest (more than forty-two thousand full- and part-time students), and most prestigious educational center and is by far the largest employer in the area.

According to the visitor's bureau, Gainesville is the "Archery Capital of the World." They bestowed this title on themselves because they are home to the world's largest archery manufacturer and also the Fred Bear Museum that is filled with bowhunting trophies and exhibits on archery. This part of the state is also a major agricultural area. *Money* magazine has repeatedly ranked Gainesville as "one of the best places to live in America."

If you want to experience more of Old Florida, go to the nearby town of High Springs. Founded in 1884, it is now popular with visitors for its historic downtown and its antique, art, and curio shops.

Another historic town near Gainesville is Micanopy (MIK-uh-no-pee). This popular small town attracts visitors and antique collectors.

Micanopy was built on the former site of a Timucuan Indian village and named after one of that tribe's chiefs. The town borders Payne's Prairie, an area named after another Indian chief, a Seminole who lived here about two hundred years ago. The prairie is now a twenty-one-thousand-acre state preserve of freshwater marshes, woods, hammocks, swamps, ponds, and even a small herd of buffalo.

GAINESVILLE

Bed tax 9 percent

Magnolia Plantation Bed & Breakfast Inn

College students had lived in this house for thirty years before Joe and Cindy Montalto bought it in 1990, so it's not hard to imagine what they mean when they say it was in bad shape. With hard work, and the help of both their families and neighbors, they restored it to its original 1885 grandeur and opened as Gainesville's first bed-and-breakfast in 1991. One of the things that Cindy recalls about the restoration is that during it she discovered both espresso and Ben & Jerry's ice cream.

Located in the historic district, the house is singled out by architects as one of the few examples of a French Second Empire Victorian-style mansion in the South. That's a mouthful, but even if you don't know the style, one look and you'll recognize that this eye-catching beauty would look just as much at home in New Orleans.

The house, with its four-story tower, mansard roof, and old-fashioned verandahs front and back, is named for the many magnolia trees that surround it. Interestingly, although magnolia trees are all over Gainesville, there were none here when the Montaltos moved in. They planted them all.

Inside the main house, the décor and furnishings support the overall Victorian ambiance. The five themed guest rooms are named for flowers: Azalea, Gardenia, Heather, Jasmine, and, of course, Magnolia. All are decorated with antiques and collectibles, have private baths with claw-foot tubs and stand-up showers, gas-log fireplaces, and non-Victorian-era CD players with a large assortment of CDs.

Next to the main house are the Garden House and Miss Huey's Cottage. The Garden House offers modern lodging ideal for couples traveling together. It is divided into two separate one thousand-square-foot suites with a full kitchen. It also features a glass sun-room overlooking a garden, a living room with television/VCR, two bedrooms, and a bathroom with an oversized Jacuzzi tub and a stand-up shower. Miss Huey's is an 1880s cracker-style house converted into two bedrooms with living room, kitchen, dining room, and one bath.

Among the many accolades this bed-and-breakfast has earned are being voted the best bed-and-breakfast in the state by *Florida Living* magazine, and the most romantic lodging in Florida by *The Most Romantic Escapes in Florida.* A good part of the reason for the latter designation is that Cindy is an irrepressible and incurable romantic.

MAGNOLIA PLANTATION BED & BREAKFAST INN

Address:	309 S.E. Seventh Street, Gainesville 32601
	www.magnoliabnb.com
Phone:	800/201-2379; 352/375-6653
Fax:	352/338-0303
Rates:	$90 - $160
Units:	9

Sweetwater Branch Inn

While Cornelia Holbrook was planning to open this bed-and-breakfast, she wrote in her mission statement that she wanted "to provide an exceptional experience surrounded by beauty." She has accomplished her mission. Her inn was among the few that were featured in a nationwide PBS broadcast, "Inn Country USA." More proof of her achievment is evident in the decorative rooms, and the garden that is decorated with seven unique fountains and a pond filled with exotic fish.

Cornelia has wanted to be an innkeeper since she was young. She grew up in Gainesville and traveled with her mother's tour company. During her trips she made note of the good and bad in the places she stayed. Here she has incorporated the good and scrupulously avoided the bad.

The inn consists of two main houses and two smaller buildings. The Cushman-Colson House and the McKenzie House, both built in 1885, offer a total of fifteen themed rooms and suites that highlight their Victorian heritage. Although all the rooms are unique in style and décor, all five rooms and two suites in the Cushman-Colson House (usually called the main house) have a private bath with claw-foot tub and shower, antique furnishings, sitting chairs, a writing desk, a television, and a telephone. All except the Blue Moon Room have queen-size beds. Each of the five rooms in the McKenzie Home, which is listed in the National Register of

Historic Places, are not quite as Victorian in style—Aurora's Room has an art deco bathroom—but all have some antique furnishings and a queen-size bed. In addition to these two houses, the Honeymoon Cottage, also built in 1885, has a bedroom, full bath, kitchen, living room with fireplace, and Jacuzzi tub, and the Carriage House is a turnkey rental furnished apartment that sleeps five.

SWEETWATER BRANCH INN

Address:	625 E. University Avenue, Gainesville 32601
	www.sweetwaterinn.com
Phone:	800/595-7760; 352/373-6760
Fax:	352/371-3771
Rates:	$67 - $150
Units:	15

HIGH SPRINGS

Bed tax 9 percent

The Rustic Inn

The Rustic Inn lives up to its name with its ranch setting. It is located on ten acres in a quiet, rural area just two miles from the small town of High Springs. The guest rooms are behind the main house in converted horse stalls, and

30

there are no televisions in the rooms. (They are available on request.)

Other than the setting there is really nothing rustic about it. Don't let the term "horse stalls" fool you. The six rooms all have a private entrance and are extra large with twelve-foot ceilings and private baths that are artfully decorated. Each room has a queen-size bed made of western red cedar by a local artisan, futon couch, table and chairs, refrigerator stocked with sodas and juices, microwave, and coffeemaker. There are extra touches like lace-trimmed sheets and cloth napkins that make it more comfortable. The extra space is enough for a small family, and innkeepers Larry and Diana Zorovich welcome well-behaved children.

The rooms are themed after wild animals or nature: the Cat Room (not house cats), Everglades Room, Panda Room, Sea Mammal Room, Tropical Room, and Zebra Room. All the rooms share the wide common front porch on which to sit 'n' rock, and the Zebra Room also has a private deck.

Facilities include an outside pool and a library in the main house.

THE RUSTIC INN

Address:	**P.O. Box 2610, High Springs 32643**
Phone:	**904/454-1223**
Fax:	**904/454-1225**
Rates:	**under $100 to $110**
Units:	**6**

MICANOPY

Bed tax 9 percent

The Herlong Mansion

Architecturally, this historic mansion is a house over a house. It had humble beginnings around 1845 as a cracker-style farmhouse with a detached kitchen. In 1910 the original structure was completely encased in brick designed like a southern colonial home with four two-story carved wood Corinthian columns and a wide verandah in front.

Now listed in the National Register of Historic Places, it is a three-story mansion with high ceilings, leaded glass windows, ten fireplaces, mahogany inlaid floors, mission oak woodwork, and floor-to-ceiling windows in the dining room. There are nine guest rooms and suites in the main house and additional guest quarters in two separate cottages. All the rooms are named for people who were part of the history of the mansion, and they are individually decorated with furnishings and antiques such as brass beds, carved furniture, and patchwork quilts. Overall, the ambiance is that of a wealthy southern home where you'll experience both elegance and exceptional hospitality. On a more modern note, four of the rooms and the cottages have Jacuzzis.

Two extras at the Herlong Mansion include the obvious collection of more than 150 walking sticks and the elusive Inez, the mansion's ghost. Inez was the oldest daughter of the family that once owned the house. After a family fight that lasted eighteen years, she finally won possession of the mansion in 1968. As it turned out, the day she took possession she died in one of the upstairs bedrooms. Obviously, after all that effort to win her right of possession, she had no intention of leaving her home. According to those who have experienced her presence, she is a friendly ghost.

The mansion is surrounded by a lovely garden with ancient giant oak and pecan trees. The garden gazebo is especially popular for weddings. *Florida Trend* magazine has called it, "the most elegant inn in the state of Florida."

THE HERLONG MANSION

Address:	P.O. Box 667, Micanopy 32667
	www.herlong.com
Phone:	800-HERLONG (437-5664); 352/466-3322
Fax:	352/466-3322
Rates:	$70 - $179
Units:	11

Shady Oak Bed & Breakfast

Frank James, an artist and a teacher, moved to Micanopy in 1988 because he wanted to settle in a town that was still Old Florida. Although it looks old, he actually designed it that way to be in harmony with the architecture of this historic nineteenth century small town. The large three-story building has double-decked wraparound verandahs, a Florida room, and a widow's walk. The structure is named for the four-hundred-year-old live oaks that provide a canopy for it.

The rooms are on the upper floors while several shops occupy the first floor with Frank's stained glass studio, where he conducts classes. He also holds a woodworking workshop in the back. Frank specializes in artistic glass creations, so, as you might expect, there are museum quality examples in every one of the seven themed rooms and suites. The Master Suite, for example, has stained-glass shower windows, while Victoria's Suite, which is decorated in an 1890 bordello theme, includes stained-glass windows and lamps, and a private Jacuzzi with a wall of mirrors.

If we had to pick a favorite, it would be Melody's Suite, which features a four-poster bed with etched, mirrored headboard; a large wall of stained glass wild roses; a tiled shower; and stained glass lighting. A private balcony offers a view of the main street, and the widow's walk and common living room are just outside the suite. All rooms have cable television, and some have stereo systems with CDs available.

SHADY OAK BED & BREAKFAST

Address:	P.O. Box 327, Micanopy 32667
	www.shadyoak.com
Phone:	352/466-3476
Fax:	352/466-9233
Rates:	$85 – $175
Units:	7

MONTICELLO

Sales tax 7 percent

Named after Thomas Jefferson's Virginia home, this is not only the largest city in Jefferson County, it is also the only incorporated city in the only county in Florida that extends from the Georgia state line on the north to the Gulf of Mexico. Historic sites here include the 1890 Perkins Opera House and the 1906 County Courthouse. The county is largely agricultural, sparsely populated, and relatively undiscovered by tourists.

Palmer Place

If you want evidence of how well this house was built, all you need to know is that the downstairs walls are two feet thick. It was built around 1830 by Martin Palmer, a prominent planter, and was the family home until the early 1900s. (The family, by the way, eventually included fourteen doctors.) Beautifully and authentically restored, this three-story, seventy-five hundred-square-foot antebellum home is listed on the National Register of Historic Places. Sitting on ten acres of manicured lawns, natural gardens, and ancient trees, it presents the picture of the ideal southern plantation mansion.

John and Eleanor Hawkins bought the house in 1993. They wanted to live in the big old house, but decided the only way they could afford to was by making it into a bed-and-breakfast. So they did.

There are five spacious guest rooms and suites that have color themes. They all have sitting areas, private baths, cable television, and private phones. All are furnished with antiques. In fact, antiques abound in the house. The Gold Room, for example, contains a beautifully carved rosewood four-poster bed brought to Jefferson County by the Palmers in 1829, a nineteenth century rolltop desk, and an empire butler's desk. The Red Room has a carved mahogany Victorian dresser and a mahogany four-poster bed from the Empire period.

PALMER PLACE

Address:	**P.O. Box 507, Monticello 32345**
	www.palmerplace.com
Phone:	**850/997-5519**
Fax:	**850/997-2863**
Rates:	**$70 – $120**
Units:	**5**

QUINCY

Sales tax 7 percent

Established in 1828, it owed its early prosperity to tobacco. In the early 1900s, a wise officer in the Quincy State Bank persuaded some of his patrons to invest in the then-young Coca-Cola Company. The result was an economic boom for the patrons and the town. By the early 1940s, two dozen Quincy residents were millionaires, making it, at that time, the richest town per capita in the United States. The thirty-six block historic distric contains homes dating from the 1840s to the 1880s.

The McFarlin House Bed & Breakfast Inn

John McFarlin, one of Quincy's prominent tobacco planters, built this fine looking three-story Queen Anne Victorian mansion for his family in 1895. Sparing no expense, he put in hand-carved woodwork and mantels from France, stained glass window pieces, pressed ceilings, an impressive staircase, and a wraparound porch.

By 1994, however, when Richard and Tina Fauble bought it, it had been empty for twenty years and was in such disrepair and so overgrown that Tina recalls: "We didn't know we had a driveway."

Today the artfully restored house, listed in the National Register of Historic Places, has nine spacious guest rooms, all with private baths, some with fireplaces and Jacuzzi tubs, and all furnished with carefully selected Victorian antiques and reproductions. They also have cable television and private phones. The names of the rooms—like Gentlemen's Quarters, Southern Grace, and Ribbons and Roses—reflect southern Victorian heritage and hospitality. One of our favorites is the King's View

Room, which is in the many-windowed round turret. It also features a bath with a two-person Jacuzzi.

THE MCFARLIN HOUSE BED & BREAKFAST INN

Address:	**305 E. King Street, Quincy 32351**
	www.macfarlinhouse.com
Phone:	**877/370-4701; 850/875-2526**
Rates:	**$110 – $175**
Units:	**9**

STEINHATCHEE

Bed tax 9 percent

Steinhatchee is a quaint fishing village located at the mouth of the Steinhatchee River in Taylor County, which is named after our twelfth president, Zachary Taylor. Located on the sparsely populated Nature Coast, it has long been a favorite destination of hunters, sport fishermen, and other lovers of the outdoors. Seventy-five percent of the land area in the county is in commercial forests, which is why the local chamber of commerce calls it the Forest Capital of the World. It also claims to be the Scalloping Capital of Florida because the estuaries remain healthy and the supplies are plentiful.

Steinhatchee Landing Resort

Dean and Loretta, his wife, own and manage this charming resort that is located on the banks of the Steinhatchee River. When Dean developed Steinhatchee Landing, he wanted to capture the spirit of Old Florida as it was in the time of the fashionable resorts that were popular more than a hundred years ago. So, he patterned it to resemble a small southern town in the early twentieth century. That means it not only has Victorian and cracker-style homes, it has the things essential to small town and farm life at those times: horses for transportation, home gardens (you can gather your own vegetables in season), chickens (you can gather eggs for your own breakfast), and other farm animals. There's also a petting zoo for the kids. Although it doesn't advertise itself as such, in some ways the resort provides a living history lesson of a simpler time and place. To some that may sound

hokey, but the steady stream of guests proves that the Fowlers' goals are the goals of many.

Of course, the resort is not limited to families. In fact, most of the guests are couples looking to get away from it all for a time. So, the twenty-one comfortable and attractively furnished Victorian and tin-roofed cracker-style cottages offer choices from one to three bedrooms with a kitchen, living area, and an appropriate number of baths. Former President Carter and his family stayed in one of the three-bedroom cottages in 1994. Located on thirty-five acres, the cottages are all spacious and can accommodate from four to ten people. Every cottage has all the modern conveniences and amenities, a screened porch, and a charcoal grill. The resort has a casual restaurant that has won several awards. It also has a seventeen-suite motel nearby.

Tranquillity permeates the atmosphere here, but that doesn't mean there's nothing to do. There is swimming, tennis, archery, cycling, horse-back riding, canoeing, fishing, and boating.

STEINHATCHEE LANDING RESORT

Address:	P.O. Box 789, Steinhatchee 32359
	www.steinhatcheelanding.com
Phone:	800/584-1709; 352/498-3513
Fax:	352/498-2346
Rates:	$115 – $615
Units:	21

TALLAHASSEE

Bed tax 10 percent

Tallahassee has been recognized as a capital center for more than eight hundred years: first as a ceremonial center for the Native Americans at the Lake Jackson Indian Mounds, later for the Apalachee Indians at San Luis Mission, and today as the capital of the Sunshine State.

The city is located in an area described as the Big Bend, just fourteen miles south of Georgia at the juncture of Florida's panhandle and peninsula. Nearer to Atlanta than Miami, it is "the other Florida" in topography, with its rolling hills; in climate, with four distinct seasons; and in its southern-persona lifestyle. It boasts five "official" canopy roads created by moss-draped giant oaks that are listed among the Top Ten Scenic Byways in America.

In addition to its many natural and historic attractions, Tallahassee is the home of two universities: Florida State and Florida A&M. While both are well-known educational institutions, Florida State is also known nationwide for its sports program and for a unique student show: the FSU Flying High Circus. The first and most prestigious big-top student circus in the country, it has been giving performances for more than fifty years. Florida A&M has also gained an international reputation for its fabulous 100 Marching Band. Both *60 Minutes* and *20/20* call this band the nation's best marching band, and it was the only American group invited to perform at France's Bicentennial Bastille Celebration.

Governors Inn

In discussing Tallahassee lodgings, someone described this inn as "the one with glass, brass, and class." Located just a block from the new state capitol, the inn, which was formerly a warehouse, fits in well with its setting in the delightfully rehabilitated historic section now known as Adams Street Commons. With its prime location it is bustling with politicians, lobbyists— especially when the state legislature is in session—the press, and business travelers, and on weekends it's a favorite of tourists. (Note: In addition to the area's regular high season, it's also busy during the legislature's session and the university football season.)

The original building is more than seventy-five years old and over

the years served as a warehouse and finally as two narrow and deep hardware stores. In 1983, the building was gutted so it could be remodeled into the inn. Fortunately, the renovators kept the exterior walls, the high ceilings, and the massive interior heart-of-pine trusses and beams, for these now add greatly to the ambiance of the place.

To reach most of the guest quarters there is a winding staircase and a walkway that resembles a bridge through a corridor that connects what was once the two old stores. The thirty-two rooms and eight suites are all so different in both size and décor that you may feel that each had its own architect and interior designer. There are many mahogany and brass antique reproductions. Some have sitting rooms on one level and sleeping lofts above, some have skylights, while others have wood-burning fireplaces and Jacuzzi tubs. Appropriately, each room is named after and contains a framed drawing and a brief biography of a former governor.

Be sure to take advantage of the location and take a short stroll down the street to the new high-rise capitol. The twenty-second floor offers what is probably the best panoramic view of the city and, on a clear day, the Gulf of Mexico twenty-five miles away. Also visit the house and senate chambers on the fifth floor. And don't miss the historic old capitol next door.

GOVERNORS INN

Address:	**209 S. Adams Street, Tallahassee 32301**
Phone:	**800/342-7717(FL Only); 850/681-6855**
Fax:	**850/222-3105**
Rates:	**$129 – $229**
Units:	**40**

WAKULLA SPRINGS

Bed tax 10 percent

In 1513 Ponce de Leon thought this was the site of the fountain of youth. In the 1940s movies were filmed here showing Tarzan swinging through the trees and swimming in the springs. Today visitors come for the unspoiled beauty of the area and find it is one of the best getaway places in Florida. Wakulla County is one of the most sparsely settled in the state, with a population of around fifteen thousand.

The primary attraction are the springs themselves, which are reputed to be the largest and deepest freshwater springs in the world. The water is so clear you can see the bottom hundreds of feet below. It flows at a rate of more than six hundred thousand gallons per minute and is the source of the Wakulla River, a nine-mile-long waterway that is home to thousands of birds, mammals, and reptiles.

Wakulla Springs State Park Lodge

In 1937 financier and world traveler Edward Ball built a lodge of quiet elegance in the most serene place he could find—Wakulla Springs. He hired artisans in iron and stone and imported marble and tile to create this unique two-story retreat. The architecture is a blend of Spanish and Moorish with art deco motifs. To his credit Ball bought the land around the springs to make certain the natural state was preserved.

Today the lodge is the centerpiece of the almost six thousand acres in the Edward Ball Wakulla Springs State Park and the only lodge in a Florida state park. Changed only for improvements in comfort and safety, it stands much as it was when first opened, with its red tile roof, stucco exterior, generous archways, and wrought-iron grillwork surrounding windows and doorways, offering visitors a glimpse into Florida's past.

Listed in the National Register of Historic Places, the lodge has twenty-seven spacious guest rooms all comfortably furnished with sitting areas and modern private bathrooms. Many rooms still have their original ornate old-world-style furnishings, including brass beds, dressers with inlaid wood, and some antiques. All the rooms have telephones, but the only television is in the lobby.

Among the items of interest in the impressive lobby are the massive fireplace and designs painted on the ceiling, which is made of deadhead cypress—cypress that had been under water for at least fifty years, making it impervious to rot. Another impressive feature of the lobby is Old Joe. Now in a plexiglass case, Old Joe, an alligator more than eleven feet long and weighing 650 pounds, was a local legend and the source of much folklore. At one end of the lobby is the lodge restaurant and at the other is the gift shop that features an old-time soda fountain that has a seventy-foot marble top.

There are several ways to enjoy the spring waters. The easiest is to go in for a swim. If you're brave, you can just jump into the clear water off the diving tower. For a more sedate view, take one of the glass bottom or jungle boat tours.

WAKULLA SPRINGS STATE PARK LODGE

Address:	550 Wakulla Park Drive, Wakulla Springs 32305
	www.dep.state.fl.us/parks/wakulla/wakulla.html
Phone:	850/224-5950
Fax:	850/561-7251
Rates:	$85 – $280
Units:	27

For Additional Information on the North Central Region

ALACHUA COUNTY CVB
30 East University Avenue
Gainesville, FL 32601
352/374-5231
Fax: 352/338-3213
www.co.alachua.fl.us/acvacb

GAINSVILLE COC
235 S. Main Street
Suite 206
Gainsville, FL 32601
352/334-7100
Fax: 352/334-7141
www.gainsvillechamber.com

QUINCY COC
P.O. Box 389
Quuincy, FL 32353
850/627-9231
Fax: 850/875-3299
www.gadsdencc.com

CEDAR KEY AREA COC
P.O. Box 610
Cedar Key, FL 32625
Phone/fax: 352/543-5600

TALLAHASSEE AREA VISITOR INFORMATION CENTER
106 E. Jefferson Street
Tallahassee, FL 32301
800/628-2866; 850/413-9200
Fax: 850/487-4621
www.co.lean.fl.us/visitors

*High Season: Varies considerably by lodging
but generally is from March through May.*

(Note: All lodging rates are for high season. Off-season rates can be
significantly lower.)

3 NORTHEAST

Bed tax 9 percent

A little over thirteen miles long and two and a half miles wide, this barrier island protects the northeast corner of the state. Amelia Island offers all the pleasurable vacation activities you might want. The waters teem with all kinds of fish. Offshore are the annual calving grounds of right whales, and each summer loggerhead and green turtles (see page 19) come ashore to leave their eggs in the sand. Behind the beach dunes you'll find majestic oaks and palmettos and other lush vegetation providing a home to a diverse population of birds.

Called the Isle of Eight Flags, the island lays claim to being the only place in the United States that has been under eight different flags. Although some were short-lived, the island has been under flags of the French; the Spanish; the British; the American patriots who overthrew the Spanish in 1812 but were diplomatically forced to give the island back; the Green Cross of Florida who overthrew the Spanish again in 1817 but gave it up to the Mexican rebels; the Mexicans; the Confederates; and the United States. The English named it after Princess Amelia, a daughter of King George II.

Addison House Bed & Breakfast

It took awhile for John and Donna Gibson to find the right place to open a bed-and-breakfast. When they lived in the Midwest, mostly Indiana, where John worked in the automotive industry and Donna taught high school science, they spent their vacations for fifteen years looking. The break came when they found out about Amelia Island at an innkeepers conference in San Antonio, Texas. When they finally came to see for themselves, they quickly decided this was the place.

The house they bought was a Victorian built in 1876. It had

always been a single-family home, but they hired a historic architect to convert it to a bed-and-breakfast. They now have five guest rooms in the main house and four each in a connecting cottage and house, all surrounding a small garden courtyard. All the rooms have private baths. Those in the main house have fireplaces and two have whirlpool tubs. Our favorite is the Camellia Room, a large, sunny room on the second floor that has a four-poster bed and a large private porch. All the rooms in the Garden House and Coulter Cottage have whirlpools and either a private porch or access to a porch.

The Gibsons' daughter, Jennifer, is the third innkeeper here. She has a degree in hotel and restaurant administration, and got her practical training as an innkeeper in Nantucket.

ADDISON HOUSE BED & BREAKFAST

Address:	**614 Ash Street, Amelia Island 32034**
	www.addisonhousebb.com
Phone:	**800/943-1604; 904/277-1604**
Fax:	**904/277-8124**
Rates:	**$99 – $165**
Units:	**13**

Amelia Island Plantation

Environmentally sensitive are not just buzz words here. They are part of the master plan and a way of life on this 1,350-acre resort and residential community on the southern end of the island. The result of that plan is a resort that offers guests a setting of abundant lush vegetation among palms and ancient oak trees, three and a half miles of uncrowded, shell-strewn Atlantic beach, high protective sand dunes, and an abundance of birds and wildlife.

As proof that man and nature can coexist beautifully, this natural setting is a resort with all the trimmings. That includes fifty-four holes of golf and a golf school that *Golf* magazine named one of the twelve best golf resorts in America. (On the environmental side, even the golf courses have won certification as an "Audubon Cooperative Sanctuary.") Not to be outdone by the accolades for the links, its Racquet Park's twenty-three Har-Tru tennis courts and tennis program have won it recognition as one of the top fifty tennis resorts by *Tennis* magazine. In addition, there are twenty-three swimming pools, a health and fitness center, more than seven miles of bike and nature trails, horseback riding, and nature tours with an on-site naturalist. If you want to fish, you have a choice of freshwater in on-property lagoons stocked with bream, bass, and catfish, or the staff can make arrangements for charter deep-sea and back-country fishing.

The resort was also voted Best Family Beach Resort of the Year by readers of *Family Circle* magazine. Kids Camp Amelia offers supervised activities for children from three to ten years old. Amelia Explorers provides activities designed for eleven to fourteen year olds, and Teen Adventures for youths aged fifteen to nineteen years old.

Lodging opportunities are as varied as the activities. There are a variety of hotel rooms or one- to three-bedroom villas with either ocean or resort views. The 249 rooms in the Amelia Inn and Beach Club, for example, all have ocean views.

AMELIA ISLAND PLANTATION

Address:	**3000 First Coast Highway, Amelia Island 32034**
	www.aipfl.com
Phone:	**800/874-6878; 904/277-6161**
Fax:	**904/277-5945**
Rates:	**$130 - $705**
Units:	**1,000+**

Amelia Island Williams House

Built in 1856 by a banker from Boston, this antebellum mansion was bought by Marcellus Williams in 1859. His wife was related to the Spanish royal family, which attracted royal visitors and other important figures such as Jefferson Davis, president of the Confederate States of America. Davis even stored some of his personal effects here during the Civil War. It's doubtful, however, that he would have been pleased if he knew that, during that war, Marcellus freed his slaves, and the house was used as a station on the underground railway for runaway slaves. The secret room used to hide the slaves is still in the house today. As a result, the house is a treasure trove of history recognized by the National Register of Historic Places, and the state of Florida has listed it as a Heritage Landmark Site. Perhaps more pertinent, from a guest's point of view, is that it frequently has been listed as one of the top inns in the country.

The Williams family lived in the house for a hundred years. Once they left, it was neglected and fell into a deplorable state. After partners

Richard Flitz and Chris Carter bought it in 1993, they not only restored it to its original splendor, but enhanced both its appearance and its historical significance by decorating it with Richard's large collection of antiques and collectibles from around the world. Many of these are museum quality, such as the prints and paintings commissioned by the Japanese imperial family in the 1500s. Over the piano in the downstairs parlor hangs a robe worn by the last emperor of China, and a rug given to one of Richard's distant relatives by Napoleon hangs on the wall in the upstairs hall.

Flitz and Carter also bought and restored the 1859 Hearthstone House next door and connected the two, so together they offer eight guest rooms and both a downstairs and upstairs verandah. Each of the rooms is decorated with period antiques in its own distinctive style. If you like the color blue, for example, the Chinese Blue Room is for you. This large room has a king-size solid cherry bedroom suite, a love seat in a large bay window, and four oriental rugs, all decorated in calming shades of blue. For an entirely different décor, the Camelot Room, featuring a bay window and seat, has an English wrought-iron bed with a mushroomed canopy. The bathroom contains the original built-in armoire, and this room also has a private verandah and a private four-person hot tub.

AMELIA ISLAND WILLIAMS HOUSE

Address:	**103 S. Ninth Street, Fernandina Beach 32034**
	www.williamshouse.com
Phone:	**800/414-9257; 904/277-2328**
Fax:	**904/321-1325**
Rates:	**$175 – $225**
Units:	**8**

Bailey House Bed & Breakfast

According to local oral history, Effingham W. Bailey looked at his budget when he offered his bride, Kate, a choice for the home he was going to have built for them. She could either have a small house and all the furniture she needed, or a mansion with a minimum of furniture.

As soon as you see the Bailey House you'll know her choice. So, in 1895, Effingham had what is now this historic Queen Anne Victorian built

with heart-of-pine floors, a grand staircase, ten fireplaces, stained glass windows, pocket doors, and turrets. He hired local boat builders and ship carpenters to do the work, and the precision of their construction is still evident today. Also still evident is the large oak tree in front of the house on an island in the middle of Ash Street. The city wanted to cut it down so they could pave the road, but Kate Bailey fought them. According to legend when they sent the crew to cut it down, she stopped them, not with words but with a shotgun. The Bailey family occupied the house for almost seventy years. Their history can be traced in the family Bible on display in the entry hall.

Tom and Jenny Bishop were living in Jacksonville, where Tom worked in real estate. They bought this house, which is listed in the National Register of Historic Places, in 1993 in order to fulfill Jenny's dream of having a historic house bed-and-breakfast. It already was a bed-and-breakfast—in fact, the first bed-and-breakfast in town—but had only four guest rooms. Since then they have made additions and now offer guests nine rooms and a carriage house suite.

The overall décor is Victorian—eclectic Victorian. It includes furnishings and antiques from the American, Italian, and French Victorian periods. One of our favorites is the French Garden Room with its antique French country bedroom suite, oriental carpet, a working fireplace, and a two-person whirlpool tub with a separate shower.

BAILEY HOUSE BED & BREAKFAST

Address:	**P.O. Box 805, Ferdinandina Beach 32035**
	www.bailey-house.com
Phone:	**800/251-5390; 904/261-5390**
Fax:	**904/321-0103**
Rates:	**$95 – $140**
Units:	**10**

Elizabeth Pointe Lodge

Two old sayings come to mind when we think of this lodge: "Looks are deceiving" and "Practice what you preach."

The deception, and it's a beautifully executed one, is that this looks like a large 1890s shingle-sided Victorian beach house transplanted from Nantucket. And while Tim Duke, the assistant innkeeper, says he sometimes makes up wild stories about the lodge's early history to amuse guests, he always admits that the main building was deliberately designed and built in that style in 1991 by Susan and David Caples.

The Caples do practice what they preach. Their lodge is an outstanding example of how to do it right for the many potential innkeepers who attend their three-day seminars titled, "How to Acquire and Start Up a Bed-and-Breakfast." They have been providing consulting and educational services to the bed-and-breakfast industry for more than twenty years. No surprise that they are now known as the innkeepers' gurus.

David and Susan both had solid hotel experience before they came to

Amelia Island. Their first venture was the 1735 House, a small bed-and-breakfast that they restored, ran successfully, and eventually sold to open this lodge.

Their meticulous attention to detail resulted in a comfortable, guest-friendly inn with twenty-five rooms and suites ideally located on an uncrowded ocean beach. Although all the rooms are different, they all have an oversized tub, some with Jacuzzi jets, and decorations with a strong maritime flavor. There are twenty rooms and suites and a lounge with a stone fireplace in the main house. Outside is a large wraparound porch where you can sit 'n' rock. If you're an early riser, this is a great place to watch the sunrise over the water. Four larger sitting rooms are available in the adjoining Harris Lodge. Another option, a fine choice for a family or two couples, is the two-bedroom, two-bath Miller Cottage.

The lodge is named after Beth Ann, one of the Caples' daughters. For families, small groups, or honeymooners who want seclusion, they also have Katie's Light, named after their other daughter. Located nearby, this is a replica of a Chesapeake Bay Lighthouse that appeared in the movie *Pippi Longstocking*. A beachfront house, it has three bedrooms, two and a half baths, and a deck that extends from the beach all the way around the house.

ELIZABETH POINTE LODGE

Address:	**P.O. Box 1210, Amelia Island 32034**
	www.elizabethpointelodge.com
Phone:	**800/772-3359; 904/277-4851**
Fax:	**904/277-6500**
Rates:	**$150 - $245**
Units:	**25**

Fairbanks House Bed & Breakfast

Today, we would probably call George R. Fairbanks an overachiever. Among other callings, he was a historian, a major in the Civil War, a citrus producer, a state senator, and a newspaper editor. And the home he built in 1885 was much like him. A four-story, Italianate- style mansion with a fifteen-foot tower, it had such innovations as a telephone and indoor running water. It also had ten fireplaces, two with English tiles depicting scenes from Shakespeare's plays and Aesop's fables.

This turned out to be just what Bill and Theresa Hamilton were looking for when, in 1997, they decided to leave their businesses in

Baltimore and carry out their long-term plan to become innkeepers. "We wanted warm weather, water, and a friendly small town where we could walk to the shops. We didn't even know where Amelia Island was, but when we saw this house we knew it had everything on our checklist."

There are nine rooms and suites in the main house, which is listed on the National Register of Historic Places, and an additional three rooms in two cottages out back. The most intriguing room is the tower suite. It has two bedrooms furnished with iron beds and antiques, a bath with a Jacuzzi tub and shower, a large living room, and a sitting room. And then there are the stairs to the tower room where you can see long distances in every direction.

On the other hand, Room 3 on the first floor is a bright, large, comfortable suite furnished with antiques, oriental rugs, and period pieces; it also features a Jacuzzi with a separate shower, a private entrance, and a private porch overlooking the swimming pool.

FAIRBANKS HOUSE BED & BREAKFAST

Address:	**277 S. Seventh Street, Amelia Island 32034**
	www.fairbankshouse.com
Phone:	**800/261-4838; 904/277-0500**
Fax:	**904/277-3103**
Rates:	**$150 – $250**
Units:	**12**

Florida House Inn Bed & Breakfast

The Florida House is listed in the National Register of Historic Places as the oldest operating tourist hotel in Florida. Built in 1857 by the Florida Railroad, it hosted such notables as President Ulysses S. Grant, who gave a speech from the balcony (you can sit 'n' rock there now); some members of the Carnegie and Rockefeller families, who frequently came here to eat; and a number of silent film stars. Perhaps its most important long-term guest was Jose Marti, the Cuban hero of Cuba's second war of independence against the Spanish. Marti is internationally recognized. There is a statue of him in New York's Central Park, another in a square named for him in Paris, and today Radio Marti is the name of the U.S. broadcast to keep the Cuban people informed of what's going on both inside and outside Castro's regime.

By the late 1980s the hotel had become a cheap boarding house, a derelict that the city planned to tear down. Karen and Bob Warner rescued it, spent a year rehabing it ("In some places we scraped off twenty-eight coats of paint," Bob recalls), and had the grand opening of their restored bed-and-breakfast in 1990. It was truly a GRAND opening because it was just in time for Fernandina Beach's annual Shrimp Festival.

Of the twenty-five rooms in the original hotel, eleven remain. All the rooms were enlarged, have baths—some with Jacuzzi tubs—and working fireplaces. Each room is furnished with antiques, or period reproductions, and handmade quilts. These original historic rooms are joined by four rooms added in what's called Tree House Row, overlooking the courtyard and shaded by a 250-year-old giant oak. The new rooms all have two-person Jacuzzi tubs, wood-burning fieldstone fireplaces, and are individually decorated with outdoor themes.

The inn's restaurant, is extremely popular with the locals. Where else can you find a place that serves all-you-can-eat, hearty country-style meals (no menu), boarding-house style on long, oilcloth-covered tables seating twelve, at unbelievably reasonable prices? The inn also has an English-style pub.

Fittingly, the oldest active tourist hotel in Florida is downtown just a short walk from the Palace Saloon, the oldest bar in the state still in the same location.

FLORIDA HOUSE INN BED & BREAKFAST

Address:	P.O. Box 688, Amelia Island 32034
	www.floridahouse.com
Phone:	800/258-3301; 904/261-3300
Fax:	904/277-3831
Rates:	$65 – $159
Units:	15

Hoyt House Bed & Breakfast

There are more giraffes scattered throughout this house than in all the zoos in the United States—hundreds of them are in the stately parlor alone. They range from miniature ones to one that is six feet tall. They are all part of Rita Kovacevich's ceramic collection that looks quite at home in this comfortable Queen Anne Victorian.

Rita started her collection while she and her husband, John, were running businesses in Connecticut and thinking of owning a bed-and-breakfast. They found this house for sale by accident, while visiting a friend on the island. Originally built as a banker's family home in 1905, it was then a lawyer's office. They bought it and spent six months converting the original five rooms. Then they added five more guest rooms and private baths to all the rooms. The inn opened in 1993.

Fred Willis Hoyt, the original owner, was a native of New Hampshire, which may explains some of the interesting architectural features in this house that seem more suited to a colder climate. The "Yankee doors," for example, are double doors separated by a small entranceway to provide extra insulation from the cold. The house also has seven fireplaces, all with intricately carved mantels framed by colorful tiles.

One of the most popular rooms with guests is the Lavender Suite. Once the original owner's room, it's the largest room in the house, furnished with a four-poster rice bed, a wing chair, an inlaid-wood secretary, a settee and a selection of antiques. It also has a fireplace and a separate dressing area.

Other features of the house are a wraparound porch with a glider and porch swing, and a gazebo that is a popular spot for weddings. One room is devoted to Rita's antique shop.

HOYT HOUSE BED & BREAKFAST

Address:	804 Atlantic Avenue, Amelia Island 32034
	www.hoythouse.com
Phone:	800/432-2085; 904/277-4300
Fax:	904/277-9626
Rates:	$114 – $159
Units:	10

Ritz-Carlton Amelia Island

Too often when we check out a hotel we find that their restaurant serves mediocre food to a virtually captive audience. Not this time. This hotel's Grill Room is one of only three restaurants in the state that have earned AAA's top rating of Five Diamonds.

Want to get behind the scenes to know why? Make a reservation for dinner at "A Seat in the Kitchen." You (and only three others) will literally be seated at a table set up in a small room in the kitchen where you can watch through a picture window while you interact with the chefs and

dine on five courses paired with selected wines. This might be one of the most expensive dinners you've ever had, but it also will be a culinary experience. If you are truly a culinary aficionado, you can also enroll in the Ritz-Carlton's cooking school, held for two days each month.

This restaurant, of course, is just one of the many examples of the excellent facilities at this hotel. In addition to the Grill Room, there are two other restaurants, an eighteen-hole golf course, a nine-court oceanside tennis complex, an indoor lap pool, an outdoor pool and whirlpool, and a fitness center and day spa. For children, there is the Ritz Kids program of well-planned and well-supervised activities. And of course, we can't forget the beach, with white sand that goes on and on. (May through September is turtle-hatching season on the beach.)

Its 404 rooms and forty-five suites all have either a balcony or patio with an ocean or coastal view. And this is one of those cases where it would pay to get a room on the concierge floor. For just a few dollars more, you can stay on this private Ritz-Carlton Club floor with special amenities including a private lounge, five complimentary food-and-beverage presentations throughout the day, and the personal services of a concierge.

More than a million dollars worth of museum-quality art and furnishings are located throughout the hotel. If you want to check them out, the concierge will lend you a self-tour guide. In spite of the luxurious surroundings and attentive staff, the ambiance is casual. After all, it is a beach hotel.

RITZ-CARLTON AMELIA ISLAND

Address:	4750 Amelia Island Parkway, Amelia Island 32034
	www.ritzcarlton.com
Phone:	800/241-3333; 904/277-1100
Fax:	904/261-9063
Rates:	$249 – $1,500
Units:	449

CRESCENT CITY

Bed tax 8 percent

The older section of the city sits in a grove of live oak trees on a narrow neck of land between Crescent Lake and the smaller Lake Stella. In the late 1800s it was the center of one of the state's major citrus-growing areas. The citrus was shipped out on steamers that brought back tourists, including wealthy northerners who built their winter homes here. The evidence of this "Golden Age of Tourism" can be seen in the number of homes in the historic downtown area that reflect the Victorian architecture of that time. A series of freezes forced most of the citrus growers to move south, and by the early 1900s the area's primary cash crop changed to ferns.

Sprague House Inn

Built in 1892, this is the one remaining inn from the city's "Golden Age." When the great freeze of 1895 destroyed the local citrus industry, the owner went bankrupt. Katie Sprague, the wife of the city's first mayor, bought it and continued to operate it for a number of years. Many famous people stayed here, including Theodore Roosevelt and William Howard Taft.

Because Crescent City is not in today's general tourist flow, it is relatively undiscovered. The town retains its charming atmosphere, and this inn fits in perfectly. Its architecture is classic Steamboat Gothic adorned with gingerbread accents and deep wraparound porches offering lake views. One of the features of the house is the number of stained glass windows installed by previous owners who were glass crafters.

The six rooms and suites are all on the second floor. Among the most popular of these with repeat visitors is the DeLuxe Suite with its exposed cypress beams in a vaulted ceiling, skylights, and several stained glass windows. Furnishings include a four-poster bed. There is a separate sitting room, a dining area, and French doors that open onto a private balcony with lake views. The large bathroom also has stained glass windows and an extra large his-and-her shower.

Downstairs, Terry Moyer, the innkeeper, operates a popular restaurant that is open to the public for lunch and dinner. An antique shop shares the ground floor with the restaurant.

Bikes are available to explore the town. With the lake less than a block away, you can also rent boats for pleasure or fishing. There is excellent crappie, bass, bream, and catfish fishing on the lake, and fishing guides are available upon request.

SPRAGUE HOUSE INN

Address:	**125 Central Avenue, Crescent City 32212**
Phone:	**904/698-2430**
Rates:	**$50 – $115**
Units:	**6**

FLAGLER BEACH

Bed tax 9 percent

Although developers are moving in, Flagler Beach is not fully discovered yet. About six miles long and only a few blocks wide, it still has an aura of a Florida beach town of fifty years ago. Perhaps this is because, although it is named after Henry Flagler whose railroad was a prime instrument in the development of this part of the state, in its early years his railroad never came here.

Topaz Motel/Hotel

As the "motel/hotel" in its name implies, these beachside accommodations definitely have a split personality. Built as a family mansion in 1926, the structure has gone though several lives as an inn, a coast guard station during World War II, apartments, and now a motel/hotel.

The majority of the rooms and efficiencies are in the motel sections that flank the original hotel. With all the standard motel conveniences, they are more than adequate for a beach vacation, but are generally indistinguishable from hundreds of other motel rooms that line the coast. The motel rooms are all oceanfront. The Topaz also has a swimming pool and a restaurant.

Then there's the hotel section. Ah, this is something different! First, there's the lobby/parlor, which resembles a small museum with display cases filled with everything from a Shirley Temple doll and toys from the 1920s and '30s to a letter signed by President Grover Cleveland. There are eleven hotel rooms, all decorated with a Victorian or 1920s flair and housing other antique and collectible treasures from the family's collection. Several hotel rooms have a balcony with an ocean view and some have hot tubs.

TOPAZ MOTEL/HOTEL

Address:	1224 S. Ocean Shore Blvd. (AIA), Flagler Beach 32136
Phone:	800/555-4735; 904/439-3301
Fax:	904/439-3942
Rates:	$62 – $106
Units:	58

JACKSONVILLE

Bed tax 12.5 percent

Jacksonville is located on the St. Johns River, which is the longest river in Florida (310 miles long) as well as one of the few rivers in the United States that flows north. The city's location on this river makes it a major seaport as well as one of the more important business centers in northern Florida.

In 1820, after centuries of trading hands between the French, British, and Spanish, Florida became part of the United States, and a tiny settlement was started at a cattle crossing on the St. Johns River. Originally called Cowford, it was later renamed Jacksonville after General Andrew Jackson, hero of the Seminole Wars. Covering 844 square miles, Jacksonville today is the fifteenth-largest city in the United States and the largest city in land area in the forty-eight contiguous states.

Hilton Jacksonville Riverfront

Since this Hilton is located on the south side of the river, from a river view room balcony you can look across the river at the Jacksonville Landing— a downtown riverfront marketplace with over fifty shops, restaurants, and entertainment spots. You can also watch the water taxis ferrying people to the marketplace and other points of interest. If you are there at the right time, you'll see the fascinating process by which the huge center span of the Main Street Bridge draws up to let ships pass under it. This happens every day at noon and sporadically on most days, depending on the port traffic. Also from your river view balcony you can look down at *The Jacksonville Princess,* the hotel's yacht that is available for weekend sunset dinner and Sunday brunch cruises.

The hotel has 263 rooms and twenty-nine suites, all with balconies. More than half of the rooms have river views and the rest have views of the city. Facilities include an outdoor swimming pool, a fitness center, a complimentary business center, a bar, a Ruth's Chris Steakhouse, and a hotel restaurant. The hotel is within easy walking distance of the Skyway Riverplace Station and the Museum of Science and History. This is another hotel where it may be worth paying the difference for the club floor.

HILTON JACKSONVILLE RIVERFRONT

Address:	1201 Riverplace Boulevard, Jacksonville 32207
	www.jacksonvillehilton.com
Phone:	800/HILTONS (445-8667); 904/398-8800
Fax:	904/398-9170
Rates:	$89 – $460
Units:	292

House on Cherry Street

In 1901, after a great fire destroyed more than twenty-four hundred buildings in downtown Jacksonville, a number of wealthy merchants, bankers, and professionals decided to seek a less congested area to live that was still convenient to downtown. They soon discovered that the old plantation lands along the St. Johns River west of town were ideal, so they built their stately homes and mansions there.

This is one of those stately homes, located on a cul-de-sac at the quiet end of a tree-lined street. It was built in 1909, but on a lot away from the river. Ten years later it was cut into two pieces and moved to its present location at the end of Cherry Street where guests can now sit 'n' rock on the screened back porch and look out over the shaded green lawn that gently slopes down to the river.

Three of the four rooms in this three-story Georgian Colonial style home have water views. All are furnished with owner Carol Anderson's

collection of period antiques, including canopy beds and oriental rugs, and all four have a comfortable sitting area. On a more whimsical note, scattered throughout the house is a collection of about four hundred duck decoys and dozens of other duck representations in every form. If you want to go out on the river at your doorstep, Carol has a canoe and a kayak for guests.

When not actively running this charming bed-and-breakfast, Carol is a tennis official who has been the chairman of all tennis officials in Florida and is still the chief umpire at Amelia Island tournaments.

HOUSE ON CHERRY STREET

Address:	**1844 Cherry Street, Jacksonville 32205**
	www.1bbweb.com/cherry
Phone:	**904/384-1999**
Fax:	**904/384-5013**
Rates:	**$85 – $105**
Units:	**4**

Plantation Manor Inn

For a number of years, Jerry Ray bought old homes, then restored and sold them while his wife, Kathy, worked for an insurance company. Finally they

decided they wanted to spend more time together, and since they'd always enjoyed staying in bed-and-breakfasts, they thought that would be the way to go. Jerry bought a condemned three-story mansion that was built in 1905 on a corner lot in the historic Riverside District. His original plan was to turn it into offices, but they changed that plan to make this their bed-and-breakfast. It took just a year to rehabilitate the outside and three years to finish the rest. With its massive Doric columns at the entrance and wrap-around porches on both floors, it definitely looks like a grand manor house.

The nine guest rooms are all attractively decorated with a mix of antiques, carefully selected reproductions, and some contemporary pieces. All the rooms have a private bath, and some have canopy beds. One of our favorites is Room 1, which is a large corner room upstairs. It has both a fireplace and an especially large bathroom. Several of the rooms have a fifty-two-inch television that are so well placed they fit in without disturbing the plantation manor house décor.

Outside is a colorful secluded garden with a lap pool and hot tub. The house sits behind a gated fence with guest parking inside the gate. In addition to the comfortable and cozy surroundings, this extra security is perhaps one of the reasons the Rays find that many of their repeat guests are women who come to town on business. This includes some women celebrities who look at this as a snug getaway to ensure privacy.

PLANTATION MANOR INN

Address:	**1630 Copeland Street, Jacksonville 32204**
	www.plantationmanorinn.com
Phone:	**904/384-4630**
Fax:	**904/387-0960**
Rates:	**$120 – 175**
Units:	**9**

ORANGE PARK

Bed tax 10 percent

Club Continental Bed & Breakfast

In the 1880s, Palm Beach and Miami had not yet become popular winter resorts, but pleasure boats cruised the St. Johns River. B. J. Johnson, who owned the Johnson Soap Company, came on one of those cruises and decided this would be a good place for his family to get away from the Wisconsin winters. For years, the family wintered here in a leased country home. Then, in 1906 one of Johnson's daughters bought a waterfront estate and named it Winterbourne. In the meantime, the Johnson Soap Company had grown into the Palmolive Soap empire.

Winterbourne, which is listed in the National Register of Historic Places, is still in the family as part of a lovely complex of Mediterranean-style buildings on the secluded thirty-acre estate on the river that makes up the Club Continental resort run by Johnson's heirs. Today Winterbourne is used mostly for weddings and parties and its four housekeeping suites are generally reserved for guests staying a week or more. The two other club buildings are a 1920's mansion, called Mira Rio, and the Riverside suites.

Although the Mira Rio is now the clubhouse and restaurant for club members, its six guest rooms and suites and one apartment are a bed-and-breakfast. The downstairs décor features baronial chandeliers, tapestries, and huge carved fireplaces. The upstairs rooms are all themed and each was designed by a different decorator. The decorators were given a free hand, except they all had the same budget and they had to furnish the rooms from the extensive collection of furniture and antiques accumulated by the family in its world travels. Most of the rooms look like film sets and the themes are clear from their names, like the French Room, the Mexican Room, and the English Room. The Tower Apartment on the third floor was originally the servants' quarters. It has a full kitchen and a large balcony with a river view.

The Riverside suites were built in 1992 in the same Mediterranean style as the mansion. True to its name, all fifteen rooms have a balcony with a river view and, while more modern in décor, each has its own distinct style, some with Jacuzzis and fireplaces.

Rounding out the resort are lush gardens, three swimming pools, seven tennis courts, an eighty-five-slip marina, and a pre-Civil War cottage moved to the property and converted to a pub.

CLUB CONTINENTAL BED & BREAKFAST

Address:	**P.O. Box 7059, Orange Park 32073**
	www.bbonline.com/fl/clubcontinental
Phone:	**800/877-6070; 904/264-6070**
Fax:	**904/264-4044**
Rates:	**$99 – $145**
Units:	**22**

PONTE VEDRA BEACH

Bed tax 9 percent

Ponte Vedra Inn & Club/
Ponte Vedra Lodge & Club

These two resorts, about a mile and a half apart, are owned by the same company. Transportation is available between them, and guests at either can use the facilities of both. The larger of the two is the Inn and Club. Started in 1928 as a single cottage, it's now a three hundred-acre ocean-front resort with a campus-style layout of 160 rooms and forty suites in nine low-rise buildings. In all the buildings most of the rooms and suites offer a private patio or balcony, and some of them have kitchenettes.

In addition to the palm-fringed white sandy beach the resort also offers two eighteen-hole golf courses, and its fifteen-court Racquet Club has been rated one of the top five greatest tennis resorts in the U.S. by *Tennis* magazine. Other facilities include a well-equipped gym and oceanfront pools: a lap pool, an Olympic-size pool, an adults-only pool, and a children's wading pool. From June through August, there is a summer camp for four to twelve year olds and the rest of the year the Recreation Department conducts numerous activities for children.

Deep-sea fishing and charter boats can be arranged. Or, on a smaller scale, you can fish or boat in more than four miles of lagoons. If you want to just cool it on the lagoons, a fleet of pedal boats are available.

The full-service spa, offering more than a hundred different personal and pampering services for both women and men, is popular enough to have its own ten-thousand-square-foot building, including a private garden oasis with a cascading waterfall and an oversized Jacuzzi.

The club also offers the Mayo Ponte Vedra Seaside Program in conjunction with the nearby branch of the world-renowned Mayo Clinic. Guests check into the inn, get an in-depth checkup at the clinic and receive fitness guidelines that can be carried out in conjunction with the staff at the inn's gym, restaurants, and other facilities.

If you want a more boutique hotel on the beach, the Lodge and Club, just down the road, has just forty-two rooms and twenty-four suites, all with ocean views. All the suites have gas fireplaces and Jacuzzi tubs. Its fountain courtyard, classic archways, Spanish tile roofs, ornamental turrets, trellises, and balconies all combine to make it a romantic setting.

PONTE VEDRA INN & CLUB

Address:	200 Ponte Vedra Boulevard, Ponte Verde Beach 32082
Phone:	800/234-7842 ; 904/285-1111
Fax:	904/285-2111
Rates:	$200–$395
Units:	200

PONTE VEDRA LODGE & CLUB

Address:	607 Ponte Vedra Boulevard, Ponte Vedra Beach 32082 www.pvresorts.com
Phone:	800/243-4304; 904/273-9500
Fax:	904/273-0210
Rates:	$230 – $250
Units:	66

Sawgrass Marriott Resort

The name of the game at this forty-eight-hundred-acre resort is golf, golf, GOLF!

The nation's second largest golf resort, it offers ninety-nine holes on five courses, including the famous 6,857-yard TPC Stadium course, home of The Players Championship. And you won't have to scurry around trying to get a tee time at any one since the golf shop makes tee times for all of them. By the way, No. 17 of the Stadium—the famous par-three Island hole—is reportedly one of the most photographed holes in the world. They even have

an eighteen-hole miniature golf course that is a replica of the Stadium course.

Although golf is king here, it is not the only sport you can play at this sports-oriented resort. Tennis comes in a close second with eight clay courts at the resort and eleven at the ATP (Association of Tennis Professionals) International Tour Headquarters, home of the men's professional tennis tour and the ATP University. This complex includes two grass courts, seven cushioned hard courts, and two European red clay courts.

Golf. Tennis. What else?

Well, there's two and a half miles of white sandy Atlantic beach, three swimming pools, two kiddie wading pools, two health clubs, jogging and walking trails, and bike rentals. The staff can also make arrangements for deep- sea fishing, sailing, horseback riding, and, if all these strenuous sports cause some stiff muscles, massage and spa services are available.

Naturally, there are a number of restaurants ranging from fine dining to a pizza place, including a poolside one that carries on a golf club tradition of the nineteenth hole, except this one is appropriately called the Hundredth Hole.

You have a choice of lodgings. The resort hotel offers 324 rooms and twenty-four suites, about half with golf course views and all with a view of one of the fifteen acres of alligator-inhabited lagoons that surround the hotel. Serpentine shaped, the hotel is encased in emerald glass, has a seventy-foot atrium with a view of the thirteenth hole on the Stadium Course, plus cascading waterfalls both inside and out. Or you can choose one of the villas that offer eighty suites and eighty guest rooms that can be combined to make two-bedroom suites. (It only costs about fifty dollars to upgrade from a villa room to a suite.)

During the summer, the resort has the Grasshopper Gang children's program, providing supervised fun for kids ages three to twelve.

SAWGRASS MARRIOTT RESORT

Address:	**1000 PGA Tour Boulevard, Ponte Vedra Beach 32082**
	www.marriott.com/marriott/jaxsw
Phone:	**800/457-GOLF (457-4653)**
Fax:	**904/285-0906**
Rates:	**$125 – $700**
Units:	**508**

ST. AUGUSTINE

Bed tax 9 percent

In 1513 Juan Ponce de Leon claimed La Florida, named after the many flowers, for Spain. However, it was the French in 1562 who were the first to establish a colony in this area. This infuriated the Spanish king who, three years later, sent Don Pedro Menendez de Aviles, an experienced admiral, with about a thousand settlers to drive out the French and start a Spanish colony. Since he first landed on the Feast of St. Augustine, he named the colony *San Augustin.*

For more than four centuries, the town was alternately destroyed and rebuilt, surviving pirate raids, wars, hurricanes, fire, and epidemics. During those years, Florida changed hands among the European powers several times.

Henry Flagler, one of the founders of the Standard Oil Company, came to St. Augustine in 1883 and decided this was a tropical paradise he could develop as a winter resort for his wealthy friends. And develop he did, not just St. Augustine, but all the way down the coast, bringing the tourism industry to the state—an industry that has made Florida the nation's number one winter vacation destination.

Fortunately, some early city fathers were wise enough to recognize the historic treasure they had. In Old Town itself there are 144 blocks of restored and preserved historic structures, many of them listed in the

National Register of Historic Places. (With the exception of the World Golf Village, all the irresistible lodgings listed in St. Augustine are in the historic Old Town.) Although a little spread out, the Old Town is basically a walking city, which is good since streets are narrow and parking is at a premium.

As one might expect with a city this old, there are so many tales of ghosts that there's a nightly Old Town ghost tour. One other interesting historic tidbit about this city is that although oranges are one of Florida's most important cash crops, the orange is not native to the state. The Spanish brought oranges with them, planting the first groves here in St. Augustine in the late 1500s.

Carriage Way Bed & Breakfast

As we walked up to the front of this bed-and-breakfast, we could just see ourselves sitting and rocking on the front porch or the upstairs verandah. A vernacular Victorian, it looks as homey as when it was built as a family home for Edward and Rosalie Masters in the mid 1880s. Today it is run by a father and son, Bill and Larry Johnson, who offer guests a choice of nine rooms in the main house and two bedrooms in a cottage a few doors down the street. All rooms have a private bath.

The rooms are named after former owners of the house and furnished with antiques and reproductions. The Masters Room, for example, is a large upstairs room with floor-to-ceiling windows, a four-poster oak bed, and a Ben Franklin stove. The Elizabeth Gould Room, also upstairs, is in the back of the house and has its own hallway so it's very quiet. This room is bright, has a four-poster mahogany bed, a cathedral ceiling with two skylights, and a large bathroom with a double wide shower.

The Cottage, also built in the mid-1880s, has two bedrooms, two baths (one with a whirlpool), a common living room, and a kitchenette. You can rent one bedroom or, for a small family or two couples, the entire cottage for under three hundred dollars.

CARRIAGE WAY BED & BREAKFAST

Address:	**70 Cuna Street, St. Augustine 32084**
	www.carriageway.com
Phone:	**800/908-9832; 904/829-2467**
Fax:	**904/826-1461**
Rates:	**$89 – $175**
Units:	**11**

Casa de Solana Bed & Breakfast

Don Manuel Solana, a Spanish military official, built this elegant house of sturdy coquina bricks in 1763, just in time to be ordered out of St. Augustine as Florida was turned over to the British in exchange for Havana. Today, his house is as sturdy as when he built it and as lovely. It was restored and eclectically decorated by Faye and Jim McMurry, making it even more striking and elegant.

In typical Old Spanish style, the two-story house and its garden are enclosed by a thick, high wall with a small entryway on the narrow cobblestone Aviles Street. Since it is the seventh oldest house in town, as well as one of the most attractive, it is a lure for both history buffs and tourists. So much so that, while we were visiting, several stepped through the entryway into the private garden to take photos of it.

It was the mayor's house when the McMurrys bought it in 1983 and turned it into a bed-and-breakfast. Now guests have a choice of four suites, each named for a period in the house's history: British, Minorcan (Spanish), Colonial, and Confederacy. Some have fireplaces, others have balconies overlooking the garden or Matanzas Bay. All are decorated with fine antiques, family heirlooms, and oriental rugs, and all have private baths and sitting rooms.

CASA DE SOLANA BED & BREAKFAST

Address:	21 Aviles Street, St. Augustine 32084
	www.oldcity.com/solana
Phone:	904/824-3555
Fax:	904/824-3316
Rates:	$125 – $145
Units:	4

Casa de Sueños Bed & Breakfast

It's called the House of Dreams because it was Sandy and Ray Tool's longtime dream to open a bed-and-breakfast. Sandy was a creator of gourmet cuisine for nationally known restaurants, and Ray was a chemist. Tired of being separated due to their work, they wanted to do something together and this was it.

The house was built in 1904 by James Colee, a friend and surveyor to oil baron Henry Flagler. At that time it was a plain, story-and-a-half clapboard. About twenty years later, it was transformed into its present Mediterranean style by Pantalina Carcaba. Carcaba emigrated from Spain to Cuba and then to the United States where he opened cigar factories in New York and Cincinnati and eventually founded one in St. Augustine. The cigar business was good, and he wanted his home to reflect his wealth and position. So, he completely redid the home, furnishing it with antiques and chandeliers. The Tools bought the house in the mid-1990s, and have carried on the tradition of elegance set by the Carcabas.

The inn has four guest rooms and two suites, four with whirlpool baths. All are named after streets in St. Augustine, which, of course, were named after cities in Spain. One of the more popular, especially for honeymoons and anniversaries, is the Cordova Suite. It features a large wrought-iron bed with a heart-shaped headboard, a cherry dresser with a marble top, and a number of antiques, plus an enclosed balcony with a whirlpool.

Weddings and honeymoons are a big thing in the House of Dreams. In the hallway leading to the dining room is a photo gallery of five generations of Tool family pictures starting with Ray's great-grandparents in 1879 and spanning well over a hundred years. In keeping with that tradition, Ray, who is a notary, has performed more than sixty weddings in the house, and there has been a honeymoon couple in the house almost every weekend since they opened it.

CASA DE SUEÑOS BED & BREAKFAST

Address:	20 Cordova Street, St. Augustine 32084
	www.casadesuenos.com
Phone:	800/824-0804; 904/824-0887
Fax:	904/825-0074
Rates:	$95 – $180
Units:	6

Casa Monica Hotel

If early Florida developer extraordinaire Henry Flagler could see the latest rebirth of this hotel, he would undoubtedly be mighty pleased. The Casa Monica was first opened in 1888 and sold to Flagler three months after its opening. Flagler already had two other grand hotels within a block of this hotel, the Ponce de Leon and the Alcazar. He renamed this one the Hotel Cordova, and the triumvirate soon had a guest list that included kings,

presidents, lords of industry, famous authors and artists, and Broadway stars.

As with most old hotels, once its golden days were over, it went downhill and was forced to close during the Depression. This one lay dormant from 1932 until the mid-1960s when it was converted and served for a time as the St. John's County Courthouse. (The two other Flagler hotels of the time were also converted: the Ponce de Leon is now the Ponce de Leon Hall of Flagler College, and the Alcazar is the Lightner Museum.)

In 1997 Richard Kessler bought it to add to his growing portfolio of Grand Theme Hotels. It fit perfectly into the unique theme concept since the building resembles a Moorish Revival castle with intricate kneeling balconies, an arched carriage entrance, hand-painted Italian tile, arched windows, five majestic towers, and a red tile roof. No detail was overlooked in restoring the hotel to its golden days of Flagler grandeur while preserving its historic status that is recognized by the National Register of Historic Places. Once again named the Casa Monica, in January 2000, 102 years after its first opening, it had its second grand opening.

Typical of the elegance of the restorations are the ceiling of the Gold Room of the Cordova Restaurant which is inlaid in twenty-four-karat gold, the Baldwin grand piano in the lounge, and the handmade brass chandeliers and light fixtures from Syria throughout the hotel.

Although each of the eighty-eight guest rooms and fifty suites is different, they all are decorated with variations of Spanish-style furnishings, including Picard-pattern window treatments and mesh sheers, natural sisal-like carpets, wrought-iron beds, mahogany tables and wicker lounge chairs. Four of the five hotel towers, ranging from two to four stories, contain one- to three-bedroom suites. Our favorite is the Ponce de Leon Suite that has a bedroom downstairs, a bedroom upstairs, a Jacuzzi in the tower, and a walkway that goes all around the tower offering great views in every direction. The hotel also has an outdoor pool, a hot tub, a fitness center, and valet parking.

CASA MONICA HOTEL

Address:	95 Cordova Street, St. Augustine 32084
	www.casamonica.com
Phone:	800/648-1888; 904/827-1888
Fax:	904/827-0426
Rates:	$139 – $599
Units:	137

Casablanca Inn Bed & Breakfast

This Inn not only offers a downtown waterfront location with a gorgeous view of Matanzas Bay, it also has a ghost. According to local tales, the ghost is a woman who was in love with a member of a gang of rumrunners during the Prohibition era in the 1920s. The inn was a boardinghouse then and—at different times, of course—had as guests both the gang members and the revenue agents trying to catch them. If the agents were in the house, the woman would go to the widow's walk at night and signal with a lantern to tell the gang it wasn't safe to come ashore there. The story goes on to say that later her boyfriend was lost at sea, and she is still trying to signal him to a safe landing.

The 1914 Mediterranean-style home, listed on the National Register of Historic Places, cannot offer you the thrills of watching rumrunners versus revenue agents anymore. And the appearance of the ghost (if she shows) isn't guaranteed. It does offer a dozen large rooms and suites in the main house furnished with fine antiques and private baths, some with Jacuzzis, some with private balconies, and some with panoramic views of the bay. It doesn't have phones or televisions. If you prefer those, you can ask for one of the eight rooms in the Coach House. Located directly behind the main house, all the Coach House rooms have televisions and phones as well as the antique furnishings, plus all of the rooms have Jacuzzis and either a covered first-floor outside patio, or a second-floor private covered porch overlooking historic Caroline Street. No matter where you stay in the inn, of course, you can always sit 'n' rock on the front porch.

CASABLANCA INN BED & BREAKFAST

Address:	**24 Avenida Menendez, St. Augustine 32084**
	www.casablancainn.com
Phone:	**800/826-2626; 904/829-0928**
Fax:	**904/826-1892**
Rates:	**$89 – $179**
Units:	**20**

Kenwood Inn Bed & Breakfast

Like many bed-and-breakfasts, this started out as a private home in the 1860s, but as early as 1886 it was advertised as a guest house. Over the years, pieces were added on, and by 1911 it had become the Kenwood Hotel.

Mark and Kerrianne Constant sold a bed-and-breakfast in New England in 1988 to buy this one. Their daughter, Caitlin, grew up in the house and now is part of the family staff. Located just a block from the bay, the three-story inn has ten guest rooms, three two-room suites, and one three-room suite: the Bridal/Special Occasion Suite. This suite is the highest in two ways—it is located on the third floor and is the most expensive. But for your money you get a huge apartment-size suite with views of both the bay and much of the historic district. All the rooms have private baths and four-poster beds, and are furnished with period antiques, many of which the Constants brought with them from New Hampshire. Some have televisions, but none has a phone.

Space is tight in Old Town, so it's unusual to find that this inn not only has a swimming pool, nicely walled off for privacy, but also a courtyard with a koi pond. Both are great places to relax after touring the town.

KENWOOD INN BED & BREAKFAST

Address:	**38 Marine Street, St. Augustine 32084**
	www.oldcity.com/kenwood
Phone:	**800/824-8151; 904/824-2116**
Fax:	**904/824-1689**
Rates:	**$85 – $175**
Units:	**14**

Old Mansion Inn

This three-story house lives up to its name. Not only is it old (built in 1872), it is also a lovingly maintained mansion that, with its extensive gardens, could easily be a home on an English estate.

That's appropriate because Vera Kramer and her husband came from England. They first came to St. Augustine to visit relatives, fell in love with the area, and bought the mansion in 1980. At that time it was "old" in the worst sense of the word. It was a defunct restaurant that needed lots of tender loving care and creative restoration. That's what they gave it, and their labor of love took thirteen years. For several of those years they commuted between England and St. Augustine. They finally decided to make the big move and settled permanently into the mansion, bringing with them their lovely English antiques, art, collectibles, and other furnishings that provide an aura of gracious English manor formality. Also very much at home is Vera's sizable doll collection that is on display in the formal dining room. If you want, she can tell you the delightful history of each doll.

While guests are welcome in the main house, the two guest rooms are actually in the attached coach house. Furnished more casually than the rooms in the main house, both are spacious, with canopy beds and kitchenettes, while still offering the ambiance of a genteel English country inn. We especially liked the upstairs room, which has a sitting area overlooking the garden.

OLD MANSION INN

Address:	14 Joiner Street, St. Augustine 32084
Phone:	904/824-1975
Rates:	$175
Units:	2

Old Powder House Inn

Shortly after Katie and Kal Kalieta bought this bed-and-breakfast, they added a room. About this time Katie found an old print in a closet of a young woman in a rowboat in a storm rowing toward a sinking ship. Intrigued, she researched it and discovered it was a classic print of the

British heroine Grace Darling, a lighthouse keeper's daughter who rescued several people from a shipwreck. Digging further, she went onto the Internet. The result was that people sent her all sorts of stories and memorabilia about Grace Darling, as well as eight books recounting her heroism. Wordsworth even wrote a poem about her. So, they named their new room after her. And if you stay there, you'll find the print and the memorabilia. You'll also find you are in a Victorian setting with lace curtains, a four-poster bed, and a corner fireplace. In deference to the modern world, there's also a two-person whirlpool tub.

The eight other themed rooms and suites are also decorated in Victorian style. All the rooms have private baths—several with deep soaking tubs. Towering oaks and pecan trees shade both the downstairs and upstairs verandahs where you can sit 'n' rock. Of course you'll have to watch out for the elephants. About two hundred of them, from Katie's eighteen-year collection, have found homes all over the inn.

While many lodgings in St. Augustine offer bicycles for guests to use, this one also has a bicycle-built-for-two.

OLD POWDER HOUSE INN

Address:	**38 Cordova Street, St. Augustine 32084**
	www.oldpowderhouse.com
Phone:	**800/447-4149; 904/824-4149**
Fax:	**904/825-0143**
Rates:	**$85 – $195**
Units:	**9**

St. Francis Inn

The St. Francis, built in 1791, is one of the oldest guest houses in continuous use in the nation. So it's appropriate that guests are given complimentary admission to the oldest house in the city, which is right down the street. Built of native coquina limestone, the St. Francis has been a public guest house since 1845. Because the house was constructed on land at the junction of two old streets that did not meet at right angles, the Spanish colonial building is shaped like a trapezoid rather than a rectangle, meaning there are no right angles in the main building.

Like most old lodgings, this one has been added to and altered again and again until now it has three floors. Each of the rooms is truly individualized in both size and shape, and there are twelve fireplaces (all with electric flame). The lodgings range from the least expensive Graham Room to the spacious two-room Elizabeth Suite. The Graham Room has a stained glass and hammered-tin ceiling and is the only one with its private bath down the hall. The Elizabeth Suite has a kitchenette, fireplace, a two-person whirlpool tub, and a view of St. Francis Park across the street. All the rooms are furnished with antique or reproduction furniture and have cable television.

A good choice for families or two couples is the two-bedroom, two-bath cottage that overlooks the courtyard. Formerly the cookhouse/slave quarters for the main house, it has an eat-in kitchen and a living room with fireplace. Also for families or small groups is the Wilson House across the street. A Victorian built around 1800, it has one guest room, a two-room suite, and a three-room suite. The inn has a small swimming pool, a courtyard garden, and complimentary bicycles for touring downtown.

ST. FRANCIS INN

Address:	279 St. George Street, St. Augustine 32084
	www.stfrancisinn.com
Phone:	800/824-6062; 904/824-6068
Fax:	904/810-5525
Rates:	$70 – $179
Units:	15

Westcott House Inn

Typical of the refinements and attention to detail in this bed-and-breakfast is its turndown service, which includes a snifter of brandy and chocolates beside your bed. Located bayfront, the Westcott House offers sweeping and unobstructed views of Mantanzas Bay and the nearby Bridge of Lions from the wraparound verandahs and many of the rooms. The two-story Victorian was built in the late 1880s by Dr. John Westcott, who was one of the developers responsible for dredging the Intracoastal Waterway linking the St. Johns River to Miami.

The beautifully maintained house has a front porch and two verandahs, one in the front and one in the back. It is all detailed with Italian gingerbread work. Inside is a fine combination of both polished pine floors and lush carpeting, working or decorative fireplaces, and rooms furnished with American and European antiques. Several travel writers have called them among the best-kept rooms in town. All the rooms have cable television, a private phone, and a private bath—some with Jacuzzi tubs. Of the nine, the Isabella and the Anastasia are two of the more popular guest rooms. Both have fine views of the Bay and easy access to the second floor porch for better views. Outside there is a shaded courtyard and a large garden. For boaters, the inn is just half a block from the city's marina.

WESTCOTT HOUSE INN

Address:	**146 Avenida Menendez, St. Augustine 32084**
	www.westcotthouse.com
Phone:	**800/513-9814;904/824-4301**
Fax:	**904/824-4301**
Rates:	**$95 – $175**
Units:	**9**

World Golf Village Renaissance Resort

World Golf Village is a sixty-three-hundred-acre mixed use development that features golf (of course), a resort, several family-oriented attractions, retail shops (including the PGA Tour Stop, one of the largest golf shops in the nation), restaurants, and residential housing. Located just eight miles north of St. Augustine, it has its own exit (95A) on I-95.

The World Golf Hall of Fame is the centerpiece and heart of the Village. Golf's rich heritage and growing popularity are showcased here with exhibits spanning five centuries from the sport's inception on the links of Scotland to today's Tigermania. Appropriately, the hall is laid out like a golf course into eighteen separate areas that take you through the many facets of the game. Many of the exhibits are interactive so you can experience some of golf's most exciting elements. For example, you can feel the pressure of putting under the eyes of cameras and spectators as well as the sensation of victory as you sink the final putt in the "World Golf Hall of Fame Open." Or discover which professional player your swing most resembles in the swing analyzer.

Separating the front and back nines is the actual Hall of Fame honoring seventy-six male and female members from around the world. Be sure to take the elevator up to the Tower Shrine, which memorializes the

people who have carried golf from its ancient game to its present level. The tower also offers a spectacular 360-degree view of Golf Village.

If you really want to swing a club, the village has the Slammer and the Squire. Famed golf course architect Bobby Weed tapped golf legends Sam Snead and Gene Sarazen as player consultants for the eighteen-hole course that bears their nicknames. This is the first of three planned golf courses at the village.

Real enthusiasts can even play a round of golf indoors at the Renaissance Resort. Using a computer screen and infrared beams that track the speed and flight of the ball, you can "virtually" play a game with real clubs and balls on any one of thirty-two famous golf courses all over the world. The simulator will keep score for up to eight people playing eighteen holes on the selected course. This virtual game costs a lot less than greens fees at just about any course.

When you want to settle down and relax, the hotel has 270 rooms and thirty suites with all the comforts and amenities you'd expect in a resort. Each room has an armoire carved with replicas of the very first PGA cup and paintings that convey the beauty of the game. About half the rooms and suites have balconies. The hotel has a fitness center with sauna and an outdoor swimming pool with a Jacuzzi.

If you are traveling with children aged three to twelve, the Little Legends Kids' Club has a supervised program of activities for half a day, all day, or even weekend evenings. And the IMAX Theater, next to the Hall of Fame, is always popular with children of all ages. Young people are also the focus of the nationwide First Tee program that is headquartered here. This program, an initiative of the World Golf Foundation, which also operates the Hall of Fame, is focused on making golf accessible for people from all walks of life and especially on introducing young people to golf.

WORLD GOLF VILLAGE RENAISSANCE RESORT

Address:	**500 S. Legacy Trail, St. Augustine 32092**
	www.wgv.com
Phone:	**888/446-5301; 904/940-8000**
Fax:	**904/940-8008**
Rates:	**$129 – $899**
Units:	**300**

WELAKA

Bed tax 8 percent

Some of the more ardent boosters of Putnam County claim it is the "Bass Capital of the World." More conservative boosters just say it's "the Greatest Bass Fishing in the Country." In either case, freshwater fishing, especially bass fishing, is one of the biggest attractions of this area, and Welaka, on the St. Johns River, is one of the centers of that attraction. Fittingly, this is also the home of a U.S. Fish and Wildlife Service National Fish Hatchery and Aquarium, a warm water hatchery with forty-one ponds that raises between four and a half and five million fish each year. This hatchery stocks lakes and streams in Florida and several neighboring states. Guided tours are available by appointment, but you can get a good overall view from the hatchery's observation tower.

With a resident population of just a little over five hundred people, Welaka is the smallest of the five incorporated cities in Putnam County. Of course locals say that if you count the resident bass, it would rank up there with Miami. One other interesting connection to the river in Welaka is the Fort Gates Ferry. Florida's oldest continuously operating ferry, it connects Welaka with Salt Springs.

Floridian Sports Club

The St. Johns River has often been called "a river of bass." Marinas and fish camps abound along the river, and as any fisherman knows, there are rustic fish camps and then there are not-so-rustic fish camps. This definitely falls into the second category, a former private club that not only offers great fishing but also comfortable, clean resort-type lodging for when you finally have to leave the water.

The Floridian Sports Club is what fishermen's dreams are made of. But then what else would you expect from a club owned by the same guy who owns the Bass Pro Shops? Bass is the top catch, of course, but the waters around here also contain snook, shad, crappie, and bream.

The club's lodge and restaurant are on a bluff overlooking Welaka Springs where manatees often spend the winter. Standard rooms have two queen-size beds, a full bath with a Jacuzzi, a small refrigerator, and a wet bar. The suites have a king-size bed, a full bath, a Jacuzzi, a sauna, a living room with fireplace, a half bath, a wet bar, a refrigerator, and a screened porch where you can sit 'n' rock and tell fish stories as you look out on the river. Naturally, they can hook you up with a fishing guide, and all their fishing packages include guide service.

For families or groups there are two houses: the three-bedroom, two-bath Harris House, and the two-bedroom, two-bath Riverview House. Both have all the amenities, including a screened porch on the river.

Don't fish, or want a break? The resort has canoe and pontoon boat rentals, two tennis courts, and a swimming pool. They can also arrange back-country sightseeing. Or, according to the manager, Roberta Rominsky, many guests come just for what she calls "the sound of peace and quiet."

FLORIDIAN SPORTS CLUB

Address:	**P.O. Box 730, Welaka 32192**
	www.floridiansportclub.com
Phone:	**904/467-8826**
Fax:	**904/467-8383**
Rates:	**$85 – $239**
Units:	**11**

For Additional Information
on the Northeast Region:

**AMELIA ISLAND TOURIST
DEVELOPMENT COUNCIL**
102 Centre Street
Fernandina Beach, FL 32034
800/2-AMELIA (226-3542);
904/277-0717
Fax: 904/261-2440
www.ameliaisland.org

**JACKSONVILLE AND
THE BEACHES CVB**
201 East Adams Street
Jacksonville, FL 32202
800/733-2668; 904/798-9111
Fax: 904/798-9103
www.jaxcvb.com

PUTNAM COUNTY COC
P.O. Box 550
Palatka, FL 32178-0550
904/328-1503
Fax: 904/328-7076
www.putnam.special.net/chamber

ST. JOHNS COUNTY CVB
88 Riberia Street, Suite 400
St. Augustine, FL 32084
800/418-7529; 904/829-1711 ext 306
Fax: 904/829-6149
www.aug.com

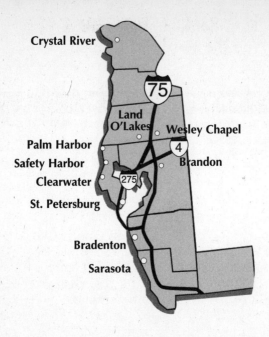

High Season: Usually December through Spring.

(Note: All lodging rates are for high season. Off-season rates can be significantly lower.)

CRYSTAL RIVER

Bed tax 8 percent

This small town has been restored to its nineteenth-century ambiance with ornate brass streetlights, covered walkways, and houses with verandahs. Once a bustling fishing and mill town, tourism is now its main industry. Many of the visitors are scuba divers from around the world who come to dive in the underground springs. These springs pump millions of gallons of fresh water daily. The water temperature is a constant seventy-two degrees Fahrenheit, creating ideal diving conditions year round. The constant water temperature also attracts manatees, which need water of at least sixty-eight degrees Fahrenheit to survive. As a result, from around November to March, depending on the weather, Crystal River and Kings Bay become the winter home for the largest herd of manatees in North America. There is also a major pre-Columbian archaeological site in this town.

Best Western Crystal River Resort

Location, location, location! That's the shining star of this small resort that is located on Kings Bay. The two-story facility offers ninety-six rooms and eighteen efficiencies. All are casually and comfortably furnished. The heated swimming pool and whirlpool look out on Kings Bay. The boat dock has twenty slips, and you can rent pontoon and motorboats and canoes there. Guests are offered a complimentary one-hour sightseeing boat ride on the Crystal River. The only airboat tour on the Crystal River is also available here. For divers and snorkelers, there's a full-service dive shop and guided dive tours.

BEST WESTERN CRYSTAL RIVER RESORT

Address:	**614 NW Hwy 19, Crystal River 34428**
	www.seawake.com
Phone:	**800/435-4409; 352/795-3171**
Fax:	**352/795-3179**
Rates:	**$80-$105**
Units:	**114**

Plantation Inn & Golf Resort

When you drive up to this resort, with its pillared portico, it gives the feeling of a gentler, more peaceful time in the Old South. That was precisely the goal of W. W. Caruth when he founded this inn on the banks of the Crystal River on the Nature Coast.

Of course, when you're on the resort's eighteen-hole championship golf course or nine-hole executive course, the feeling you get when driving might be entirely different. This resort is the winter home of the Original Golf School, which they claim as the first in Florida and now America's most successful golf program.

There is a choice of 126 guest rooms, twelve golf villas, or five condominium units at this 232-acre resort. The hotel rooms are in the wings of the main building, while the villas and condos are located on the golf course. The villas are two-story units with a living/dining room, kitchen, a sleeping area, and a full bath downstairs, and the bedroom and a second bath upstairs. The family-size condos have living and dining rooms, a kitchen, three bedrooms, and two-and-a-half to three baths.

In addition to the golf, the resort has restaurants, two swimming pools (one heated), four lighted tennis courts, and a dive shop providing boat and equipment rentals plus instruction for scuba diving or snorkeling. If you want to stay on top of the water, kayaks, canoes, and small boats are available to rent and boat tours can be arranged.

If you are looking to escape from the fast lane, you can just stroll the extensive grounds and river areas.

PLANTATION INN & GOLF RESORT

Address:	**9301 West Fort Island Road, Crystal River 34429**
	www.plantation.com
Phone:	**800/632-6262; 352/795-4211**
Fax:	**352/795-1368**
Rates:	**$90-$310**
Units:	**142**

SARASOTA AREA

(Bradenton Beach, Holmes Beach, Longboat Key, Saratoga, Siesta Key)

In 1885 the Florida Mortgage and Investment Company promoted the new town of Sarasota in Scotland with promises of fertile fields, fine housing, and profitable citrus groves. Scottish families came with hopes of fulfilling that promise, but like television infomercials of today, there was only a little bit of truth and a lot more hype. Many Scottish families left, but those who stayed worked hard to turn the hype into reality. So the Scottish influence remains, and it was a Scotsman, of course, who around 1900 built the first golf courses here, giving the city the right to claim the title of "America's Cradle of Golf."

Wealthy Americans discovered the area by 1910. Probably the most famous of them, and the one who left the biggest mark on the community, was John Ringling of the Ringling Brothers and Barnum and Bailey Circus. In the 1920s, he and his wife, Mabel, built a magnificent Venetian-style estate on Sarasota Bay as well as an art museum to house their collection. By 1927 he had made Sarasota the winter quarters for his circus, thereby marking it as "Circus City."

The circus tradition lives on here, but the area from around Venice north to around Bradenton is now called Florida's Cultural Coast. It boasts a bevy of professional theaters; a professional symphony, ballet, and opera; the Ringling Museum of Art and the Florida State Museum; art galleries; and artist communities. A good way to explore this area is to follow the sites on the Gulf Coast Heritage Trail. Maps of the trail are available from the Sarasota Visitor Information Center (see address at end of this region).

BRADENTON BEACH

Bed tax 10 percent

Bungalow Beach Resort

This mini-resort revives those pleasant days before the high-rise mania with a group of thoughtfully restored and modernized bungalows located on the beach on Anna Maria Island. The sixteen bungalows were built in the 1930s with hardwood floors, cathedral-beamed ceilings, private screened porches, and skylights. All have a private entrance just steps from a beach of sugar-white sand dunes, sea oats, and coconut palms. Lounge chairs and beach umbrellas are provided for those who just want to sit on the beach and relax.

Each bungalow has either an efficiency or a full kitchen with microwave, a bath (some with whirlpool tubs), cable television, and phone. Choices range from poolside or gulffront studios to one- and two-bedroom units. Furnishings are causal wicker and rattan that fit in with the beach setting. We especially liked Room 1, which has a stunning gulf view.

BUNGALOW BEACH RESORT

Address:	**2000 Gulf Drive North, Bradenton Beach 34217**
	www.bungalowbeach.com
Phone:	**800/779-3601; 941/778-3600**
Fax:	**941/778-1764**
Rates:	**$140-$290**
Units:	**16**

HOLMES BEACH

Bed tax 10 percent

Harrington House Bed & Breakfast

There are three houses in this lovely bed-and-breakfast complex developed by owner and innkeeper Jo Davis on Anna Maria Island. All are beach houses, so even as you drive up the bougainvillea-bordered drive to the main house you can see the gulf waters through the trees.

The three-story main house was built in 1925 of coquina shell block. It has a huge stone fireplace in the living room and is the essence of Old

Florida. The seven rooms in this house are all large, comfortably furnished with antiques and collectibles, have private baths, cable television, a phone, and a small refrigerator. On the grounds is the cottage, a former garden house remodeled into a bedroom with a bath that features a heart-shaped Jacuzzi. A favorite with honeymooners, it has a private deck with a great view of the gulf.

The two other houses in the complex are just a short walk in either direction down the beach. The Spangler Beach House, built in the 1940s, has four rooms that are superior to what you might expect in a beach house. They all have beach views, and remote-control fireplaces, which you can turn on or off from your bed, adding to the romantic setting.

For real romance and the coziest of rooms, however, our choice is the Huth Beach House. Also a short beach walk away, all three rooms here have a remote-control fireplace; two have a Jacuzzi and the other a shower built for two. But the real prize is the gorgeous water view from the two gulffront rooms. What a beautiful sight to wake up to!

Other amenities include a heated pool and free use of bicycles and kayaks.

HARRINGTON HOUSE BED & BREAKFAST

Address:	**5626 Gulf Drive, Holmes Beach 34217**
	www.harringtonhouse.com
Phone:	**941/778-5444**
Fax:	**941/778-0527**
Rates:	**$179–$239**
Units:	**15**

LONGBOAT KEY

Bed tax 9 percent

Colony Beach & Tennis Resort

"Tennis, anyone?"

If that's your call, this resort should be irresistible for you. Consistently rated among the top tennis facilities, the Colony can now boast that *Tennis* magazine has named it the number one tennis resort in the nation.

It is more than just tennis, of course, but let's cover that first. The twenty-one courts consist of ten soft courts (two lighted) and eleven hard-surface courts, and court time and adult tennis matchmaking services are always free to guests. Whether you're a beginner or an advanced player, to help improve your game there are ten pros available for lessons, clinics, and even exhibition games with visiting tennis celebrities you can watch.

No age group is neglected. There are all levels of play and instruction for juniors, and Tiny Tots Tennis for kids ages six and under.

Now let's get to the other part of the name—the Beach Resort. All the amenities—lodging, cuisine, and off-court recreational activities—were considered when *Tennis* magazine named it number one. These include a fitness center; a health spa with a whirlpool, a sauna, and a steamroom; restaurants including the dining room overlooking the gulf; a beachside swimming pool; and of course, the beach with sun, white sand, and a water sports center.

Family owned and operated since it was started by Dr. M. J. "Murf" Klauber in 1969, the Colony is definitely a family-friendly resort. Kidding Around is a complimentary daily program of supervised fun-filled activities designed especially for children ages seven to twelve and Kinder Kamp caters to three to six year olds. In season, they offer a selection of programs for parents and children to participate in together.

Choices of lodging range from 208 one- and two-bedroom villa suites to twenty-six cottages and a duplex penthouse, all attractively furnished and close to the beach.

COLONY BEACH & TENNIS RESORT

Address:	**1620 Gulf of Mexico Drive, Longboat Key 34228**
	www.colonybeachresort.com
Phone:	**800/282-1138; 941/383-6464**
Fax:	**941/383-7549**
Rates:	**$395-$1,195**
Units:	**234**

Holiday Inn Hotel & Suites Longboat Key

This Holiday Inn is irresistible because it is the only lodging on the magnificent Longboat Key with Kidsuites (see page 134), and we found Kidsuites irresistible for families with children.

With the Kidsuite, the parents get a double guest room and the kids get an attached but essentially separate room. The kids' room is colorfully and whimsically decorated and furnished with bunk beds, a television, a VCR, a Nintendo, and other things that will let them have fun in their own place. While designed for those under ten, kids a little older will probably enjoy these special rooms, too.

While the Kidsuites add to the fun for families, there's also plenty to do outside the rooms for all the guests. There's the private beach, a heated pool with a kiddie pool, four lighted tennis courts, and a volleyball area. Indoors, the typical Holiday Inn Holidome has an indoor heated pool and whirlpool, a sauna, an exercise facility, a putting green, and a video arcade. There are also restaurants and a lounge.

The three-story inn has 146 rooms and suites, of which more than a dozen are Kidsuites. You can chose from a standard room to twenty-five two-room suites, some with kitchens, and a gulf or Holidome view.

HOLIDAY INN HOTEL & SUITES LONGBOAT KEY

Address:	**4949 Gulf of Mexico Drive, Longboat Key 34228**
	www.hilongboat.com
Phone:	**800/465-4436; 941/383-3771**
Fax:	**941/383-7871**
Rates:	**$299-$425**
Units:	**146**

The Resort at Longboat Key Club

In the 1920s, circus owner John Ringling started to build a grand hotel at this site on Longboat Key. Before he could finish it, the real estate boom fizzled, and he dropped the project. If he could see this resort today, he would probably think it is grander than even he could have imagined. Two of the major national lodging rating systems agree: Mobil rates this a Four Star and the AAA rates it a Four Diamond. With a top rating of five, that's not quite perfect, but almost.

Golf, tennis, and the sun and sand on the beach of Longboat Key are the main attractions here. There are forty-five holes of championship golf. The Islandside Course offers eighteen holes bordered by the Gulf of Mexico. The Harborside Course, bordered by Sarasota Bay, has three nine-hole courses. The pros in the Golf School on the resort offer instruction and clinics as well as computerized swing analysis. If tennis is your game, there are thirty-eight Har-Tru courts in two centers, all open on a complimentary basis to guests, and lessons and clinics are available.

But you don't have to be into either of these sports to enjoy your stay here. The Fitness Center features aerobics classes, personal trainers, and massage therapy. There are nine miles of bicycle and jogging trails, a swimming pool, and a ten-person Jacuzzi. Not to forget that long and pristine beach where you can relax or have fun in the water by renting a variety of water toys from a Hobie Cat to Aqua Cycles to Boogie Boards.

You have a choice of lodgings ranging from the spacious guest rooms to one- and two-bedroom suites, some with full kitchens, washer/dryers, and all with private balconies.

The seasonal Kids Klub program has well-supervised activities for children ages five to twelve. Options include full day, morning, or afternoon programs featuring educational and fun field trips, arts and crafts, outdoor games, and water sports.

After all those activities, you are bound to be hungry. For the famished, the club offers four restaurants, giving you a choice of fine to casual dining, plus room service.

THE RESORT AT LONGBOAT KEY CLUB

Address:	**P.O. Box 15000, Longboat Key 34228**
	www.longboatkeyclub.com
Phone:	**800/237-8821; 941/383-8821**
Fax:	**941/383-0359**
Rates:	**$250-$1,210**
Units:	**232**

SARASOTA

Bed Tax 10 percent

The Cypress, A Bed & Breakfast Inn

Let's start with its great location. Sarasota's only downtown bed-and-breakfast overlooks the bay and is just a couple hundred yards from the downtown marina. It is within easy walking distance to the Marie Selby Botanical Gardens, the Sarasota Opera House, and the nearby shops on Palm Avenue. Just a few minutes drive will take you to St. Armand's Circle, the Ringling Museum of Art and the Museum of the Circus, Asolo Theatre, the white sands of Lido Beach, and several other of the more popular places to visit.

The tin-roofed, Florida Vernacular-style building sits on extensive grounds among large oak trees, palms, and tropical fruit trees. It is surprising that all this lies on a street lined with high-rise condos. It survived the developers because the original owner loved to sail and would not give up her home close to the marina. So now you can sit on the front porch in a comfortable rocking chair and look out at the sailboats in the bay and watch the sunset.

All four guest rooms and suites are named after members of the owners' families and are furnished with European and American antiques—mostly from family collections—oriental area rugs, and a television. Our favorite was the Martha Rose Suite, with its French mansion bed, plantation armoire, sitting area with love seat and Corinthian marble coffee table, private bath and separate powder room, and a balcony with a bay view.

The three owners/innkeepers include two teachers from New Jersey and a professional photographer. Nina Belott has a masters in anthropology, and her background is reflected in the artifacts she has collected and now shares with her guests. Her husband, Robert, is an artist and photographer who was one of the nineteen photographers worldwide whose work was chosen for the Kodak "Professional Photographer's

Showcase" at EPCOT Center. You can see samples of his work in many of the rooms in the house. The third owner is Vicki Hadley. She is the one who always wanted to have a bed-and-breakfast and talked about it so much that she convinced her friends to join in her plan. They originally wanted a place on the beach, but once they saw this house, they all fell in love with it.

THE CYPRESS, A BED & BREAKFAST INN

Address:	621 S. Gulfstream Avenue, Sarasota 34236
	www.bbonline.com/fl/cypress
Phone:	941/955-4683
Rates:	$150-$210
Units:	4

SIESTA KEY

Bed tax 10 percent

Turtle Beach Resort

Siesta Key is an eight-mile-long barrier island across the bay from Sarasota. Residents claim that their island is the best-kept secret in all of Florida, and the innkeepers of this resort say theirs is a hidden jewel. The high-rise condos on the north end of the key detract from the best-kept secret—the

resort on the quiet south end. While not really hidden, it lives up to its claim of being a jewel.

In 1991 Gail and David Rubenfeld bought what was then a fishing camp dating from the 1940s with the idea of transforming it into a bed-and-breakfast. The restoration project was a natural for them since David was in construction and Gail was into interior design. The result is a charming waterfront inn with a Key West ambiance. The name of the resort comes from the turtle nesting area on the beach across the street, but they could just have easily named it for the dolphins, manatees, blue herons, or pelicans you have a good chance of seeing from the dock.

The resort has two studios, two one-bedroom cottages, and six family-size two-bedroom cottages with full kitchens. Gail decided on a theme for each and used her decorating skills to fit the décor to their names, which range from Southwest and Bahama Breeze to Country Cottage and Victorian. Each one has a private patio with a hot tub, and all but one has a bay view.

Guests have use of the docking facilities, as well as free use of a rowboat, a canoe, a paddleboat, fishing poles, and bicycles There's no restaurant in the complex, but there are three restaurants nearby, including a fine-dining one right next door.

TURTLE BEACH RESORT

Address:	**9049 Midnight Pass Road, Siesta Key 34242**
	www.turtlebeachresort.com
Phone:	**941/349-4554**
Fax:	**941/312-9034**
Rates:	**$200 -$325**
Units:	**10**

TAMPA BAY AREA

(Brandon, Clearwater, Palm Harbor, Safety Harbor, St. Petersburg,
St. Pete Beach, Tampa)

When Hernando de Soto sailed into the bay in 1539, the native tribes called it "Tanpa," which meant "sticks of fire." On maps made by the early explorers, that spelling became Tampa, and the name stuck.

Today, the Tampa Bay area is Florida's fastest-growing area, and the eighth fastest growing in the country. And why not? The many cities around the bay offer tremendous attractions for both residents and visitors. There are all sorts of activities on the water from sailing or scuba diving to charters and pampered cruises. There is theater: St. Petersburg's Bayfront Center/Mahaffey Theater, Tampa Bay Performing Arts Center, and Clearwater's Ruth Eckerd Hall. In St. Petersburg Fort De Soto Park offers nine hundred acres including a beach that has been rated one of the top ten in the continental United States. There are museums, including St. Petersburg's Salvador Dali Museum, Florida International Museum, the Museum of Fine Arts, Tampa's Museum of Science and Industry, and the Children's Museum. Other attractions include Tampa's Busch Gardens and the Florida Aquarium.

For baseball fans, Clearwater is the spring training home of the Philadelphia Phillies, and Tampa has the New York Yankees in the spring and is the permanent home of the Tampa Bay Devil Rays. For professional football, it's the Tampa Bay Buccaneers; hockey, the Tampa Bay Lightning; and soccer, the Tampa Bay Mutiny. Golf, tennis, thoroughbred and greyhound racing, and even a rodeo are all in the Tampa area. If you want a place to jog, bike, or skate without interruption, Tampa's Bayshore Boulevard borders Tampa Bay for four-and-a-half miles without a break.

In other words, you can come and relax on that twenty-eight miles of white sand beach, or find a wide variety of other things to do and places to go.

BRANDON

Bed tax 11.5 percent

Behind the Fence

This authentic replica of an 1800s salt-box house stands on extensive grounds at the end of a residential street. Although it's just fifteen minutes from Tampa, it is like stepping back in time. Inside there is a large brick fireplace with a hanging iron pot that makes you feel as though you have left the modern world behind.

In 1977 when Carolyn and Larry Yoss came to Florida, they couldn't find a house that would be compatible with their collection of American antiques, which included pre-Civil War and Amish furnishings. So they built this two-story home to recreate the one Carolyn had

grown up in. They raised their four children in the home, as Carolyn says, "so they would understand their heritage and learn simple values."

In 1993 after the children were all out on their own, Carolyn and Larry, eager to share their passion for the early 1880s lifestyle, turned their unique home into this bed-and-breakfast. They frequently invite spinners and weavers to demonstrate their old trades and crafts, and invite school tours to "teach the children what their history texts leave out." Guests, too, feel as if they've entered history when they come to the inn.

There are five guest rooms. The three upstairs in the main house reflect Amish influences with authentic antique maple or pine-rope beds (some built high enough that you need a stepping stool to get in), armoires, colorful quilts, and Shaker pegs on the wall that hold Larry's hand-dipped candles. One room has a private bath; the other two share a bath.

The two other guest rooms are in the cottage in the rear by the pool that looks like a natural pond. Each has a private bath, and the same simple and authentic furnishings and décor are carried out here.

Perhaps they are holding to an era when such things didn't exist, but for whatever reason, Carolyn and Larry don't accept credit cards.

BEHIND THE FENCE

Address:	**1400 Viola Drive, Brandon 33511**
Phone:	**800/44-TAMPA (448-2672/ Tampa Outdoor Adventures); 813/685-8201**
Rates:	**$60-$75**
Units:	**5**

CLEARWATER

Bed tax 11 percent

Belleview Biltmore Resort & Spa

This huge, multigabled, clapboard building is reputed to be the largest occupied wooden structure in the world. It has two miles of corridors to prove it.

The fabulous Victorian-era hotel, perched on a picturesque bluff overlooking the bay, was built in 1896 by railroad baron Henry Plant for his wealthy northern friends who liked to winter in Florida. Among its long list of distinguished guests are Thomas Edison, the Duke of Windsor, Babe Ruth, and Joe DiMaggio. More recently, Presidents Gerald Ford and George Bush and Prime Minister Margaret Thatcher slept here. In the early days, some of its guests arrived by private railway cars. If you take the historic tour, run daily at 11 A.M. ($5), one of the stops is the underground railway.

The hotel, which is now on the National Register of Historic Places, is set on the resort's twenty-two acres amidst water oaks, cabbage palms, citrus trees, palmettos, and orchids. Resort facilities include a swimming pool, a Donald Ross-designed golf course, four red-clay tennis courts, a fourteen-thousand-square-foot day spa and fitness center,

jogging and walking trails, bicycle rentals, and restaurants. Harking back to the days of the tycoons, the staff can even arrange for yacht charters.

The hotel offers 243 guest rooms that include forty junior, one- and two-bedroom suites. While there are forty-seven different room types, the common elements are that most rooms are spacious, some have two closets (after all, Mr. Plant's guests used to come for the full season), period furniture, and all the modern conveniences.

BELLEVIEW BILTMORE RESORT & SPA

Address:	**25 Belleview Boulevard, Clearwater 33756**
	www.bellviewbiltmore.com
Phone:	**800/237-8947; 727/442-6171**
Fax:	**727/441-4173**
Rates:	**$149-$1,500**
Units:	**243**

PALM HARBOR

Bed tax 11 percent

Westin Innisbrook Resort

Ninety holes of golf, a tennis center, and the Loch Ness Pool and Spa are a few of the highlights of this family oasis set in a thousand acres of towering pines, citrus groves, cypress trees, and colorful hibiscus. The ninety holes of golf are on five award-winning courses laid out over six-hundred acres of natural lakes, woodlands, and hilly terrain that's unusual for Florida. Two of the courses, Copperhead and Island, have been rated "America's Top 50 Resort Courses" by *Golf Digest*. If you want to improve your game, the Innisbrook Troon Golf Institute provides instruction for all levels of play, including a summer program for juniors. If you don't want to hit those little golf balls around, you can stroll over to the Tennis and Racquet Center and hit other balls on the eleven Har-Tru courts or indoors on the three rac- quetball courts.

While the resort has always been family friendly, it is reaching out more to families with young children whose interests are not necessarily golf. Camp Innisbrook provides supervised activities for youngsters ages four to twelve. For teenagers there are special activities like pool parties and dances. And the Loch Ness Pool, which features two water slides (the longest 110 feet in length), a fifteen-foot cascading waterfall, and spontaneous pop jets, is a kids' favorite. (Adults watching the kids can do so from the free-form monster spa that seats thirty-six.)

The one thousand guest rooms and suites are in twenty-eight lodges nestled around the resort's golf courses. There is a swimming pool within walking distance of each lodge cluster. Each suite has a kitchen and a private balcony and can vary in size up to two bedrooms. Five restaurants cover the gamut from snack bar to fine dining.

And you won't need your car to get around this spread-out resort because there is a free shuttle service.

WESTIN INNISBROOK RESORT

Address:	**36750 US Hwy 19 N, Palm Harbor 34684**
	www.westin-innisbrook.com
Phone:	**800/456-2000; 727/942-2000**
Fax:	**727/942-5298**
Rates:	**$260-$485**
Units:	**1,000**

SAFETY HARBOR

Bed tax 11 percent

Safety Harbor Resort & Spa

Spanish explorer Hernando de Soto discovered five natural sulfur springs here in 1539. According to the legend, the waters cured some of his sailors of beriberi, a disease caused by a vitamin deficiency common among sailors on long voyages. The "miracle" waters led him to believe he had found what Ponce de Leon had missed—the legendary Fountain of Youth.

By the early 1900s, Safety Harbor had become known as the "Health Giving City," and people came to "take the waters." At that time three of the five springs were named for their supposed specific healing properties for stomach, liver, and kidney ailments. The other two were called the Beauty Springs and the Pure Water Springs. Today, the idea that the waters have specific healing properties has been completely discounted.

Instead the emphasis is on the general health and rejuvenating qualities the spa offers its guests.

Built in 1926 on twenty-two acres of tranquil waterfront property on Old Tampa Bay, Safety Harbor Resort and Spa is one of America's oldest and best-known spa resorts. The Zagat Survey has named it one of the top ten spas in the country, and the U.S. Water Fitness Association has cited its water fitness program as the best in Florida.

The fifty-thousand-square-foot spa, which has been renovated several times since its founding, has forty rooms for Swedish massage and other types of body treatments, including sports, shiatsu, reflexology, and aromatherapy. There are two pools and more than thirty-five hydrofitness classes a week. Nonaquatic options include yoga, tai chi, boxercise, movement relaxation, and total-body conditioning. There is also a skin-and-body-care institute.

For outdoor exercise, the resort has nine tennis courts and is the home of the Phil Green Tennis Center and Academy. There is also the Quinzi Golf Academy that has a driving range overlooking the bay.

Naturally (no pun intended) the spa's restaurants offer nutritious meals that emphasize American fusion cuisine, with both kosher and vegetarian menus available.

All 193 colorful and attractively decorated rooms, suites, and one-bedroom apartments have private baths, televisions, and phones. Some have balconies or patios overlooking either the bay or a pool.

SAFETY HARBOR RESORT & SPA

Address:	**105 N. Bayshore Drive, Safety Harbor 34695**
	www.safetyharborspa.com
Phone:	**888/237-8772; 727/726-1161**
Fax:	**727/726-4268**
Rates:	**$129-$189**
Units:	**193**

ST. PETERSBURG

Bed tax 11 percent

Bayboro House

When Sandy and Dave Kelly spent their first anniversary in a bed-and-breakfast in Maine, they realized a bed-and-breakfast could be the answer to their problem: that Dave's work as a captain in the Merchant Marine kept them apart a great deal of the time. So, in late 1999 they bought the Bayboro House, where they could live and work together.

Located in a quiet residential neighborhood, Bayboro House was St. Petersburg's first bed-and-breakfast and is still the only one offering an unblocked view of Tampa Bay. The gabled, nineteen-room Victorian mansion was built in 1907 as a family home by Charles Harvey, one of St. Petersburg's founding fathers. Like most older homes, it has had many lives, including being a bank and the winter home of some north Florida cattle ranchers.

Now restored to its original splendor, with a swimming pool added, it offers guests five spacious rooms in the main house, plus a garage apartment and a cottage at the rear of the house. All are furnished with quality antiques Sandy and Dave collected over the years, and all have private baths, televisions, and other modern conveniences. There are two lovely sitting rooms downstairs, a formal dining room and a verandah where you can sit 'n' rock and watch the sailboats, fishing boats, and occasionally even cruise ships pass on the bay.

BAYBORO HOUSE

Address:	**1719 Beach Drive S.E., St. Petersburg 33701**
	www.bayborohousebandb.com
Phone:	**877/823-4955; 727/823-4955**
Fax:	**727/823-4955**
Rates:	**$115-$145**
Units:	**7**

Holiday Inn Sunspree Marina Cove

The two things that set this Holiday Inn apart from many of the others in the chain and make it irresistible to us are its four Kidsuites (see page 134) and the fact that it's the home of the St. Petersburg branch of the famed Annapolis Sailing School.

The Kidsuites are a great idea for families with children up to about ten years old. Part of the parents' room, they are separated by a wall, so the kids feel they are on their own. Colorfully decorated, each has bunk beds, a television, a Nintendo game system, and other goodies to keep the kids happily engaged when they're in the room. When they are not in the room, there is an organized children's activity program they can attend.

Located on eighteen acres overlooking Tampa Bay, the Inn is a

perfect location for a branch of the oldest and largest sailing school in the country. The emphasis at the Annapolis Sailing School is on basic sailing with courses that can make you a sailor over a weekend or a vacation. But if you already know the basics, they also offer advanced courses and instructional cruises that last up to eight days. And since the Inn is family oriented, they also offer a Kidship Program to teach youngsters ages five to fifteen how to sail.

Other facilities at the inn include two pools (one heated), a Jacuzzi, a private beach, a playground and playroom, five tennis courts with a pro available, a fitness center, and the marina.

In addition to the regular rooms and the Kidsuites, the inn offers a number of two-story units with kitchen and space to sleep six people.

HOLIDAY INN SUNSPREE MARINA COVE

Address:	**6800 Sunshine Skyway Lane, St. Petersburg 33711**
	www.holiday-inn.com/marinacove-ss
Phone:	**800/227-1151; 727/867-1151**
Fax:	**727/864-4494**
Rates:	**$109-$159**
Units:	**156**

Renaissance Vinoy Resort

As the story goes, in 1923 Aymer Vinoy Laughner decided the ideal place to build a hotel in St. Petersburg was where the Williamson house stood on the water's edge. Mr. Williamson agreed to sell the property, but only on the conditions that the hotel would be the finest in the city and have the best views of St. Petersburg's waterfront. Mr. Laughner agreed, and the sale was signed right there, on the back of a brown paper bag.

The hotel was a fantasyland for the rich and famous from the time it opened in 1925 until around World War II. Then lack of repairs and air-conditioning led to its decline. Finally closed in 1974, it remained closed for eighteen years until, in 1992, after a ninety-three-million-dollar renovation, it was reopened. Faithfully restored to its original elegance and grandeur, the Mediterranean Revival-style hotel today has many exquisite details from its early years. In the lobby, for example, there is a glazed quarry tile with colorful hand-painted decorative inserts and huge stenciled pecky-cypress beams, frescoed ceilings and walls in the dining room, and intricate ornamental plaster work on the observation tower, main entrance door, and arched dining room windows. Even the salmon shade of the exterior replicates that of the original. An interesting aside is that during the renovation a vault containing several thousand silver pieces stamped with the Vinoy's 1925 logo was discovered. Some of these are now on display in a case at one end of the lobby.

Today, the Renaissance Vinoy continues to live up to the sale conditions set by Mr. Williamson. Elegant, grand, but by no means stuffy, the hotel offers 258 rooms and suites in the main building and 102 rooms in the added guest tower. All the rooms and suites are spacious and tastefully furnished and decorated in keeping with its history, but with all the modern amenities. From our room we could see a beautiful expanse of Tampa Bay dotted with sailboats; we could also see the marina and the St. Petersburg Pier, a local attraction.

The resort has twelve Har-Tru tennis courts, two outdoor heated pools, three outdoor spas, a fitness center, a day spa, a seventy-four-slip marina where you can book sunset cruises or deep-sea fishing, and two croquet courts for tournament or individual play. Its eighteen-hole golf course is a short distance away, and free shuttle service is provided. Two of its five restaurants have earned *Florida Trend* magazine's Golden Spoon Award, which means they are among the top twenty restaurants in the state.

The hotel is in the National Register of Historic Places, and if you want to see why firsthand, a guided Resort History Tour is given Wednesday through Saturday at 10:30 A.M. ($7).

RENAISSANCE VINOY RESORT

Address:	501 Fifth Avenue N.E., St. Petersburg 33701
	www.renaissancehotels.com
Phone:	727/894-1000
Fax:	727/894-1970
Rates:	$259-$1,500
Units:	360

Sunset Bay Inn

When Martha and Bob Bruce came from Atlanta to visit Martha's mother in St. Petersburg in 1996, they did what many of us do when we revisit our

old hometown. They drove by Martha's childhood home. When she was young, her parents were innkeepers and ran the house as a guest house from 1947 to 1967. All Martha saw now was that the house was in disrepair and there was a For Sale sign out front. Bob saw it as a house that could be restored into a prized bed-and-breakfast inn.

So they bought it, and after almost two years of restoration work, Martha followed in her parents' footsteps and became an innkeeper. Their own thirty years of traveling on business made the Bruces especially sensitive to the needs of travelers, especially business travelers. So one of their goals in the restoration was to incorporate all the good things they had learned about lodgings during those years of business travel. Their guests' comments are evidence they have reached this goal.

There are five rooms and one suite in the main house, all named for places that have a special meaning in their lives and decorated to carry out that theme. They include places like Augusta, reflecting their love of golf; Highlands, named for the town in North Carolina where they were married; and Marthasville, because this was Martha's childhood room. Marthasville was also the original name for Atlanta, which was Bob's childhood home and home to both of them for a number of years. The room we found most interesting was the Kihei Room, named for the little town on the island of Maui in Hawaii where Martha and Bob honeymooned. The décor is tropical, with birds, flowers, and beach accents. Several pictures in this room depict scenes from Kihei. What's unusual is they are the needlework of Martha's mother. In fact, you'll find her mother's needlework throughout the house.

All rooms have a private bath and all but the Marthasville Room have a whirlpool. (The Marthasville Room has the original clawfoot soaking tub dating from 1909.) Modern conveniences include televisions, VCRs, and phones. In addition, the carriage house has two large suites with small kitchenettes and a small conference room, which, when not used for meetings, doubles as a guest library and reading room.

SUNSET BAY INN

Address:	**635 Bay Street N.E., St. Petersburg 33701**
	www.sunsetbayinn.com
Phone:	**800/794-5133; 727/896-6701**
Fax:	**727/898-5311**
Rates:	**$160-$210**
Units:	**8**

ST. PETE BEACH

Bed tax 11 percent

Don Cesar Beach Resort & Spa

Thomas Rowe built this ten-story hotel on the Gulf of Mexico in 1928 to resemble the Royal Hawaiian in Waikiki Beach. He named it after a hero of a light opera who miraculously escaped sure death when the guns of a firing squad misfired. While the architecture is a blend of Mediterranean enhanced with turrets and Moorish bell towers, the thing most people remember is the flamingo pink exterior that makes it look like a grand wedding cake with pink icing, a fact leading to such affectionate nicknames as the Pink Palace and the Pink Lady. (The color is registered, so you can ask for Don Cesar Pink.)

The hotel soon became a favorite playground for such celebrities as F. Scott Fitzgerald and his wife Zelda; Clarence Darrow; Lou Gehrig; and even Al Capone. In the early 1930s, the New York Yankees made it their spring training site. The hotel remained a darling of high society until the depression and World War II sent it into decline. It was finally stripped and closed in 1967.

In 1973 the first of several multimillion-dollar restorations brought it back to life as a luxury hotel, and it has reigned ever since. Today it is affectionately known simply as "The Don" and is on the National Register of Historic Places.

Its interior emulates European elegance with rich English Exminster carpets, Italian crystal chandeliers, French candelabras, and fountains. There are 275 guest rooms, fifty suites, or, if you want to go all the way, two two-story penthouses. All have pastel- draped furnishings, Carrara marble accents, and spectacular views of either the gulf or Boca Ciega Bay. A short distance down the beach, the Beach House offers an additional seventy condo-style suites with full kitchens.

All the facilities you'd expect in a resort are here: two swimming pools, a beach with aquabikes and other water toys for rent, a boardwalk, a fitness center, a spa, restaurants, and for vacationing families, the Kids Ltd. program to entertain the children.

Two of the more unusual items about the resort are the Chef's Table and its ghosts. For about $75, up to eight guests can watch and talk with the chef and his staff as they prepare dinner in the kitchen of the fine dining Maritana Grille. The guests then have a meal that is a sampling of appetizers and a medley of entrees. As for the ghosts, so the story goes, Thomas Rowe fell in love with Lucinda when he was in Europe in the 1890s. Her family forbade the relationship, but Rowe never stopped loving Lucinda. In the lobby of his new hotel, he built a replica of the fountain where they secretly met. Before Lucinda died, she wrote him a deathbed letter saying they would meet again at the fountain. Rowe died in the hotel in 1940 and the fountain no longer exists, but employees tell tales of seeing a loving couple in vintage clothes who appear to be walking hand in hand and then simply disappear.

DON CESAR BEACH RESORT & SPA

Address:	**3400 Gulf Boulevard, St. Pete's Beach 33706**
	www.doncesar.com
Phone:	**800/637-7200; 727/360-1881**
Fax:	**727/367-6952**
Rates:	**$294-$1,944**
Units:	**345**

Island's End Resort

This hideaway is located on the southernmost tip of St. Petes Beach in the little village of Pass-a-Grille Beach, where the Gulf of Mexico and Tampa Bay and the Intracoastal Waterway merge. It would be hard to find a place that's not an island with more water surrounding it.

The village was originally named Passe-aux-Grilleurs for the fishermen who grilled their catch here. The Cubans and Bahamians were here several hundred years ago, then the British and Spanish arrived. Its history is such that just about the whole town, which is only a little more than a block wide and thirty some blocks long, is listed as a historic district in the National Register of Historic Places.

Island's End claims it has the perfect combination of sand, sea, sky, and rustic charm. We don't know if the combination is perfect, but we agree it is a most pleasant one, and a bargain getaway besides. The tiny resort offers peace and quiet in five one-bedroom cottages and a three-bedroom cottage with its own private pool that's great for a family or several friends. The cottages are linked by wooden walkways that meander through tropical foliage with gazebos and decks scattered throughout. All the cottages have great views of both sunrises and sunsets over the water.

Each gray weathered cottage is slightly different, but all have full kitchens, simple casual furniture, cable television with VCR, phones, and, of course, water views. There are hammocks, a fishing dock, a small private beach, and the five-mile-long public beach is just a short stroll away.

The staff speaks English and four eastern European languages: Latvian, Lithuanian, Russian, and Czech.

ISLAND'S END RESORT

Address:	1 Pass-a-Grille Way, St. Pete's Beach 33706
	www.islandsend.com
Phone:	727/360-5023
Fax:	727/367-7890
Rates:	$99-$120
Units:	6

Tradewinds Island Resorts

Three resorts, just a short stroll from each other, combine to create the Tradewinds Island Resorts. The trio's total of thirty-one acres make it the largest beachfront resort complex on Florida's central west coast. The three resorts are the Tradewinds Island Grand, Tradewinds Sandpiper, and the Tradewinds Sirata Beach. Since each has its own unique features, the synergy works for you. The sum of the whole is much greater than any of the parts, and, as a guest of one, you have access to the facilities and amenities of all.

Our favorite is the Island Grand. Its trademark is the waterway that meanders a quarter mile through the property, passing lush tropical landscaping, lily ponds, and white gazebos. You can share this waterway with the

swans, ducks, egrets, and herons by taking a complimentary paddleboat, or for a more romantic tour, you can schedule an evening gondola ride. This resort is the largest of the three with 577 rooms and suites and nine restaurants and lounges. As with all three resorts many of the rooms offer a water view.

The Sandpiper is a six-story building with 159 units, the majority of which are one-bedroom suites. Two- and three-bedroom suites and penthouse units are also available. The unique feature of this resort is that it provides the only year-round kosher kitchen in the Tampa Bay area that's established in accordance with conservative Judaism kosher standards.

The Sirata's four buildings all have a Mediterranean flair. Although primarily designed as a conference center, it offers 150 rooms and 230 suites on thirteen beachfront acres. The three add up to all the beach you could want, all the water toys you could want to rent, heated pools—one that's enclosed—a sauna, a putting green, tennis courts with an on-site pro, a fitness center with complimentary aerobics classes, croquet, life-size chess, a total of thirteen restaurants, and a salon offering massage therapy.

If you want to give your kids something extra, you can KONK them. Family oriented, the resorts have a kids program called KONK (Kids Only, No Kidding) that offers supervised activities for their guests between the ages of three and twelve.

Europeans discovered this complex years ago, so members of the staff are available who can speak French, German, and Spanish.

TRADEWINDS ISLAND RESORTS

Address:	**6000 Gulf Boulevard, St. Pete's Beach 33706**
	www.tradewindsresort.com
Phone:	**877/300-5519; 727/360-5551**
Fax:	**727/562-1215**
Rates:	**$159-$899**
Units:	**over 900 in three resorts**

TAMPA

Bed tax 11 percent

Hyatt Regency Westshore

One of the great things about this hotel is that it's located in the center of a thirty-five-acre mangrove and wildlife preserve overlooking Tampa Bay with magnificent views of the bay and the city's skyline. Combine this delightful setting with an interior featuring marble floors, hand-painted ceilings, and guest rooms with equally gorgeous views, and you have a gem. In fact it got four diamonds, according to the AAA, and four stars in Mobil's book—just one step below their top rating.

The hotel received a well-deserved Florida Audubon Society Corporate Award for its environmentally sensitive development of the site. Prior to site planning, the susceptible wetlands in the area were identified and targeted for protection. Then all construction was on upland areas. A million and a half dollars were spent for additional land acquisition to protect the wetlands. To verify that this effort was all worthwhile, take a stroll on the Nature Trail boardwalk into the preserve and observe the wide variety of birds that nest there.

The fourteen-story hotel offers 377 guest rooms and twenty-three suites, many with bay views. In addition, there are forty-five one- and two-story Spanish-style Casitas, like small condos, on the Bay. It might be worth your while to look into paying the little extra to get your own private Casita or a room on the concierge floor, which offers many extra amenities.

Facilities include two swimming pools, a private beach area, two tennis courts, a health club, meeting rooms, and three restaurants, including a seafood restaurant by the bay and a fine-dining one atop the roof.

HYATT REGENCY WESTSHORE

Address:	**6200 Courtney Campbell Causeway, Tampa 33607**
	www.hyatt.com
Phone:	**813/874-1234; (reservations 800/233-1234)**
Fax:	**813/286-9864**
Rates:	**$225-$250**
Units:	**445**

Wildlife on Easy Street

This place is for the cats, and we don't mean the cute little domestic kind. The "Wildlife" in the name is accurate, because this is an exotic cat sanctuary. You can have the memorable experience of staying in a cabin with some of these wild cats as backyard neighbors. Set up for your safety, of course, it allows you the opportunity to interact with the cats.

The forty-acre nonprofit sanctuary is hidden down a dirt road across from a mall. It is home to more than two hundred animals that were saved from being abandoned or abused, including bobcats, caracals, servals, ocelots, jaguars, Siberian lynxes, tigers, mountain lions, and leopards.

The sanctuary was founded by Carole Lewis. Carole always loved cats of all sizes, and in 1992 when she discovered that a farmer in

Minnesota was going to slaughter more than fifty bobcats and lynxes for their fur, she bought him out to save their lives. Then she had to figure out what to do with them. It took awhile, but the end result is this sanctuary.

Carole and her husband Dan subsidize much of the expenses of the sanctuary with the earnings from their real estate business. But that can't pay all the bills. Just one example of expenses is that these animals eat about four hundred pounds of beef and chicken daily at a cost of around six hundred dollars. The rest of the bills are paid from donations and fees from such programs as tours, photo safaris, and bed-and-breakfast with the cats.

The beds in the bed-and-breakfast are in three rustic cabins set in the cages of some of those exotic felines. The host and hostess cats have been carefully chosen from among the smaller cats (no tigers or leopards) that have learned to accept humans and are relatively tame. These include various wildcats, bobcats, lynxes, servals, and caracals. Each cabin is actually in a cat cage, but separated from the cats by another cage around the cabin. Cabins are small, but can accommodate two adults (no children under eighteen years old), have twin beds, a bathroom and shower, a television, a VCR, and a kitchenette with a small refrigerator.

Guests are given a two-hour orientation that includes how to properly interact with the animals. After that they are on their own to come and go as they please, and play with the cats. If you can't stay overnight, this is such a unique place it's worth putting on your personal list of Tampa attractions to visit, but reservations are required.

WILDLIFE ON EASY STREET

Address:	12802 Easy Street, Tampa 33625
	www.wildlifeeasyst.com
Phone:	813/920-4130
Fax:	813/920-5924
Rates:	$100 all year
Units:	3

Wyndham Harbour Island Hotel

Usually when we write about a hotel on an island it's well offshore. This island, however, is conveniently located just off downtown Tampa. Harbour Island is a 177-acre urban complex of businesses, condos, shops, the hotel, and a marina. Although the twelve-story luxury hotel is just across the bridge from the heart of downtown, being on an island separates it nicely from the traffic and the hurried pace. At the same time, if you want to go downtown, a free trolley makes frequent stops at the door.

The lobby is pleasing to the eye, with its dark green marble floor with deep pile area rugs and furniture upholstered in bright fabrics in classic Florida colors. Adding to the feeling of elegance are the massive ballroom doors made of tiger maple. You have a choice of 279 guest rooms or twenty-three suites, including seven one-bedroom suites. All are bright and elegantly furnished, and all offer outstanding views of the city and the waters surrounding the island.

Facilities include a large heated swimming pool overlooking the fifty-slip marina, and a restaurant where you can watch the boats glide by as you dine. Guests also have privileges at the Harbour Island Athletic Club, which has fitness equipment, tennis, racquetball, and squash.

WYNDHAM HARBOUR ISLAND HOTEL

Address:	725 S. Harbour Island Boulevard, Tampa 33602
	www.wyndham.com
Phone:	800/WYNDHAM (996-3426); 813/229-5000
Fax:	813/229-5022
Rates:	$199-$259
Units:	299

LAND O' LAKES

Bed tax 8 percent

Paradise Lakes Resort

This is the largest clothing-optional/nudist resort in rural Pasco County, which reportedly has more clothing-optional/nudist resorts than any other county in America. Altogether they are the second-largest employer in the county. Paradise Lakes is one of the 225 membership clubs affiliated with the American Association of Nude Recreation.

Clothing-optional means you can wear clothing, but most of the six thousand members and residents of the resort and the more than eighty thousand annual visitors opt for nudism as their lifestyle while here.

Who are these members and visitors who choose the philosophy that "nude is natural?" According to the Trade Association for Nude Recreation, they are teachers and students, doctors and medical professionals, computer programmers and mechanics, homemakers and lawyers. They are singles, couples, and families, both from the United States and abroad. In other words, they are a wide variety of people from all walks of life who just enjoy many activities, in appropriate settings, without the restriction of clothing. The Association also emphasizes that clothes-free facilities are legal, safe, and secure.

This seventy-six acre resort, which was established in 1981, includes a large residential community of more than five hundred permanent residents who live in more than 350 homes, apartments, condos, townhouses, and mobile homes. Visitor accommodations include hotel rooms, cottages, and one- and two-bedroom condominiums. There's also a full-service RV park and tent camping area.

Facilities are what you'd find in any resort: a great beach on a spring-fed lake with canoes, kayaks, and paddleboats available; five pools plus a seventy-foot Jacuzzi conversion pool (think of it as a giant whirlpool tub); two hot tubs and a sauna; five tennis courts; an exercise room; a miniature golf course; a variety of sports courts; a day spa; a salon; a restaurant; and a nightclub with live entertainment.

PARADISE LAKES RESORT

Address:	P.O. Box 750B, Land O' Lakes 34639
	www.paradiselakes.com
Phone:	800/ 237-2226 (Outside FL); 813/949-9327
Fax:	813/949-1008
Rates:	$65-$110 all year
Units:	47

WESLEY CHAPEL

Bed tax 8 percent

Saddlebrook Resort-Tampa

S is for Sports, and Saddlebrook is for Sports with a capital *S*.

Let's get the big picture first. This internationally known golf and tennis resort is located on 480 acres of beautifully wooded countryside north of Tampa. Facilities include golf courses, tennis courts, world famous golf and tennis schools, swimming pools, a full-service spa, a fitness center, a great program for children, and a five-acre Executive Challenge Course.

Now to flesh that out, this is the home of the Arnold Palmer Golf Academy World Headquarters and two championship golf courses. Features include the Harry Hopman Tennis Program, as well as forty-five tennis courts with a range of surfaces that match all the major open tournament courts in the world.

Saddlebrook's Sports Village features a large glass-enclosed fitness center; a variety of sports fields and courts, including soccer; fourteen of

the resort's tennis courts; a swimming pool; a whirlpool; and a fitness trail. The centerpiece of the Village is the SuperPool, 270 feet long with twenty-five-meter racing lanes. The seven-thousand-square-foot spa offers a variety of body treatments for both men and women—they have rooms for couples. Guests can select treatments à la carte or choose from a variety of full- and half-day packages. And while you are off doing your own thing, kids ages four to twelve can enjoy the day of supervised activities at the S Kids Club. Theme programs are presented each day of the week, many of them are off property to area attractions.

Not forgetting the stomach, there are five dining options. There's plenty to do and lots of space to do it in.

If you see a number of very talented young people playing golf or tennis, they are probably from the Prep School. (You might want to get their autographs because some of them will undoubtedly be stars in those games in the near future.) These students are taking a full-time college preparatory program in their own schoolhouse on the property, which offers a combination of academics and intense golf and/or tennis instruction.

As for places to stay, there are eight hundred attractively decorated and comfortably furnished guest rooms or in one- two- or three-bedroom suites that are in clusters among the greenery throughout the resort.

SADDLEBROOK RESORT-TAMPA

Address:	5700 Saddlebrook Way, Wesley Chapel 33543
	www.saddlebrookresort.com
Phone:	800/729-8383; 813/973-1111
Fax:	813/973-4504
Rates:	$277-$370
Units:	800

For Additional Information
on the Central West Region:

BRADENTON AREA CVB
P.O. Box 1000
Bradenton, FL 34206
941/729-9177
Fax: 941/729-1820
www.floridaislandbeaches.org

SARASOTA VISITOR
INFORMATION CENTER
655 N. Tamiami Trail
Sarasota, FL 34236
800/522-9799; 941/957-1877
Fax: 941/951-2956
www.cvb.sarasota.fl.us

ST. PETERSBURG/CLEARWATER CVB
14450 Forty-Sixth Street North, Suite 108
Clearwater, FL 33762
727/464-7200
Fax: 727/464-7222
www.stpete-clearwater.com

TAMPA/HILLSBOROUGH VISITOR
INFORMATION CENTER
400 North Tampa Street, Suite 1010
Tampa, FL 33602
800/826-8358; 813/223-1111
Fax: 813/229-6616
www.gotampa.com

5 CENTRAL

LAKE COUNTY

(Howey-in-the-Hills and Mount Dora)

This county is appropriately named. Within its borders are more than a thousand lakes covering more than two hundred of the county's twelve hundred square miles. Many of these are part of the Ocklawaha Chain of Lakes which, through a series of locks, canals, and lakes, connects to the St. Johns River and provides boaters access to the Atlantic Ocean.

While nature is the big attraction here, there are also adventure attractions. The Seminole Lake Gliderport in Clermont offers introductory sailplane rides. Also, two of the top water ski schools in the country are in Okahumpa, and Quest Air, in Groveland, offers parasailing via aerotow. According to the Guinness Book of World Records, the world's largest dollhouse is in Lake County. It's the sixty-foot miniature replica of the White House at the National Presidents Hall of Fame in Clermont.

Two of the several towns in the county are Howey-in-the-Hills and Mount Dora. William J. Howey came here around 1916 and bought sixty thousand acres with the intent of building a horticultural empire. The Great Depression killed that ambitious plan, but Howey's name stuck on this tiny village.

Mount Dora has been referred to as a place right out of a Norman Rockwell illustration. Visitors often say it reminds them of the town where they grew up—or the place where they wished they had. The town is located at one of the highest elevations in the state. It's less than two hundred feet, but in a state where the terrain rarely gets much above sea level, that's high. Residents poke fun at this with bumper stickers and T-shirts that read "I Climbed Mount Dora." The ambiance of the town has also been compared to a New England village with rolling hills, historic buildings, picket fences, large porches, and a quaint downtown with antique shops and gourmet restaurants.

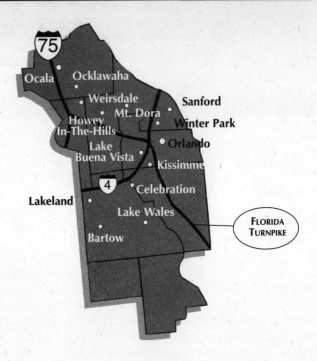

High Season: Spring

(Note: All lodging rates are for high season. Off-season rates can be significantly lower.)

HOWEY-IN-THE HILLS

Bed tax 9 percent

Howey-in-the-Hills Mission Inn Golf and Tennis Resort

This resort looks like it was once a Spanish mission since all the buildings conform to that theme with Spanish tiles, buff-colored stucco, terra cotta tile roofs, arched walkways, and lovely fountains and courtyards. Actually, the decision to create the Spanish Colonial theme was made in 1969, not long after Nick Beucher responded to a Wall Street Journal ad and bought what was then the run-down Floridan Country Club, which dated back to the 1920s. At that time, the club had two great assets going for it. It was secluded and tranquil, and it had a golf course built by Charles E. Clarke of the famous Troon Golf Course in Scotland.

Nick's family still owns and operates the resort, but now the extensive grounds include two golf courses, the Bill Skelley School of Golf, eight tennis courts, an outdoor heated pool, an exercise room, a lakeside pavilion, restaurants, jogging trails, and a playhouse for children that resembles the Mission Inn.

This is Lake County, so it's natural that there is also a lake here. Lake Harris is one of the largest of Florida's seventy-eight-hundred lakes, and the Inn has a marina on it where you can arrange for guided fishing trips, rent bass and pontoon boats, charter powerboats, and rent slips. When you tire of all the other activities, you can take a cruise on the lake on the Inn's 1930s antique yacht, *La Reina*.

Your lodging choices here range from hotel rooms and one- two- and three bedroom suites to two-bedroom villas. These are located in three inns (called posadas) and a villa complex. All the accommodations are spacious, tastefully decorated, and most have screened porches that overlook one of the golf courses. Shuttle service is available.

HOWEY-IN-THE-HILLS MISSION INN GOLF AND TENNIS RESORT

Address:	10400 County Road 48, Howey-in-the-Hills 34737
	www.missioninnresort.com
Phone:	800/874-9053; 352/324-3101
Fax:	352/324-2636
Rates:	$225–$480
Units:	190

MOUNT DORA

Bed tax 9 percent

Darst Victorian Manor Bed & Breakfast

This Victorian manor is both a beauty and a deception. When Nanci and Jim Darst decided to fulfill their longtime dream to open a bed-and-breakfast, they started looking for a Victorian house with character in an ideal location. After several years traveling up and down the east coast, they found the ideal location: Mount Dora. And here's where the deception comes in. Although the Darsts are in no way trying to deceive, when they could not find the Victorian house they wanted, they built one. It looks like it's right out of the Victorian era while actually they built it in the 1990s as their modern three-story interpretation of an 1880s-style Queen Anne with traditional gabled roofs, corner turrets, and a spacious verandah.

The manor overlooks Lake Dora. It offers four guest rooms and two suites, all decorated with Victorian-style furniture, both antiques and reproductions, and each has a private bath. Our favorite is the Queen Victoria suite. Located on the third floor (not for those who have difficulty climbing stairs), this three-room suite is decorated in cranberry and hunter green. It includes a sitting room in the turret that overlooks the lake and a remote control fireplace.

There are advantages to building your own Victorian home. For one thing it eliminates potential guest horror stories that sometimes result from stays in real Victorian buildings where the modern conversion doesn't always resolve problems inherent in old buildings.

DARST VICTORIAN MANOR & BREAKFAST

Address:	495 Old Highway 441, Mount Dora 32757
	www.bbonline.com/fl/darstmanor
Phone:	888/53-DARST (533-2778); 352/383-4050
Fax:	352/383-7653
Rates:	$135-$220
Units:	6

POLK COUNTY

(Bartow, Haines City, Lakeland, Lake Wales)

Polk County is a large (2,048 square miles) county located in the geographic center of Florida, between Orlando and Tampa. More citrus is produced here than in the entire state of California. Mainly rural, it has pine forests, rolling hills, pasturelands, more than six hundred lakes, and colorful citrus groves. Tourism is one of its major industries with ecotourism as a prime ingredient.

Among the major attractions here are: the "Water Ski Capital of the World" at Cypress Gardens; Bok Tower Gardens, a national historic landmark near Lake Wales; the largest single site collection of Frank Lloyd Wright architecture in Lakeland; the world's largest private collection of vintage aircraft at the Fantasy of Flight in Polk City; and major league baseball spring training camps for the Cleveland Indians in Winter Haven, Detroit Tigers in Lakeland, and Kansas City Royals near Haines City.

BARTOW

Bed tax 10 percent

Stanford Inn

Even if you have never heard of Bartow, you may still recognize this 1905 house with its brilliant exterior colors of yellow and blue. It was in the movie *My Girl*, and the colors that were painted for the movie still make it stand-out. It has also been in several television commercials and people frequently come by to photograph it, which probably makes it one of the most photographed homes in central Florida. Even if it wasn't famous, this house would still stand out. Everything about it is as close to perfect as you could get in a bed-and-breakfast.

Angie and Bob Clark gutted it and started over (Bob is in the construction business). They now offer their guests a choice of six rooms: four in the main house and two cottages. The main house rooms are beautifully themed and named: Cabbage Rose, Azalea, Victorian Rose, and our favorite, the Francesca Suite, which has ornate gold wall covering with matching bedding, colonnade-faced fireplace, and a sunroom. The two-story Rosie's Cottage, which was the original servants' quarters, and one-story carriage house have the same elegant décor and comfortable ambiance. Both cottages have kitchens. All the rooms have private baths and are delightfully decorated with fine antiques. Some rooms have fire-places, and the Azalea and Victorian Rose have Jacuzzi tubs. Outside, there is a large verandah, a lush tropical hidden garden, and a heated pool.

STANFORD INN

Address:	**555 East Stanford, Bartow 33830**
	www.wbus.com/stanfordinn
Phone:	**941/533-2393**
Fax:	**941/533-2393**
Rates:	**$125-$165 all year**
Units:	**6**

HAINES CITY

Bed Tax 10 percent

Grenelefe Golf & Tennis Resort

A character in Robin Hood inspired the name, and although the type of trees aren't the same, Robin himself might feel right at home among the natural beauty of the tall pines and sprawling oaks on this thousand acre resort. And if he had taken up the Scottish game of golf, he'd be in heaven since there are three championship courses here. In keeping with the "nat-ural" Florida ambiance of the resort, all three are part of the National Audubon Society's program to preserve and enhance the environmental quality of golf courses. The Ken Venturi Golf Academy is also here.

Besides golf, the "tennis" in the resort's name refers to the twenty tennis courts. If that's not enough, there's a sixty-four-hundred-square-foot lake offering fishing (Big Bass world fishing tournaments are held here) and wildlife cruises, four pools, Jacuzzis, saunas, a fitness center, hiking and nature trails.

The nine hundred guest accommodations range from hotel-style rooms to one- and two-bedroom villas clustered in low-rise buildings, many of which overlook the golf courses. The traditional rooms have either a balcony or patio. Each villa includes a living/dining area and a fully equipped kitchen. For dining, there are a number of restaurants that offer both fine dining and snack items.

GRENELEFE GOLF & TENNIS RESORT

Address:	3200 S.R. 546, Haines City 33844
	www.grenelefe.com
Phone:	800/422-5333; 941/422-7511; 941/421-5000
Rates:	$190-$420
Units:	900

LAKELAND

Terrace Hotel

When it opened in 1924, this ten-story hotel was advertised as Florida's finest year-round resort and tourist hotel. The concept of year-round was novel in the days before air-conditioning when most Florida hotels were closed during the summer. During its boom years it hosted such famous guests as Henry Ford, musicians Fred Waring and Wayne King, Frank Sinatra, and legendary architect Frank Lloyd Wright, who designed many of the structures on the Lakeland campus of Florida Southern University.

After World War II, the hotel began a slow downward slide. By the 1980s it was a run-down transient hotel that was finally closed in 1986. Ten years later, an investment group purchased it. The hotel was modernized and brought back to its original grandeur in a restoration that cost more than seven million dollars.

And *grandeur* is the right word. Even its location, overlooking the small downtown Lake Mirror, fits that description. (The Lake Mirror Promenade is listed in the National Register of Historic Places.) A relatively small hotel, it is still impressive and grand on its own scale. Its large classical entrance features four Ionic columns, gargoyles, and a huge swan neck's pediment. Inside, the lobby is unusually ornate with gray marble walls, black tile floor, elegant chandeliers, huge arched windows, and a cypress ceiling with geometrical designs that have been stained in green, red, and brown.

Guest accommodations include seventy-three spacious and well-appointed rooms and fifteen suites. Many of these are decorated by local corporate sponsors and a number of them have views of Lake Mirror. The hotel's Terrace Grill, off the lobby, is a popular restaurant with Lakeland residents.

TERRACE HOTEL

Address:	**329 E. Main, Lakeland 33801**
	www.terracehotel.com
Phone:	**888/644-8400; 863/688-0800**
Fax:	**863/668-0664**
Rates:	**$109-$169**
Units:	**88**

LAKE WALES

Sales tax 10 percent

Chalet Suzanne Country Inn

The Hinshaw family, which has owned and operated the inn since it started in 1931, describe it as a Swiss-styled village. To us it's more like storybook land combined with Old Florida quirkiness.

What else can you call an inn with Tyrolean towers, terraces, turrets, gabled roofs, and balconies? No two rooms are alike. They are all painted in vivid sherbet colors and meander all over the place. This thirty-room country inn was a miniature fantasyland long before Walt Disney came to Florida.

As for the idea of it being a village, that has some merit, too. The seventy-acre estate has a private airstrip, a lake, a ceramics studio, a restaurant, specialty shops, and a soup cannery. It also has a European-tiled swimming pool, a wall of ceramic tiles designed and bought by guests, croquet, badminton, horseshoes, volleyball, jogging trails, a rare collection of art and artifacts, and—no surprise—its own National Historic District.

Unique is an overused word, but it fits here because each room is truly one of a kind. All are uniquely furnished, too, with antiques from the family collection or excellent reproductions, paintings, photographs, and ceramic figurines. Your room might be rustic or pink plush chintz. And the second story

honeymoon suite has a dumbwaiter for delivery of meals so the honeymooners don't have to leave the room.

The chalet started during the depression when Bertha Hinshaw was left a widow with two children and had to earn a living. She opened a small restaurant that soon became popular. Then she began adding rooms for guests, building them from whatever material she could find. From there, it all just grew and grew in every direction.

The award-winning restaurant that also grew and grew now has fourteen different levels. Every year for more than twenty-five years, *Florida Trend* magazine has selected this restaurant as one of its top ten in the state. The meals are exquisitely gourmet—and expensive.

There may be other inns that have their own cannery, although we don't know of any, but none of them can claim that their soups went on the Apollo-Soyuz space mission or are for sale at the Smithsonian Air and Space Museum.

CHALET SUZANNE COUNTRY INN

Address: **3800 Chalet Suzanne Drive, Lake Wales 33853**
www.chaletsuzanne.com
Phone: **800/433-6011; 863/676-6011**
Fax: **863/676-1814**
Rates: **$169-$229 all year**
Units: **30**

RIVER RANCH

Sales tax 10 percent

River Ranch

More than two hundred years before the West was won, the cowboy lifestyle—cattle raising, riding, roping, whip-cracking, and shootouts—

was already going on in Spanish Florida. America's first cattle trail was in Florida. It was used by the Confederate Army to drive cattle north to feed its soldiers. Parts of that trail are now the Florida Scenic Hiking Trail that cuts through River Ranch.

The ranch traces its history back to the Kissimmee Island Cattle Company in the 1800s. The cowboy traditions of both Florida and the Old West are carried on at this sixteen-hundred-acre country western resort that is so big it is three miles from the entrance to the inn.

One tie with its past is its claim to having the longest continuously running rodeo in the U.S. There are performances every Saturday evening, rain or shine. It also offers everything you would expect of a dude ranch from line dancing to horseback rides. Facilities include a five thousand-foot paved and lighted airstrip, skeet and gun range, golf course and golf school, marina with airboat ecotours of Lake Kissimmee, four swimming pools, tennis courts, fitness center, two restaurants, and of course, a saloon. For the kids, there's a petting farm complete with a live pony carousel. Coyotes, deer, wild turkeys, and wild boar roam the vast range, and you can take a safari tour to see them as well as learn how the cowboys and Indians lived in this area for hundreds of years.

You have a choice of regular rooms at the ranch, one- and two-room suites, efficiencies, or one- and two-bedroom cottages. All the rooms except ones at the ranch have either a kitchenette or a full kitchen, and some of the cottages have a fireplace. Our favorite was the Courtyard Suites because each has a screened porch on which to sit 'n' rock.

RIVER RANCH

Address:	**P.O. Box 30030, River Ranch 33867-0030**
Phone:	**800/785-2102; 863/692-1321**
Fax:	**941/692-1303**
Rates:	**$100-$244**
Units:	**200**

OCALA AREA

(Ocala, Ocklawaha, Weirsdale)

Ocala is in Marion County which is the heart of Florida's horse country. When it comes to white fenced horse farms, this area can easily compete with the famed Bluegrass area of Lexington, Kentucky. There are more than four hundred horse farms that raise and nurture more that forty different breeds including Arabians, Quarter horses, Paso Finos, and Thoroughbreds. You'll even find breeders of miniature horses here. What Marion County has that Lexington can't offer is a warm winter where horses can be trained for the spring racing season. The county boasts five winners of the Kentucky Derby.

OCALA

Sales tax 6 percent

Heritage Country Inn

Lao Coutts is an accomplished house designer with graduate work in housing for the physically impaired, an accomplished seamstress, a good cook, and an experienced real estate saleswoman. Her husband, Harold, is a retired engineer with building experience and a master craftsman. What a perfect team to build and run a bed-and-breakfast inn.

And that's just what they did. With Lao designing and Harold making all the inn's interior doors, mantels, beds, and other handsome furnishings in his workshop, they built their one-story ideal inn.

The inn offers six spacious guest rooms. They all have a sitting area, a fireplace, a private bath with Jacuzzi tub, a walk-in shower, and a separate private entrance. Each room is highlighted in woods native to Florida and themed to represent a different period in local history. The Plantation Room, for example, has the ambiance of a mid-1800s master bedroom with its rich cherry furnishings in traditional Queen Anne style. The Thoroughbred Room, our favorite, is decorated in English country style with rich oak panels and a handcrafted formal canopied bed with elegant red and gold paisley print fabric.

Although you wouldn't know it unless you looked closely, all the rooms are completely handicapped accessible. And, unlike many bed-and-breakfasts, children are welcome. If you are interested in touring a horse farm or riding, the Coutts can make the arrangements.

HERITAGE COUNTRY INN

Address:	14343 West Highway 40, Ocala 34481
	www.heritagecountryinn.com
Phone:	888/240-2233; 352/489-0023
Rates:	$79-$94 all year
Units:	6

Seven Sisters Inn Bed & Breakfast

It has been a number of years since Florida's Historic Preservation Society awarded its "Best Restoration Project in Florida" to this inn, but the stunning restoration job is still evident today. In fact, it may have been restored to a higher level of elegance than when it was built as a family home in 1888.

A classic Queen Anne Victorian on the National Register of Historic Places, the house has a wraparound porch, turret, and clapboard siding painted in pleasant shades of blue and pink.

Inside, the eight guest rooms are dramatically furnished with period antiques. Originally, seven of the eight rooms were named after the seven sisters of an early owner. But now, six have those sisters' names and the other two are named after the present owners, Bonnie and Ken. In any case, each of the eight guest rooms is dramatically furnished with antiques designed to match the persona of the person it's named after. All have private baths, some with Jacuzzis and others with Victorian soaking tubs, and most have a phone and television.

Our favorite is Sylvia's Room (the most expensive). It is the largest room with an attractive sitting area and an ornamental fireplace. It is richly decorated with peach moiré, chintz, and lace. In contrast to this, and perhaps to match his persona, Ken's room is painted in bold colors and has a red Jacuzzi tub for two. If you want more room, Lottie's Loft on the third floor offers twelve hundred square feet of space and includes a Jacuzzi tub for two under a large skylight. In addition to being a wedding favorite, the inn often hosts business retreats, murder mystery weekends, and a yummy chocolate extravaganza.

An interesting aside is that Ken and Bonnie are both active commercial airline pilots (for two different airlines).

SEVEN SISTERS INN BED & BREAKFAST

Address:	**820 S.E. Fort King Street, Ocala 32671**
	www.7sistersinn.com
Phone:	**800/250-3496; 352/867-1170**
Fax:	**352/867-5266**
Rates:	**$115-$185 all year**
Units:	**8**

OCKLAWAHA

Bed tax 8 percent

The Refuge at Ocklawaha

If you truly want to get away from it all, this place lives up to its name. It is a natural refuge offering the serenity of woods, waterways, and wildlife. You'll be lulled to sleep at night by the breeze rustling through the Spanish moss on the live oak trees and awakened in the morning by the birds and, perhaps, the whinny of a horse.

Although the setting is natural, the lodgings are far from rustic. From the outside, the cabins may appear that way, but they have all the modern conveniences, including air-conditioning. They are comfortable and are specially decorated to reflect the heritage of the place and the region. There are no phones, televisions, or stereos, but most rooms do have rocking chairs on the porches where you can sit and enjoy nature.

This first truly ecological resort on the U.S. mainland is a work in

progress being developed by Stanley Selengut and Florida Legacy Lodges, creator of environmentally sensitive resorts. The 1930s hunting lodge has been converted into a dining room and meeting rooms. Nearby is a pool and screened pavilion. When we visited, there were nineteen cracker-style cabins, each with two units separated by a breezeway, all built with conservation principles in mind. Additional cabins are in the works.

To give you the opportunity to fully enjoy this attractive natural setting, you can bike, hike, ride a horse, canoe or kayak, or take one of the daily pontoon boat rides. The staff naturalist here claims this is the best birding in Florida, and after touring the refuge with him, we believe it.

THE REFUGE AT OCKLAWAHA

Address:	14835 S.E. Eighty-fifth Street, Ocklawaha 32179
	www.flanaturelodge.org
Phone:	877/862-8873; 352/288-2233
Fax:	352/288-6369
Rate:	$125
Units:	38

WEIRSDALE

Bed tax 9 percent

Continental Acres Equine Resort

There are several resorts in Florida where you can vacation with your horse. This resort, however, is also for carriage drivers. It is also the home of the Austin Carriage Museum. Someone described it to us as "equine heaven" for both horse lovers and the horses.

To start with, the resort offers a wide range of opportunities for riding and training on special courses and in pastures outlined with traditional white fences. For riders, the training emphasizes classical dressage. For carriage drivers, world-class trainers offer lessons in classical driving, four-in-hand, simple, pair, tandem, and pleasure driving. The facility also includes seven barns and seventy stalls.

The resort is an outgrowth of Gloria Austin's driving hobby. Mrs. Austin had put off serious riding while she raised a family. Then, when she bought herself a horse on her fortieth birthday, a friend suggested she take up carriage driving because "that's what ladies do." She did what ladies do and became so intrigued by the sport she now travels all over the world—with her horses—to give driving demonstrations or take part in competitions.

Another result of her hobby is the Austin Carriage Museum where you can—by appointment and for a fee—learn about the more than eighty-five original and restored carriages from all over the world.

We two-legged guests have a choice of lodging that includes a cottage, one- and two-bedroom condo-style units with or without a kitchen, and several park mobiles (complete little one-bedroom mobile homes). Since this is an equine resort, most of the accommodations come with some combination of stalls, pastures, or turn-out paddocks.

CONTINENTAL ACRES EQUINE RESORT

Address:	**P.O. Box 68, Weirsdale 32195**
	www.continentalacres.com
Phone:	**352/750-5500**
Fax:	**352/753-3105**
Rates:	**$65-$85 all year**
Units:	**14**

Shamrock Thistle and Crown

Irish linens, Irish china, Irish crystal, and an 800-4-BLARNEY phone number, should give you a good hint about the heritage of your innkeeper here.

Anne is an Irish journalist who came to Ocala to visit her brother and stayed to marry Brantley Overcash, a CPA from Texas. Marriage means finding a place to live, so the couple spent Sundays house hunting. At that time, they had a tiny seed of a thought that someday they might want to open a bed-and-breakfast. When they saw this three-story 1887 Victorian on three acres, the seed started to germinate. But it still took awhile to sprout. They bought the house in 1989, worked for several years fixing it up and transforming the grounds, and finally opened their bed-and-breakfast in 1994.

Your choices here include six rooms in the house and a Victorian dollhouse cottage in the back yard. All the rooms are themed, have private baths, and are furnished with antiques. Some of the rooms have whirlpool tubs and fireplaces. Our favorite is the European Formal with its antique four-poster bed, fireplace, and whirlpool.

The front porch has two of the furnishings we love most on a porch, a swing and rocking chairs. There's also a swimming pool.

The cottage, which truly looks like a grown-up Victorian dollhouse also has a fireplace, a sitting room, a Jacuzzi on the back deck, plus porches and privacy. As you might expect, this is a favorite of honeymooners.

With a little encouragement (very little), Anne will entertain you with Irish poetry.

SHAMROCK THISTLE AND CROWN

Address:	**P.O. Box 624, Weirsdale 32195-0624**
	www.shamrockbb.com
Phone:	**(800)4-Blarney (425-2763); 352/821-1887**
Rates:	**$99-$185**
Units:	**7**

GREATER ORLANDO AREA

(Celebration, Kissimmee, Lake Buena Vista,
Maitland, Orlando, Winter Park)

Thirty years ago Orlando was a modest-sized community surrounded by citrus groves and cattle ranches. Then in the early 1970s, Walt Disney came to town and it hasn't been the same since.

Today, the Greater Orlando Area might be called "Theme Park and Attractions Heaven." It is the biggest tourist attraction in the state. The whole area has experienced unprecedented growth and is still growing. In addition to the major Disney and Universal theme parks, there are more than eighty attractions in the area. To take care of the constant flood of visitors, there are more than ninety-one thousand rooms and thirty eight hundred restaurants in the several adjoining cities that make up the area.

But it's not all fantasy attractions. Performing Arts include the Orlando Opera Company, Southern Ballet, Orlando/University of Central Florida Shakespeare Festival, the Civic Theatre of Central Florida, and the Orlando Philharmonic Orchestra. Museums include the Morse Museum of Fine Art, the Orlando Museum of Art, and the Orange County

Historical Museum. There are seven regional malls with more than seven hundred stores plus several outlet malls. And for the sports enthusiast, the Greater Orlando Area offers more than eight hundred tennis courts, 125 golf courses, and professional sports teams—the Orlando Magic of the NBA (National Basketball Association), the Orlando Miracle of the WNBA (Women's National Basketball Association), the Orlando Solar Bears of the IHL (International Hockey League), and the Atlanta Braves and Houston Astros baseball teams come here for spring training.

All this explains why the slogan of the Orlando/Orange County Convention and Visitors Bureau is: "Orlando: You never outgrow it."

CELEBRATION

Bed tax 11 percent

Celebration Hotel

Celebration is a planned community designed to combine the mood and feeling of Old Florida with the charm of small town America near big town Orlando. The community was built and is owned by the Disney company. The hotel, however, is privately owned and operated by Kessler Enterprises. It is one of Richard Kessler's unique hotels that is part of a portfolio of Grand Theme Hotels that include the Casa Monica in St. Augustine, the Sheraton Studio City, the Doubletree Castle in the theme park area of Orlando, and the Westin Grand Bohemian in downtown Orlando.

The Celebration Hotel is designed to be in harmony with that community's theme of the natural simplicity of the 1920s. It has a Florida wood frame design with clapboard siding, awnings, a tin roof, low eves, dormers, and the hotel's symbol, a lighthouse tower.

This full-service, upscale boutique hotel has 115 guest rooms and suites, some with balconies, all with views of either Celebration Lake or the town. All the rooms are attractively furnished in keeping with the 1920s theme. A number of rooms have windows that actually open on two walls. Our favorite was Room 322 with its expansive windows and view of the lake. We especially liked the rocking chairs on the hotel's back porch that also overlooks the lake.

Facilities include an outdoor heated pool and Jacuzzi, fitness center and day spa, and restaurants. Celebration is designed as a pedestrian village, so the shops, restaurants, and movie theater are all within easy walking distance. Paddleboats are available on the lake, and the town's eighteen hole golf course.

CELEBRATION HOTEL

Address:	**700 Bloom Street, Celebration 34747**
	www.celebrationhotel.com
Phone:	**407/566-6000**
Fax:	**407/566-1844**
Rates:	**$165-$470**
Units:	**144**

KISSIMMEE

Bed tax 12 percent

Holiday Inn Hotel & Suites, Main Gate East

While most businesses don't like clowning around on the job, this one encourages it and has made it part of the overall management style. All of the management and many of the staff are "certified" clowns.

It all started in 1987 when it was discovered that the full-time clown on the hotel's recreation staff couldn't meet the demand. So, Terry Whaples, a managing partner, started a clown training course for interested employees, and most of them were interested. The course leads to the creation of each student's own clown persona complete with name, personality, and costume. "Clowning not only teaches you to smile and laugh," she says, "it also teaches humility and a sense of humor about yourself—an important lesson when dealing with customers and employees in the hospitality industry."

The clowns fit in perfectly with this hotel's goal of being family friendly—making families and kids the number one priority. Other evidence of how family and kids are number one are in the fifty-five Kidsuites (see page 134), a special check-in window for kids, a specially themed kids area in the main restaurant, and Camp Holiday, which is a licensed childcare activity program for ages three to twelve. Another family-friendly offering is the extra discount for grandparents traveling with their grandchildren.

In addition to the Kidsuites, the hotel offers more than five hundred guest rooms and fifty-five two-room suites. Facilities include two heated swimming pools, two whirlpool spas, a kiddie pool, two playgrounds, and two lighted tennis courts and other sports courts.

HOLIDAY INN HOTEL & SUITES, MAIN GATE EAST

Address:	5678 Irlo Bronson Highway, Kissimmee 34746
	www.familyfunhotel.com
Phone:	800/FON-KIDS (366-5437); 407/396-4488
Fax:	407/396-8915
Rates:	$89-$225
Units:	614

LAKE BUENA VISTA

Bed tax 11 percent

Holiday Inn Family Suites Resort Lake Buena Vista

An all-suites hotel isn't a new concept, but a hotel with a bunch of out-of-the-ordinary themed suites sure is. We thought we had seen just about every variation of accommodations until we saw this one. The eight hundred suites in this resort offer such a variety that you may have a hard time making a selection.

There are the Classic Suites with two bedrooms, parlor area, bath, and kitchenette, and for longer stays there are the Residential Suites with

KIDSUITES

Although the Holiday Inn chain provides comfortable, clean, and reasonably priced lodging, most of them couldn't be classed as irresistible. However,

we thought the Holiday Inn Kidsuites would be irresistible for families.

The only entertainment for kids in most hotel/motel rooms is the television. Terry Whaples, now a partner in two Holiday Inns in Lake Buena Vista, decided to do something about that. She consulted with her partners and developed the idea of the Kidsuite: an expanded regular room for the parents with an attached but essentially separate room for the kids. The kid's room is colorfully and whimsically decorated and furnished with bunk beds, television, VCR, Nintendo, and other fun things

that make the kids feel they have their own space while the parents can still keep an eye on them. Kidsuites are designed for kids ten and under, but we found that kids a little older enjoy them, too.

This concept was so popular it has been built into

more than twenty Holiday Inns worldwide and the chain has adopted it for all their new Sunspree Resorts. Further expansion of the concept is in the works that will let the kids have their own separate fun room in a three-room suite.

The whole idea of what makes a hotel/motel room has been set for too long. The growing trend of family travel makes this type of innovation a most welcome development. We sincerely hope the other chains will take note of this and come up with guest-friendly innovations of their own.

one bedroom, a large parlor, bath, and a full kitchen. These are nice but not unusual. Next there are 474 Kidsuites, but in this hotel they aren't just an extended room, they are suites with a private bedroom, themed kid's bedroom, a parlor, bath, and a kitchenette. And then the fun begins. All the other types of suites have a bedroom, parlor, bath and kitchenette, plus another special room. Sweetheart Suites have a room with a large, heart-shaped whirlpool tub. Business Suites feature a small conference room. Fitness Suites offer you a chance to work out in your own small, but well-equipped, Nautilus Room. And the feature attraction in the Cinema Suites is a room with a sixty-inch television and a double rocker recliner.

The themes start as soon as you enter with a lobby designed to resemble an old train depot and a Kids' Check-in Desk. Other facilities include an Olympic–size lap pool, an Olympic-size zero-depth entry pool, interactive water park, kiddie pool, two whirlpools, fitness center, restaurants, and a children's recreation center.

This is such a family-friendly resort, you may find it hard to tear yourself away to go to the big theme parks.

HOLIDAY INN FAMILY SUITES RESORT LAKE BUENA VISTA

Address:	18000 International Drive South, Orlando 32821
	www.hifamilysuites.com
Phone:	877/387-KIDS (387-5437); 407/387-KIDS (387-5437)
Fax:	407/387-1490
Rates:	$139–$189
Units:	800

Holiday Inn Sunspree Resort Lake Buena Vista

You may not have noticed, but whenever we listed a Holiday Inn it was always because it had Kidsuites. Well this Holiday Inn is where it all started. It was the first in the world to offer Kidsuites, and today, out of more than five hundred rooms and suites, 231 are Kidsuites. They come in different sizes and themes. There are Kidsuites for two and Kidsuites for four. The different playhouse themes include Magic Castle, Noah's Ark, a Clown Circus Tent, Space Ship, and Fort Sunspree.

Kids are king at this resort, and to make sure they are treated like royalty all the management and many of the staff are graduates of a six-week Clown College. There's also a free daily supervised program of fun and games called Camp Holiday and a Cyber Arcade with computer and other games available to kids (and parents). By reservation, Max, the resort's (costumed) mascot will come and give your child a bedtime tuck-in. It also features Grandtravel programs designed for children traveling with grandparents. The resort has been named one of the best family friendly hotels in America by *Parents Magazine* and was featured on *Good Morning America*.

If you're not interested in a Kidsuite, there are 275 other spacious rooms on six floors, including family rooms where the parents' bed is separated from the kids' bunk beds by a divider. (They also have one Sweetheart Suite with a whirlpool built for two.) All the guest rooms have a kitchenette. Facilities include a heated pool, two whirlpool spas, kiddie pool, playground, poolside Ping-Pong, restaurants, and a fitness center.

HOLIDAY INN SUNSPREE RESORT LAKE BUENA VISTA

Address:	**P.O. Box 22184, Orlando 32830**
	www.kidsuites.com
Phone:	**800/FON-MAXX (366-6299); 407/239-4500**
Fax:	**407/239-7713**
Rates:	**$113-$202**
Units:	**507**

LODGING AT WALT DISNEY WORLD

Walt Disney World is almost like a world unto itself. And since all of the Disney resorts are themed, they fit our criteria of being irresistible. But we felt these were so well covered in other guidebooks and on television that there was nothing new we could tell you about them.

There are thousands of rooms available in the thirteen Disney-run resorts here with accommodations that range from basic (with the Disney flair, of course) at moderate prices to the top of the line in luxury and expense. What do they offer that you can't find in lodging outside Walt Disney World? Convenience. You can pick the resort that's nearest your favorite Disney theme park. Guests also can sometimes get into a theme park an hour earlier than nonguests.

For details call the Orlando Visitor Center at 800/551-0181 or Disney reservations at 407/934-7639. Disney also has a resort website at www.disney.com/disneyworld. (For a non-Disney view of Disney resorts and Disney World, try www.disneyinfo.com.)

Perri House Bed & Breakfast

This place is for the birds—in the nicest possible way.

If you're going to one of the theme parks, but want to get away from all the hustle and bustle at night, this bed-and-breakfast is on sixteen quiet and secluded country acres just minutes from all the action. Here, instead of being surrounded by glittering man-made attractions, you'll be able to relax surrounded by trees, grassy fields, orange groves, and lots of birds. The grounds are preserved in their natural state and set up as a bird sanctuary and wildlife preserve. Bird feeders, birdbaths, and fountains throughout the grounds attract the birds, making this a small scale bird watchers' paradise. Perri House is listed as a Backyard Wildlife Habitat with the National Wildlife Federation.

As far as where you'll nest here, Angi and Nick Perretti offer several interesting choices. For overnights, there are seven spacious rooms and one two-bedroom suite in the main house. Each has a private bath and private entrance. The main house also contains a Birdhouse Museum and a library filled with field guides to help identify the birds you'll see. For longer stays, there are four small Birdhouse Cottages and the Perri House Acres Farmhouse.

The Birdhouse Cottages include a marble whirlpool bath for two,

and a see-through fireplace between the master bedroom and the parlor area. There is a snack/dinette area equipped with microwave, minirefrigerator, and wet bar. There is also a stock of birdseed and a front porch overlooking the central gardens. The Farmhouse is for a large family or group. It can sleep up to fourteen people in two master bedrooms, a large third bedroom, a loft bedroom, and on sleeper sofas in the living room and family room. There are three baths, a living room, family room, fully equipped kitchen, and a wraparound porch and sundeck. Both the cottages and the farmhouse have a three-night minimum.

Angi and Nick can also offer you something you won't find in many bed-and-breakfasts. As notaries, they can both perform marriages. They even have a Birdhouse Chapel to make it more romantic.

PERRI HOUSE BED & BREAKFAST

Address:	**10417 Centurion Court, Lake Buena Vista 32830**
	www.perrihouse.com
Phone:	**800/780-4830; 407/876-4830**
Fax:	**407/876-0241**
Rates:	**$99-$1,200**
Units:	**13**

Sheraton Safari Hotel

If you want to be in Orlando and Africa at the same time, you can do it here. Well, not really Africa, but the "Safari" in the title refers to the theme carried throughout the building and grounds. The Lobby, for example, is full of African artifacts and native décor. And you'll probably hear from a couple of colorful macaws perched on a branch there. On the grounds you'll find lush jungle-like vegetation, and the feature attraction in the pool is a seventy-nine-foot Python water slide.

The six-story hotel offers 393 guest rooms, ninety Safari suites with a bedroom, parlor, and kitchenette, and six executive suites that are like a small apartment. Everything is safari themed. One room, for example, may have a picture of a jaguar on the wall and jaguar-spotted upholstery on the furniture, while another has its décor built around elephant themes. With the kids (of all ages) in mind, amenities in every room include a Sony Playstation (for a fee). All rooms above the first floor have a balcony.

Facilities include an outdoor heated pool, a kiddie pool, a spa, an exercise room, a game room, restaurants, a lounge, and meeting space.

SHERATON SAFARI HOTEL

Address:	**12205 Apopka-Vineland Road, Orlando 32836**
	www.sheratonsafari.com
Phone:	**800/423-3297; 407/239-0444**
Fax:	**407/239-1778**
Rates:	**$95-$225**
Units:	**489**

Wyndham Palace Resort & Spa

There are several interesting things about this resort that we feel deserve special attention. Although it is not a Disney resort, it is located on twenty-seven acres within the Walt Disney World Resort, in walking distance of Downtown Disney, and offers many Disney guest benefits.

Accommodations are in the main tower, which is twenty-seven stores high, and four other towers. All rooms and suites have either private balconies or patios. Rooms on the Crown Level and Presidential Floor offer additional complimentary amenities. It has a full-service,

10,200-square-foot, European-style spa that has guest rooms with special air and water purifying systems, undyed linens, and allergy-free pillows. For children four to twelve years old there is a Kids Club that provides a professionally supervised activity program year round.

Facilities include three heated swimming pools, a whirlpool, a sauna, three lighted tennis courts, an arcade, two-and three-mile jogging trails, a children's playground, lounges, and several restaurants including one on the twenty-seventh floor where you can watch nightly fireworks from the nearby theme parks.

WYNDHAM PALACE RESORT & SPA

Address:	**P.O. Box 22206, Lake Buena Vista 32830**
	www.wyndham.com
Phone:	**800/WYNDHAM (996-3426); 407/827-2727**
Fax:	**407/827-6034**
Rates:	**$209-$329**
Units:	**1,014**

MAITLAND

Bed tax 11 percent

Thurston House

Looking at this charming house you'd never know it was once so unloved it was ready for the wrecking ball. Fortunately, the city fathers bought it as part of the property for a planned park. When the park plans changed in 1991, they sold it to Carole and Joe Ballard who lovingly restored it to its original grandeur and opened it as a bed-and-breakfast.

Carole and Joe had their first real contact with a bed-and-breakfast on their honeymoon in Europe where they fell in love with the concept. After that, although both were in the corporate world in the north and west, whenever business travel allowed, they stayed in bed-and-breakfasts. Finally they decided the time was right to have their own bed-and-breakfast.

Located on five wooded lakefront acres, it has fruit trees, camellia bushes, old camphor trees, flower gardens, and an herb garden. A classic 1885 Queen Anne Victorian, the house has a cross gable roof, corbeled brick chimneys, two cozy parlors, and three spacious porches. Two of the screened porches that overlook the small lake are thoughtfully furnished with swings and comfortable rockers so you can sit 'n' rock and really relax. This is all just five miles north of the hectic pace of Orlando.

The four guest rooms on the second floor offer lake or garden views. All the rooms have a private bath and are furnished with antiques or period reproductions. Each room is named after one of the four families that have owned the house over its more than a hundred-year history. Each room also has a special soothing color theme—yellow, green, pink, and blue—all beautifully coordinated.

There is also croquet, horseshoes, fishing from the banks of the lake, or walking trails that lead to some of the other historic homes in the area.

THURSTON HOUSE

Address:	851 Lake Avenue, Maitland 32751
	www.thurstonhouse.com
Phone:	800/843-2721; 407/539-1911
Fax:	407/539-0365
Rates:	$120-$130 all year
Units:	4

ORLANDO

Bed tax 11 percent

Courtyard at Lake Lucerne

Too many times we've found the advertising slogan for a lodging is more hype than truth. That's not the case here. They say this is "A traveler's oasis in the heart of historic downtown Orlando" and that's exactly what it is.

For starters, the two-and-a-half acre courtyard is definitely in the heart of downtown, within walking distance of Orlando's business and financial district and shopping. The oasis part is also true because it is at Lake Lucerne, and there are four inns offering you a bevy of delightful choices in a surprisingly (since there are two major highways nearby) quiet setting.

Want to stay in a lavishly furnished Victorian inn? Then choose the Norment-Parry House (1883) or the Dr. Phillips House (1893). The Norment-Parry House, which, by the way, is the oldest house in

Orlando, offers six guest rooms (four with adjacent sitting rooms) all elegantly furnished with authentic American and English antiques. The six suites in the Dr. Phillips House are also Victorian in a grand manner. There are original period antiques, including the beds, working fireplaces, leaded glass windows and doors, rare oil paintings, and double whirlpool tubs. This house also has a large private deck with a great view of the Orlando skyline.

Prefer an antebellum manor house? That'd be the I. W. Phillips House with wide verandahs wrapping the inn on three sides. Three upstairs suites, furnished in authentic Belle Epoque fittings, have French doors opening onto those verandahs.

Do you like Art deco? The Wellborn offers a choice of twelve one-bedroom suites each with a living room, an eat-in kitchen and streamlined modern furnishings and art deco collectibles.

The courtyard, a favorite place for weddings, connects the buildings with tree- and flower-lined brick walkways through colorful gardens. The compound also includes a fine dining restaurant on the first floor of the I. W. Phillips House.

As you might expect with all this history in the compound it's listed in the National Register of Historic Places.

COURTYARD AT LAKE LUCERNE

Address:	211 N. Lucerne Circle East, Orlando 32801
	www.orlandohistoricinn.com
Phone:	800/444-5289; 407/648-5188
Fax:	407/246-1386
Rates:	$89-$225 all year
Units:	27

Doubletree Castle Hotel

Legend has it that wherever there is a castle, there is a castle creature who attaches himself to the castle when it is being built, claims it as his territory, and protects it from then on. All seven feet of this castle's creature stand just inside the entrance surveying all who enter and establishing the theme that you'll find carried out throughout your stay here.

Themed hotels add to the fun of overnight stays, and the more the theme is carried out, the more we enjoy it. As you may have noticed, we find them irresistible. The castle theme here is evident in the hotel's turrets and other medieval features, including the grill on the door that comes from a real European castle. The theme continues inside with the furnishings, room décor, artifacts and private collections of European art, mosaics, authentic Renaissance music, and of course the castle creature. It is understandable that the theme is so well-carried-out since this is the flagship hotel of Kessler Enterprise's Grand Theme Hotels, a portfolio of unique hotels in Florida.

You have a choice of 209 rooms and seven suites in this nine-story hotel, all designed in the fantasy castle theme while including all the modern amenities.

The hotel offers a circular outdoor pool, a hot tub, a fitness center, a game room, restaurants, lounges, and meeting space. Richard Kessler's daughter's collection of European dolls is also on display.

DOUBLETREE CASTLE HOTEL

Address:	**8629 International Drive, Orlando 32819**
	www.doubletreecastle.com
Phone:	**800/95-CASTLE (952-2785); 407/345-1511**
Fax:	**407/248-8181**
Rates:	**$199**
Units:	**216**

Hyatt Regency Grand Cypress

There are so many choices offered at this fifteen hundred-acre luxury playground that it might be easier to tell you what's not there—but we'll try to condense the choices.

Starting on the outside, the grounds look like a well-cared-for botanical garden dotted with brooks, flower beds, rock gardens, and a nature walk, jogging trails, and bike paths. The eight hundred thousand-gallon lagoon swimming pool (that's a lot of water!), which covers half an acre, has twelve waterfalls, a 115-foot waterslide, whirlpools, and a stream flowing through a rock grotto. Just beyond the pool is the beach and marina where you can get sailboats, canoes, and paddleboats to explore the twenty-one-acre private lake.

If you like land sports, there are twelve tennis courts, plus racquetball and shuffleboard courts. The golf club has been listed in *Conde Nast Traveler* magazine as one of the "50 Best Golf Resorts" in the nation. It features forty-five holes of Jack Nicklaus-designed golf including an eighteen-hole Scottish-style links and a nine-hole pitch and putt course. The resort's Equestrian Center offers instruction in both Western and English riding as well as trail rides and events.

Inside, the huge atrium lobby is almost as lush with tropical vegetation as the outside: large palm trees with orchids sprouting from their trunks and philodendrons cascading from planters several stories up, while a little brook alive with goldfish meanders through it all.

Other offerings include a health and fitness center, five restaurants (if you order from the "Cuisine Naturelle" menu they'll even count the calories and fat grams for you), lounges, shops, and even a helicopter landing pad.

The 750 rooms and suites are luxuriously decorated in tropical colors and all have balconies. The concierge staff on the Regency Club floor provides extra services and amenities to guests.

And while you are trying to choose among all these things to do, your kids can be having professionally supervised fun in the Child Care Center for ages three to twelve, or Camp Hyatt programs for children five to twelve.

HYATT REGENCY GRAND CYPRESS

Address:	One Grand Cypress Boulevard, Orlando 32836
	www.hyatt.com
Phone:	800/233-1234; 407/239-1234
Fax:	407/239-3800
Rates:	$189-$1400
Units:	750

Peabody Orlando

Among the staff at this luxury hotel are several full-time residents who, at eleven each morning and five each evening, parade through the ornate lobby on a red carpet to the tune of Sousa's "King Cotton

March," and dive into a fountain. These are the famed Peabody ducks, the mascots of this hotel where their traditional twice-a-day parades delight the guests.

The duck parade tradition started in the 1930s when the manager of the Peabody Memphis and a friend returned from a duck hunting trip where they had used live "call ducks" as decoys. They decided it would be fun to put these ducks in that hotel's ornate lobby fountain. The guests got such a big kick out of it that the ducks stayed and became such a part of the Peabody tradition that they now perform their daily ritual in every Peabody hotel. The ducks live in a penthouse Duck Palace, are trained by a duck master, and usually hold their job for about three months before they are retired and replacements are brought on board.

As you might expect, the Peabody Orlando is awash in duck art and motifs, even the soap in the rooms is in the shape of little ducks. Of course, this great duck parade is not all there is to the Peabody. The twenty-seven story hotel has 833 rooms and fifty-eight suites. (A major expansion to more than eighteen hundred rooms is in the works.) The three top floors are concierge floors offering a number of complimentary services and amenities.

It offers all the facilities, amenities, and outstanding service you'd expect in a luxury hotel. Facilities include a swimming pool, Jacuzzi, children's pool with cascading waterfall, four tennis courts, an athletic club, extensive meeting rooms, and award-winning restaurants. As part of its Executive Health Program, guests can have health screenings, workups, consultations, and briefings at the hotel. Afternoon tea is served in the Atrium lobby every weekday afternoon.

PEABODY ORLANDO

Address:	9801 International Drive, Orlando 32819
	www.peabodyorlando.com
Phone:	800/PEABODY (732-2639); 407/352-4000
Fax:	407/354-1424
Rates:	$300-$1450
Units:	891

Portofino Bay Hotel at Universal Studios Escape

How would you like to see a bit of Italy in Orlando? The façade of this resort is like a photographic image of the waterfront scene of the Italian

coastal town of Portofino Bay. To make this replica as authentic as possible, an architect was sent to live in the real Portofino Bay for several months while he created the plans. And to continue the theme, they even imported some Italians from that town, like "Mama" Della in Mama Della's Ristorante, to be on the staff here.

The thirty-acre resort offers two swimming pools, whirlpools, a wading pool, a fitness center, a full-service spa and a salon, jogging and walking paths, and eight Italian-themed restaurants and lounges.

Since this is part of the Universal Studios Escape, guest privileges include courtesy water taxi (or bus) to the theme park and early admission.

They offer three types of accommodations, all of which are charmingly furnished and decorated in warm Italian décor. You can choose from a room, Villa room, or a suite. The amenities for the Villa rooms and suites are comparable to those on a concierge floor in a luxury hotel, including access to a private lounge and pool and, in some accommodations, the extra pampering of twenty-four-hour butler service. In keeping with the Italian theme, the Villa room guests also can use the bocce ball courts.

There are also eighteen Kid's Suites with Sony PlayStations (for a fee) and other fun things in a themed room connected to the parents' room.

PORTOFINO BAY HOTEL AT UNIVERSAL STUDIOS ESCAPE

Address:	**1000 Universal Studios Plaza, Orlando 32819**
	www.uescape.com
Phone:	**888/322-5541**
Rates:	**$320-$2,000**
Units:	**750**

Renaissance Orlando Resort at SeaWorld

There are some who say the atrium lobby in this resort is the world's largest. We cannot affirm or deny that, but we can definitely say it is one of the most fascinating and colorful we have ever seen. You could spend half a day just wandering around taking in all there is to see in the ten-story atrium. This includes more than seventeen thousand plants representing 105 species, a pond filled with two hundred brightly colored Japanese koi fish, a cascading waterfall, and a fifty-foot high Venetian-style aviary that is home to a number of tropical birds. By the way, the koi and the birds are provided by an arrangement with SeaWorld, which is just across the street.

The award-winning horticultural staff takes care of all the atrium plants plus all the trees and plants on the twenty-seven acres of landscaped grounds. They use natural, pesticide-free methods to control pests. In fact, the resort management and staff is so environmentally oriented in every aspect that it is one of the few resorts in the nation to receive the American Hotel and Motel Association's Good-Enviro-Management Award.

You can chose from 716 rooms or sixty-four suites, all attractively decorated to give you a bright and festive feeling. The resort says its guest rooms are the largest of any central Florida property—five hundred square feet. Many have balconies overlooking the tropical garden atrium while others look out at either neighboring SeaWorld or the resort's landscaped grounds. There is a club floor offering a number of VIP amenities to make your stay more pleasant.

Facilities include an Olympic-size swimming pool, oversized whirlpool, wading pool, all-sand outdoor children's play yard, tennis, volleyball, and basketball courts, health club, game room, shops, lounges, and five restaurants.

RENAISSANCE ORLANDO RESORT AT SEAWORLD

Address:	**6677 Sea Harbor Drive, Orlando 32821**
	www.renaissancehotels.com
Phone:	**407/351-5555**
Fax:	**407/351-9991**
Rates:	**$199-$2,000**
Units:	**780**

Sheraton Studio City Hotel

This hotel is right out of glamorous Hollywood of the 1940s and '50s. There are classic cars parked out front, a movie marquee entrance, and a gigantic octagon ball—forty-five feet in diameter and twenty-one stories high, weighing fourteen tons—on top of the building with searchlights that swirl through the sky every night.

Obviously the theme here *is* glamorous Hollywood of the 1940s and 1950s. The lobby is tiled in classic black and white, and there are painted silhouettes of Hollywood stars on the wall. The carpeting is spotted leopard, and the elevator doors are mirrored. This motif is carried out in all 302 guest rooms with such items as zebra-striped shower curtains and circular makeup mirrors. There are Sony PlayStations (for a fee) in every room. The top two floors are the hotel's club level, offering extra amenities, and the fifteen tower rooms on the top (twenty-first) floor, which are larger than the others, give you the most spectacular views in the hotel. If this isn't enough to set the mood, almost all of the staff attends acting classes where they train to take on the persona of a famous star of the era. Humphrey Bogart or Marilyn Monroe might check you in or John Wayne could be your waiter. This is another Kessler Enterprises Grand Theme Hotel.

Facilities include a heated swimming pool with a large sundeck, a wading pool, a fitness center, a game room, shops, and a restaurant decorated with photos of the stars.

SHERATON STUDIO CITY HOTEL

Address:	**5905 International Drive, Orlando 32819**
	www.sheratonstudiocity.com
Phone:	**800/327-1366; 407/351-2100**
Fax:	**407/352-8028**
Rates:	**$139-$209**
Units:	**302**

SANFORD

Bed tax 10 percent

Higgins House Victorian Bed & Breakfast

Built in 1894, in what is now Sanford's Historic District, this charming classic two-story Queen Anne Victorian was named an outstanding restoration by the Sanford Historic Trust. It has also been featured in a number of publications including *Southern Living* magazine and *Country Living.*

The large parlor and formal dining room each have a fireplace and are furnished with antiques. An addition that may or may not have influenced the ratings is the cozy, adjoining pub room where guests may enjoy the home brew made by owner Walter Padgett.

Walter's wife, Roberta, is the one responsible for the pleasing décor in the three guest rooms in the main house and Cochran Cottage. In the main house, the Queen Anne Room overlooks the attractive Victorian box garden; the Victorian Room feels "country" with its antique brass bed, old-fashioned stenciled designs, and cedar ceiling; and the Wicker Room has a bay window sitting area that adds to the romantic ambiance.

There are rockers and swings on the front porch so guests can relax and sit 'n' rock and enjoy the slow pace of life in this small town. This town was once one of the largest vegetable shipping centers in the nation, earning it the nickname of "Celery City." Today, it is the end of the line for Amtrak's Auto Train which carries passengers and cars between here and Lorton, Virginia.

The adjoining Cochran Cottage has two bedrooms, two baths, a living room, and a full kitchen, making it ideal for extended stays by families or two couples. Lunch and afternoon tea are available Thursday, Friday, and Saturday at Mrs. Higgins Tea Room.

HIGGINS HOUSE VICTORIAN & BREAKFAST

Address:	**420 South Oak Avenue, Sanford 32771**
	www.higginshouse.com
Phone:	**800/584-0014; 407/324-9238**
Fax:	**407/324-5060**
Rates:	**$95-$150 all year**
Units:	**4**

WINTER PARK

Bed tax 11 percent

Park Plaza Hotel

As we drove onto Park Avenue, we recalled the relaxing charm of a small European village with tree-lined streets and carefully tended shops and galleries. The second floor wraparound balcony of this two-story corner hotel fits in perfectly with the chocolate and beige striped awning covering what seemed to be a floating garden of flowers in hanging baskets and flower boxes.

The lobby's dark mahogany wood-paneled walls, brass accessories, antiques and wicker furniture, reinforce the feeling of being in an intimate European hotel. Proprietor Sandra Spang likes to refer to it as a "small civilized hotel." It wasn't always such. When Sandra and her husband, John, started renovating the old building in 1975, it was a rundown, low-priced retirement home with old white hospital beds in the rooms and no balcony. Today, the quiet elegance of the lobby is carried over into the twenty-seven guest rooms that are furnished with antiques, wicker, and plants. Each room is different, but all have sitting rooms and open onto the flower- and fern-adorned balcony.

Located in the hotel, but under separate management, is the highly rated, full-service Park Plaza Gardens Restaurant, which is also filled with a profusion of greenery and bathed in sunlight coming through the glass ceiling.

PARK PLAZA HOTEL

Address:	307 Park Avenue South, Winter Park 32789
	www.parkplazahotel.com
Phone:	800/228-7220; 407/647-1072
Fax:	407/647-4081
Rates:	$85-$234 all year
Units:	27

For Additional Information
on the Central Region:

CENTRAL FLORIDA CVB
P.O. Box 61
Cypress Gardens, FL 33884
800/828-7655
941/298-7565
Fax: 941/298-7564
www.sensational.org

KISSIMMEE/ST. CLOUD CVB
P.O. Box 422007
Kissimmee, FL 34742-2007
800/327-9159
407/847-5000
Fax: 407/847-0878
www.floridakiss.com

LAKE COUNTY CVB
20763 US Highway 27
Groveland, FL 34736
352/429-3673
Fax: 352/429-4870
www.lakecountyfl.com

ORLANDO VISITOR CENTER
Gala Center
8723 International Drive
Orlando, FL 32819
800/551-0181
407/363-5872
www.go2orlando.com

OCALA/MARION COUNTY COC
P.O. Box 1210
Ocala, FL 34478
352/629-8051
Fax: 352/626-7651

SEMINOLE COUNTY CVB
105 International Parkway
Heathrow, FL 32746
800/800-7832
407/328-5770
Fax: 407/328-5775
www.co.seminole.fl.us/visit

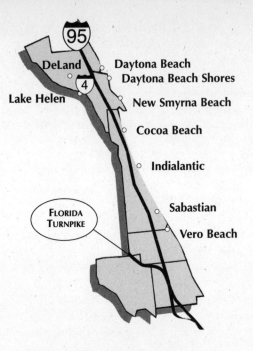

High Season: January to early summer

(Note: All lodging rates are for high season. Off-season rates can be significantly lower.)

6 CENTRAL EAST

DELAND/WEST VOLUSIA AREA
(Cassadaga, DeLand, Lake Helen)

Bed tax 11 percent

West Volusia County is away from the coastal cities and west of I-95. A relatively untouched area of the state, it offers visitors a real taste of Old Florida without the crowds, noise, or heavy traffic. At the same time, it offers a variety of opportunities for memorable experiences.

If you ever had the urge to skydive, for example, Skydive DeLand says they can train you to be ready for a tandem jump with a professional instructor in just thirty minutes. Other fun activities, although a little less thrilling, include watching the manatees. You usually can see these gentle and endangered creatures from the observation platform at Blue State Park during the months of November through March when they leave the colder waters of the St. Johns River for the comfort of the warmer spring. Or you can go for an experience of the mind at the Cassadaga Spiritualist Camp, where approximately fifty practicing psychics or mediums are available for readings. Much of the town is now a National Historic District.

Another National Historic District is the tree-lined campus of Stetson University in DeLand. The university was founded in 1883 by Henry DeLand, who also played a leading role in the foundation of the city that bears his name. DeLand envisioned this city as a center of culture, education, and beauty like the Athens of ancient Greece. The university helps continue his vision today.

This area is a nature lover's paradise, especially along the St. Johns River, which borders the area on the west. The St. Johns is one of fourteen rivers in the United States designated as an *American Heritage River*. As for fishing, the St. Johns River is well known for its bass and crappie. There are more than fifteen fish camps along the river with skilled guides and boat rentals available.

CASSADAGA AND LAKE HELEN

Bed tax 11 percent

Cassadaga Hotel & Psychic Center

As part of its full-time staff, this hotel has several psychics who will help you explore whatever your interest might be in astrology, past-life regressions, tarot, palmistry, astral projection, runes, or other areas of metaphysics and parapsychology.

The historic hotel was built in 1901, burned down in 1925, and was rebuilt and reopened in 1927. It was originally owned by the Cassadaga Spiritualist Camp. When the camp gave up ownership, in order for the hotel to survive as a business, it had to compete with the camp and this rivalry remains to this day.

The two-story hotel has twenty guest rooms, all comfortably furnished, many with handmade furniture including armoires and canopy beds. The larger rooms are upstairs, and six of them open onto a verandah.

The restaurant is appropriately called the Lost in Time Café. The hotel also specializes in murder mystery luncheon and dinner shows.

CASSADAGA HOTEL & PSYCHIC CENTER

Address:	355 Cassadaga Road, Cassadaga 32706
	www.cassadagahotel.com
Phone:	904/228-2323
Fax:	904/228-3560
Rates:	$75 all year
Units:	20

Clauser's Inn Bed & Breakfast

This Victorian house was built in 1895 as lodging for the overflow from the Cassadaga Spiritualist Camp meetings. It's listed in the National Register of Historic Places and is an excellent example of Old Florida, with its tin roof, white clapboards, slate-blue shutters, a wraparound porch, and gingerbread trim.

Innkeepers Marge and Tom Clauser were both on fast-track careers in Orlando when they decided they did not like the quality of their lives. Marge liked old houses, so in their business travels they often stayed in bed-and-breakfasts. They decided that owning such an inn would give them the life they wanted.

They saw this house when they came for a craft show. It needed work and wasn't for sale, but they could see it was what they were looking for. Marge asked the owners to call if they ever decided to sell. Three months later they gave up looking and were going to build when the call came—the owners were ready to sell. They bought it in 1989, fixed it up, and opened it in 1990. Shortly after opening, they added a six-room carriage house in the rear and Sherlock's, an English-style pub. Being innkeepers lived up to their hopes and expectations—so much so that they now teach classes on how to start and run a bed-and-breakfast.

The house sits among a variety of trees on three secluded acres. The two guest rooms in the main house and six in the carriage house are all themed. For example, among the rooms in the carriage house, the Lexington Room has colonial New England décor, including antiques and collectibles with a touch of patriotic red, white, and blue, while the Lancaster Room has Pennsylvania Dutch décor with Dutch and Amish quilts and antiques. The most expensive room is the Charlevoix Room, in the carriage house, with a décor of Old World elegance that features a fireplace and a Jacuzzi, making it a favorite of honeymooners. All the rooms have a private bath and phone, some have a television, and those in the carriage house all have screened porches.

Sherlock's Pub is open in the evenings. They occasionally run murder mystery weekends for groups that will book all eight rooms.

CLAUSER'S INN BED & BREAKFAST

Address:	201 East Kicklighter Road, Lake Helen 32744
	www.clauserinn.com
Phone:	800/220-0310; 904/228-0310
Fax:	904/228-2337
Rates:	$95–$140 all year
Units:	8

DELAND

Bed tax 11 percent

Hontoon Landing Resort & Marina

Your choices here include eighteen large rooms and suites in the resort, many with river views, or suites floating on the river itself in one of their luxurious houseboats. The resort and marina are located among ancient cypress trees on the St. Johns River. Eleven of the rooms and suites have kitchens, and all have cable television. For a family the Executive Suite offers two bedrooms and two baths, a screened porch with a river view, and a kitchen. Other facilities include a pool and a ship's store that stocks everything from food and supplies to clothing. Fishermen can get everything from bait to licenses and guides.

If you bring your own boat and stay at the resort, the full-service marina offers a free covered slip for boats up to twenty feet, and dockage for larger boats. If you stay on your boat, you may rent a slip. In addition to the houseboats, you may also rent pontoon boats, fishing boats, and canoes.

The houseboats were our favorite, especially the top-of-the-line fifty-eight-foot Camelot models, which are like a floating apartment with four separate staterooms, all with double beds, one and a half baths, a kitchen, a sun deck, and even a water slide. What a grand way for several couples or a large family to explore the natural beauty of the St. Johns River! While not cheap—the three-day weekend in high season runs around $1,900 (plus 6 percent sales tax)—when split among several couples it's about the same as a weekend at any resort. If you don't need all that room, they have fifty-two-foot houseboats with bunk beds and a few less frills for about half the amount.

The resort is across the river from the preserved natural beauty of Hontoon Island State Park. It's worth a visit, and the resort provides ferry service.

HONTOON LANDING RESORT & MARINA

Address:	**2317 River Ridge Road, DeLand 32720**
	www.hontoon.com
Phone:	**800/248-2474; 904/734-2474**
Fax:	**904/738-9743**
Rates:	**rooms $65-$175; houseboats: $425-$795**
Units:	**18 rooms and 12 houseboats**

BREVARD COUNTY AND THE SPACE COAST

(Cocoa Beach and Indialantic)

Brevard County stretches seventy-two miles along the central east coast of Florida. Cape Canaveral is in this county, and since 1953, most of the nation's space launches have been from this site.

HOUSEBOATS

Houseboats can be great alternative irresistible overnights. They come in all sizes from little more than a barebones cabin on a smallish hull to floating condos with all the comforts of home including air-conditioning and sleeping quarters for a family or a group of friends. For information on where to rent houseboats in Florida, check out www.houseboat.net on the Internet, or contact the Houseboat Association of America or Houseboat Magazine, both at 800/638-0135 (520 Park Ave., Idaho Falls, ID 83402)

The name of Cape Canaveral dates back centuries. It was renamed Cape Kennedy after President Kennedy's death, but the original name has been restored, although the NASA facilities are still called the Kennedy Space Center.

A rocket museum on the Cape, across the Banana River from Merritt Island, marks the site from which the United States launched its first satellite, Explorer I, on January 31, 1958. This is also the site from which astronaut Alan Shepard was launched into a suborbital flight on May 5, 1961.

The Canaveral National Seashore and Merritt Island National Wildlife Refuge are both just north of the Kennedy Space Center.

COCOA BEACH

Bed tax 10 percent

The Inn at Cocoa Beach

Some days the ground rumbles and the windows shake at this inn. But you'll be glad of that because it means you are in one of the prime spots on the coast to watch a launch at the Kennedy Space Center. And don't worry, no launch has ever caused any damage.

Why a prime spot? First, of course, is its location—it has 750 feet of ocean frontage looking across at the space center. Second, because forty-four of the fifty rooms and suites have ocean views, most with balconies. If you don't have an ocean view, there's an observation deck on the roof.

Karen Simpler, the owner, had been in the restaurant and hotel business for a number of years before she built this inn, and it was obvious

to us that she has used all of her experience to make it as perfect as it can be. Although its two buildings make it look like a hotel from the outside, once you step inside it's more like a large, comfortable bed-and-breakfast because of the "feel-at-home" atmosphere. It is furnished throughout with fine French country-style furniture, draperies, and bedspreads that are especially made in the inn's sewing room, and beautiful oriental rugs, all creating an aura of relaxing elegance.

In addition to the beach, the inn has a pleasant courtyard and a solar heated pool. Some of the rooms have a Jacuzzi. And for those who like to shop, Ron Jon's Surf Shop, the second most popular attraction on the space coast, is just a block away. So although launches aren't a daily occurrence, this inn stands on its own merits all the time.

THE INN AT COCOA BEACH

Address:	4300 Ocean Beach Boulevard, Cocoa Beach 32931
	www.theinnatcocoabeach.com
Phone:	800/343-5307; 321/799-3460
Fax:	321/784-8632
Rates:	$125–$250 all year
Units:	50

INDIALANTIC

Bed tax 10 percent

Windemere Inn by the Sea

This elegant two-story Italianate Victorian gives the impression of having been around for a long time. And that's exactly the impression Tom and Vivian Hay wanted to make when they built it in 1996.

When the Hays bought the original property in 1994, it came with a beach house and cottage on the oceanfront street, Wavecrest. Tom, who was in corporate real estate, and Vivian, an interior decorator, envisioned starting with the beach house and quickly expanding with a new building of their own design. And that's what they did.

So now they can offer you a choice of three rooms in the Windward Cottage Guesthouse, two rooms in the Eastwinds Carriage House, and four rooms in the old-looking new Main House, all exhibiting the best of Vivian's decorating talent and experience.

All the rooms have a private bath, six of the rooms have ocean views, and four of them have Jacuzzi tubs. The furnishings are a combination of antiques and wicker and four-poster beds. The deck with an arbor has a ramp to their private beach. A lovely courtyard connects the main

house with the Windward Cottage Guesthouse. Although all the rooms promote an ambiance of graceful comfort, our favorite is the Sweet Sentiment Suite in the Windward Cottage. It has a clear ocean view and a spacious bathroom with a Jacuzzi tub.

WINDEMERE INN BY THE SEA

Address:	815 S. Miramar Avenue, Indialantic 32903
	www.windemereinn.com
Phone:	800/224-6853; 321/728-9334
Fax:	321/728-2741
Rates:	$110–$215
Units:	9

DAYTONA BEACH AREA

(Daytona Beach, Daytona Beach Shores, New Smyrna Beach)

With more than eight million annual visitors from all over the world, Daytona Beach is one of the most popular tourist destinations in Florida. One of the area's main attractions is its white sand beach. Because the beach is so hard and expansive, it was once used as a proving ground for automobile testing and racing. Today, the quest for speed continues at the 2.5 mile Daytona International Speedway. This is the site of the Daytona 500, the world's best known and most prestigious stock car race. The race is just one day, but there is some high-speed event here every day for four months of the year. Another attraction at the Speedway is DAYTONA USA. A state-of-the art motor sports facility that not only tells the history of auto racing but offers interactive opportunities to participate in a NASCAR race—working in a pit, designing your own race car, or announcing a race. While racing is the big draw here, the area also offers family activities and a variety of sports-oriented attractions from fishing to golf. It is also rich in cultural arts, with museums, theaters, music, and festivals.

If you want to stay in a quieter area, try New Smyrna Beach. A charming small town that is pleasantly stuck in the 1950s, it is an excellent place to relax and is less than a half-hour drive to the attractions at Daytona Beach. One of the features of the town is a well-established art community that includes the North Atlantic Center for the Arts, which has artists in residence from all over the country.

DAYTONA BEACH

Bed tax 11 percent

The Coquina Inn Bed & Breakfast

The name of this charming inn comes from its building materials of coquina limestone, which nature creates by centuries of transforming sand, shell, and coral into rock. This rock-solid structure, built in 1912, is an excellent example of stone cutting and stone setting using Florida's unique coquina. For thirty-five years the building was a church parsonage.

The inn is located in Daytona's historic district and is on the National Register of Historic Places. The ambiance throughout is gracious southern comfort, which translates to "Don't let the beautiful antique furnishings intimidate you." In fact, they don't have anything too fragile to sit on.

The four themed guest bedrooms are all on the second floor. Each has a private bathroom, a television, and original artwork by Florida artists. Each room is different. The Jasmine Room, for example, features a fireplace—coquina rock, of course—and mahogany furniture, while the Hibiscus Room has wicker furniture and French doors leading to a private porch.

THE COQUINA INN BED & BREAKFAST

Address:	**544 S. Palmetto Avenue, Daytona Beach 32114**
	www.coquinainndaytonabeach.com
Phone:	**800/805-7533; 904/254-4969**
Fax:	**904/254-4969**
Rates:	**$80–$110**
Units:	**4**

The Villa

If you want a taste of how royalty lives, this is the place to stay. This seventeen-room historic Spanish-style mansion, on one-and-a-quarter acres, is the epitome of elegance and luxurious living. Inside, its impressive moldings and stenciled ceilings help make it one of the finest examples of Spanish Colonial Revival architecture in the state.

Jim Camp, the owner and innkeeper, has furnished it from his personal collection of antiques in keeping with the architecture of the period: Russian icons, Chinese jade, oriental rugs, and even a grand piano. The furnishings are sturdy and grand, with massive sideboards and carved chairs, and the spacious rooms and formal spaces express a dignified yet most comfortable lifestyle.

The Villa offers six guest rooms, four in the main house and two in what would have been the guest quarters of the mansion. All the rooms are named after Spanish grandees and Italian notables, such as Marco Polo and Queen Isabella and are individually decorated to fit the theme of that person's life. The Christopher Columbus Room, for example, has a warm nautical theme. Our favorite is the King Juan Carlos Room, which has a fireplace, a baroque canopy bed, a separate dressing room, and French doors opening onto a rooftop terrace that overlooks the private walled tropical garden and beautifully landscaped grounds.

There is a swimming pool, a sunning area, and secure parking inside the mansion's gated entrance. Naturally, it is a favorite location for weddings and other special events.

THE VILLA

Address:	801 N. Peninsula Drive, Daytona Beach 32118
	www.thevillabb.com
Phone:	904/248-2020
Fax:	904/248-2020
Rates:	$100–$190
Units:	6

DAYTONA BEACH SHORES

Bed tax 11 percent

Old Salty's Inn

The wrecked lifeboat at the entrance makes this oceanfront inn look like a fun place where you can relax. It is named after the owner's father who was nicknamed Old Salty during his time in the navy. Naturally it has a nautical theme throughout.

The present inn is a combination of two neighboring motels that the owner connected by a walkway over a fish pond. The area between the two buildings also has lots of banana and palm trees and a waterfall.

The seventeen rooms and two suites are all right next to the beach. The suites are on the beach end of each building and have ocean views. All of the rooms are simply furnished with beach-type furniture, cable television, refrigerators, and microwaves, and some have full kitchens. It has a Gilligan's Island setting around the oceanfront heated pool.

The owner's advertise that "We are the cleanest motel on the ocean." We didn't visit enough other places to know if it is the cleanest, but we will vouch for the fact that the rooms were immaculately clean. Perhaps this is one of the reasons the inn claims that 90 percent of its business is from repeat guests.

They offer a lot of little freebies here: morning coffee and cookies, weekly hot dog roasts, a guest barbecue area, and free use of beach bikes. Although it is miles from the Kennedy Space Center, another plus of this location is that its beach still provides an excellent spot from which to view launches.

OLD SALTY'S INN

Address:	1921 S. Atlantic Avenue, Daytona Beach Shores 32118
	www.visitdaytone.com/oldsaltys
Phone:	800/417-1466; 904/252-8090
Fax:	904/441-5977
Rates:	$66–$111
Units:	9

NEW SMYRNA BEACH

Bed tax 10 percent

Little River Inn Bed & Breakfast

It's easy to fall in love with the beautiful and tranquil setting of this 1883 riverfront estate's three-story home, which has been transformed into a charming inn located on two acres overlooking the Indian River Lagoon. The manicured grounds are canopied by ancient oak trees. Brick pathways lead to fountains, wishing wells, and a garden hideaway. There are also tennis and badminton courts, and a croquet field. The wide verandah on the first floor is furnished with comfortable rocking chairs, and the second-floor balcony provides an even better view of the nearby nature preserve and meandering river.

Joyce and Doug Maclean first encountered bed-and-breakfasts while Doug was in the air force stationed in England. They fell in love with the British bed-and-breakfasts and took notes on what was good and bad about each with the idea that someday they would become innkeepers. That someday arrived in 1995 when they bought this house. After a lot of work, Little River Inn opened in 1996.

The inn offers six large guest rooms, each featuring a different theme. The Library Room, on the first floor, for example, is a most elegant conversion of the previous owner's law library. The Garden Room, on the third floor, is appropriately decorated with plants. And the Parisian Room, on the second floor, is the largest and most posh of all the rooms. It is considered by many guests to be the most romantic. Four of the rooms have private baths, while the other two share a bath down the hall. Early risers have the chance to view the sunrise over the river. And if you feel like it, you might try peddling around town on their bicycle-built-for-two.

LITTLE RIVER INN BED & BREAKFAST

Address:	532 N. Riverside Drive, New Smyrna Beach 32168
	www.little-river-inn.com
Phone:	888/424-0102; 904/424-0100
Fax:	904/424-5732
Rates:	$119–$159
Units:	6

Night Swan Intracoastal Bed & Breakfast

Why Night Swan? It's an English translation of innkeepers Martha and Charles Nighswonger's classic Swiss-German family name. But night or day, the inn is as beautiful as a swan.

The three-building complex, located on the Indian River/Intracoastal Waterway, consists of a separate cottage, a lovingly restored 1906 three-story mansion with a wraparound porch furnished with rocking chairs, and the 1910 Cygnet House, which was a family home for seventy years before Martha and Charles bought and restored it. The well-maintained grounds that surround the buildings are dotted with live oaks, magnolia trees, and palms. The private dock on the river is a great place for bird, boat, and, occasionally, even dolphin watching.

All three houses are attractively furnished with antiques and collectibles. You have a choice of seven rooms and suites in the main house, seven more in the Cygnet House, and two in the cottage. All the rooms and suites have private baths, and all those in the Cygnet House have whirlpool tubs. Six of the seven rooms in the Cygnet House have a view of the Intracoastal Waterway, two of the units in the main house, and both of the cottage units also have water views.

NIGHT SWAN INTRACOASTAL BED & BREAKFAST

Address:	**512 S. Riverside Drive, New Smyrna Beach 32168**
	www.nightswan.com
Phone:	**800/465-4261; 904/423-4940**
Fax:	**904/427-2814**
Rates:	**$80–$165**
Units:	**16**

Riverview Hotel

As you drive across the North Causeway toward New Smyrna Beach, you can't miss this Old Florida-style bright pink hotel with white balconies right at the end of the drawbridge over the Intracoastal Waterway. Built in 1885 as a two-story home for the bridge tender, in the early 1900s it was transformed into a typical three-story hotel of the time with a tin roof, clapboards, railed verandahs, and gingerbread trim.

One of the interesting asides about the hotel today is that it was a surprise birthday present from Jim Kelsey to his wife, Christa. In the late 1980s, after they had spent a number of years building a successful resort on Marathon Key, they received an offer they couldn't refuse. So they sold their resort and started the search for another property that would fit Christa's dream. They soon found this one, but the price was too high, so the search went on. Unknown to Christa, the price was later reduced, and Jim, director of the Klassix Auto Attraction in Daytona, secretly bought it and presented it to her on her birthday.

Now Christa offers her guests a choice of eighteen charming guest rooms in the hotel and a two-bedroom, two-bath cottage. All the rooms have a private bath, a television, and a phone, and all but two of the guest rooms have a patio or a private balcony that overlooks the river or the heated pool. (Our choice for the best river view is Room 317 on the top floor.) Each balcony has comfortable furniture and is decorated with ferns and other tropical plants. As in most historic hotels, the rooms vary in size. Many of them have oriental rugs covering the restored old pine floors, and a number of the rooms are furnished with antiques or fine reproductions that add to the Old Florida ambiance.

In addition to the pool, the hotel has a large gift shop and a locally popular waterfront restaurant next door.

RIVERVIEW HOTEL

Address:	103 Flagler Avenue, New Smyrna Beach 32169
Phone:	800/945-7416; 904/428-5858
Fax:	904/423-8927
Rates:	$80–$200
Units:	18 and a two bedroom cottage

VERO BEACH AREA

(Sebastian and Vero Beach)

Both Sebastian and Vero Beach are in Indian River County, which offers twenty-six miles of beaches and is part of the legendary Treasure Coast. As the story goes, on July 24, 1715, a Spanish fleet and a French warship left Havana for Spain carrying a cargo of gold, silver, and jewels. A few days later, on July 31, they ran into a hurricane somewhere between what is now Cape Canaveral and Fort Pierce. Over the years salvage operations recovered about half the treasure, but the rest was never found. Periodically the tides and storms tossed blackened coins up on the beaches, drawing treasure hunters until this coastal area became unofficially known as the Treasure Coast.

When the Vero Beach community started in the late 1890s, two names were submitted for the local post office: Venice and Vero, both meaning "true." The postmaster general chose Vero. Since most of the citizens say the city is "truly peaceful, truly tropical, and truly remarkable," the name is definitely appropriate. The Los Angeles Dodgers must agree, since they come to this part of the Sunshine State for spring training.

Sebastian, on the northern end of the county, is a small town that grew up around the fishing industry, both in the ocean and on the Indian River. Fishing, boating, and other water-oriented activities are still prime attractions here. In many ways, this is still like south Florida thirty years ago.

SEBASTIAN

Bed tax 10 percent

The Angler Inn

Being an avid fisherman and former marina owner, Joe Graham long had a dream of opening a fishing lodge. When he and his wife, Debra, came to Indian River County in 1996, they were looking for a new home and a new business. This 1936 house on the Indian River Lagoon seemed ideal for that dream. Working on it part time, it took them two years to repair, renovate, and modernize the home while maintaining its stately character. When they were finished, they decided it would make a better bed-and-breakfast than fishing lodge.

Debra says the bed-and-breakfast gives them a chance to blend both their backgrounds. She was a nurse and enjoys caring for people, and Joe is into marine biology and has marina experience. In keeping with Sebastian's fishing-village ambiance and Joe's background in marine sciences, the theme of this bed-and-breakfast is nautical.

"It's still a little funky," Joe says. And its location across from the city's boat ramps and fishing pier make it an angler's paradise, so Joe rents boats and has bait and tackle available. But looking at the décor and the family antique and collectible furnishings in the three suites, it's just as easy to classify this as a romantic retreat.

Each suite has cable television, a kitchenette, and a private entrance. The common area has a brick fireplace and the front porch offers rockers on which to sit a spell. A large second-floor verandah offers an excellent view of the Indian River.

THE ANGLER INN

Address:	805 Indian River Drive, Sebastian 32958
	www.anglerinn.net
Phone:	800/317-6568; 561/589-1150
Rates:	$90 all year
Units:	3

The Davis House Inn

When Steve Wild was in the construction business in Vero Beach, he would occasionally have to drive to Sebastian and soon decided that was where he wanted to live. His parents had a rental house a half block from the water, and one day while he was repairing the roof, he took in the gorgeous view and decided this was where he wanted to build a small hotel.

In 1991 he realized his dream. He sold everything, bought his parents' rental house, knocked it down, and built his hotel. Being a golf fan, he patterned it after the clubhouse at the Augusta National. Well, he actually made it a combination of that clubhouse with a touch of New Orleans and a bit of Florida cracker, all designed to look as if the building had been there a long time. The result is a solid, unpretentious three-story building with wide overhanging roofs that provide both shade for the wraparound porches and views of the Indian River that are as good as the one Steve saw while working on the roof of his parents' house.

The Inn, a favorite of fishermen and boaters, offers twelve spacious efficiencies, each with a private bath (not as spacious), a television, and a phone. Each room is named after a famous settler of Sebastian, including Seminole Chief Billy Bowlegs.

THE DAVIS HOUSE INN

Address:	**607 Davis Street, Sebastian 32958**
Phone:	**561/589-4114**
Fax:	**561/589-1722**
Rates:	**$69–$79**
Units:	**12**

VERO BEACH

Bed tax 10 percent

Disney's Vero Beach Resort

Walt Disney World in Orlando is a two-hour drive away. What is Disney doing in Vero Beach? That's the question we asked when we researched this beautiful oceanfront property. After visitors enjoy the thrills of Disney World, some of them want to take time to slow down, unwind, and relax. Also, the Disney people found a large number of their visitors went to the beach before going home. To fill this need, they created this lovely Old Florida-style resort that bears a resemblance to the grand hotels that were found along the eastern seaboard in the late nineteenth century. To find the perfect location for this, they flew all along the coast until they found this seventy-one-acre site (only sixteen of which are developed) on a quiet barrier island with a gorgeous, uncrowded beach.

This is actually a timeshare resort that is part of the worldwide

Disney Vacation Club. It offers an average of about a hundred units in the rental pool. These include inn rooms, large studios, one- and two-bedroom villas, and even a three-bedroom beach cottage. As usual, Disney paid attention to details, so you'll find all the amenities you'd expect in a fine hotel, and each of the units is a delightfully relaxing blend of serene ocean-side color schemes and comfortable furnishings.

As you would expect, the owners are tuned in to the vacation needs of families and children. The Disney Discovery Club offers an extensive program for children between the ages of four and twelve. They describe the activities as edu-tainment, because it educates and entertains at the same time.

In addition to all that the beach has to offer, the resort facilities include a nine-hole miniature golf course, a croquet lawn, a heated pool with a two-story spiral slide, an exercise room and sauna, tennis and basketball courts, a children's play area, and several restaurants.

The beach is also a nesting area for loggerhead sea turtles (see page 19) and the resort offers organized turtle walks during the summer in the height of the nesting season to observe the nests without disturbing them. The Indian River Lagoon is also the home of a large number of manatees in season, and 310 species of birds have been recorded in this area.

DISNEY'S VERO BEACH RESORT

Address:	9250 Island Grove Terrace, Vero Beach 32963
Phone:	800/359-8000; 561/234-2000
Fax:	561/234-2030
Rates:	$240–$840
Units:	204 (about 60 percent available in rental pool)

The Driftwood Resort

Funky, eclectic, whimsical, unique, and historical are some of the words we can use to describe this resort. Proving the "historical" is easy: it's listed in the National Register of Historic Places. As for the others, once you see the Driftwood's older buildings and the original owner's collection of art, artifacts, and collectibles, we believe you'll agree with all the other descriptions, and probably add some of your own.

Waldo Sexton was a citrus farmer and businessman in the 1930s. Over the years he contributed a great deal to the growth of Vero Beach, but he is probably best remembered for the beach-house retreat he built mainly from the timbers, planks, and other driftwood that he found washed up on the shore. Since the town hadn't developed yet, there was no place for visitors to stay, so Waldo started taking in people who asked for a night's lodging. As the number of overnight guests increased, Waldo added on to his beach house. There were so many guests that his wife began to operate it as a small hotel. By the early 1940s he had a two-story hotel with balconies everywhere. Over the years other buildings were added, and today, the Driftwood is a combination old and new with each unit being individually owned.

As the original buildings grew, Mr. Sexton, a world traveler and insatiable collector, began filling them from his growing collection of eclectic objects. In fact, the buildings soon resembled a museum stocked with such things as ships' wheels, cannons from a sixteenth-century Spanish galleon, paintings and statues, stained glass, antique furniture, and a vast collection of several hundred bells from ships, cathedrals, locomotives, schools, and even sleighs. Much of this collection is still here.

Today's resort offers you a choice of excellent accommodations, ranging from a basic hotel room and suites to two-bedroom villas. Some are oceanfront, some are in the old buildings, and some in the new ones. Naturally, the décor is eclectic, and no two rooms are alike. But don't get the idea that they are rustic or an architectural mess. Different for sure, but even in the oldest buildings, all the units have been substantially updated, some luxuriously. All the rooms are well furnished and well maintained.

Facilities include two pools and Waldo's Restaurant, which was built in 1947 much as the original home had been built, with unusual found materials.

THE DRIFTWOOD RESORT

Address: **3150 Ocean Drive, Vero Beach 32963**
Phone: **561/231-0550**
Fax: **561/234-1981**
Rates: **$85–$210**
Units: **100**

For Additional Information on the Central East Region

DELAND/WEST VOLUVIA CVB
336 North Woodland Boulevard
DeLand, FL 32720
800/749-4350; 904/734-0575
Fax: 904/734-4333
www.naturalflorida.org

DAYTONA BEACH AREA CVB
126 East Orange Avenue
Daytona Beach, FL 32114
800/544-0415; 904/255-0415
Fax: 904/255-5478
www.daytonabeachcvb.org

SOUTHEAST VOLUSIA
ADVERTISING AUTHORITY
(For New Smyrna Beach)
Lanier Associates, Inc.
3599-C West Lake Mary Blvd.
Lake Mary, FL 32746
800/760-0878; 407/328-0880
Fax: 407/328-0721

INDIAN RIVER COUNTY COC
Tourism Division
P.O. Box 2947
Vero Beach, FL 32961
561/567-3491
Fax: 561/778-3181
www.vero-beach.fl.us/chamber

SPACE COAST
OFFICE OF TOURISM
8810 Astronaut Boulevard, Suite 102
Cape Canaveral, FL 32920
800/936-872-1969; 407/868-1126
Fax: 407/868-1139
www.space-coast.com

7 SOUTHWEST

BOKEELIA

Bed tax 9 percent

This small town is mainly the base for fishermen and boaters and those who want to charter fishing boats, take sight-seeing cruises of the gulf islands, or hire launches to specific islands, including the undeveloped island site of Cayo Costa State Park.

Collier Inn at Useppa Island Club

More than a hundred years old, the mansion that is now the Collier Inn was the centerpiece of the casual elegance of this private club's hundred-acre island retreat. Reinforcing this air of refinement today are the club's international croquet court (three of the top fifteen world croquet champions are club members), an outdoor chess set with two-foot tall playing pieces, and the club's own historical museum.

This inn is elegant, but not stuffy, as the island is a base for boating enthusiasts as well as for those who seek the adventure of fishing for giant tarpon or kayaking around the islands. Although the island is owned by the club members, guests are welcome at the inn, and about a dozen one- to four-bedroom cottages at the resort are available for overnights.

A true island, it's accessible only by boat. You can catch a regularly scheduled launch at the Bocilla Marina in Bokeelia. The fare is ten dollars each way and reservations are required (941/283-1061).

The inn first opened in 1898 as a tarpon fishing retreat for the wealthy, and nearby waters soon earned the title of the Tarpon Capital of the World. Barron Collier, publisher and one of Florida's single largest landowners at the time, bought the island, and in 1908 founded the Izaak Walton Club, which awarded silver, gold, and diamond buttons for members who landed tarpon that were at least 150 pounds. The club practice was to release all of the tarpons that did not weigh enough to qualify for a button.

Among the many notables who frequented the island during Collier's time were the Vanderbilts, the Rockefellers, the Rothchilds,

SOUTHWEST

- Englewood
- Cape Haze
- Pineland
- Matlatcha
- Bokeelia
- Fort Meyers
- Clewiston
- Captiva Island
- Naples

75

High Season: Mid-January through mid-April

(Note: All lodging rates are for high season. Off-season rates can be significantly lower.)

Herbert Hoover, movie stars Gloria Swanson and Shirley Temple, and author Zane Grey.

After Collier's death, the island was largely abandoned. At one point it was used by the CIA in the planning and training for the ill-fated Bay of Pigs invasion. Garfield Beckstead purchased the island in 1976 and set about the massive restoration project that led to the revival of the Ussepa Island Club and, in 1998, the opening of Collier's tin-roofed, Old Florida-style mansion as the Collier Inn.

The inn offers eleven rooms, each designed around an eclectic theme and each with a private terrace offering a splendid water view. Our favorite is the Barron Collier Room, furnished with antiques, a four-poster bed, oriental rugs, oversized leather chairs, fine chandeliers, a television and a whirlpool bath big enough for two. For fishing enthusiasts, the Izaak Walton Room features fishing photos and elaborate hand-carved furnishings.

COLLIER INN AT USEPPA ISLAND CLUB

Address:	**P.O. Box 640, Bokeelia 33922**
	www.useppa.com
Phone:	**941/283-1061**
Fax:	**941/283-0290**
Rates:	**$230 – $650**
Units:	**11 rooms/12 one- to four-bedroom cottages**

CAPE HAZE

Bed tax 10 percent

This small fishing town on the Intracoastal Waterway is a jumping-off place for several islands in the Gulf of Mexico.

Palm Island Resort

It's just a short ferry ride from the resort's landside marina to this beachfront island resort that encompasses the northern two miles of a seven-mile group of islands. No cars are allowed in the resort proper, so when you come off the ferry you'll park your car in the island parking area and settle in to the laid-back ambiance of life at the beach. Don't worry about that powerless feeling

some of us get when we have to leave our car behind; getting around is easy. Most facilities are within walking distance, and if you don't want to walk, an open-air tram will carry you throughout the resort. Or you can rent a golf cart for your own transport.

You have a choice of one-, two-, or three-bedroom villas, with a bath for each bedroom. These are grouped in low-rise two-story buildings with four or eight villas to the building set in semicircles around one of the four resort pools. All the villas are Old Florida style with tin roofs and white-railed porches, and each one has a private screened porch.

Gulffront villas offer the best panoramic view of the beach and the Gulf of Mexico and the best view of the sunsets over the water, while the gulf view rooms generally overlook a swimming pool with an indirect view of the gulf. Whichever you choose, you'll never be more than fifty or sixty yards from the pristine beach that runs the full two miles of the resort property.

Since every villa has a kitchen, you can bring your own groceries, or you can buy essentials at the resort store. If you don't want to cook, you can eat at the resort restaurant, but note that it's open only for lunch and dinner. For a change, you can also take the resort launch to the mainland to the resort's seafood restaurant, which overlooks the landside marina.

Like any resort, you can just lie on the beach or by a pool and do nothing. Or, you can take part in a wide variety of activities offered for all ages, including all types of water sports from snorkeling to kayaking to fishing, shell hunts, scavenger hunts, sand-castle contests, arts and crafts, and family bingo. Since nature is a big draw here, there are nature hunts, bicycle nature tours, and weekly programs, including presentations on the Sea Turtle Nesting Program and manatee awareness. The programs for kids include Kid Olympics and fishing tourneys.

This is also a bit of heaven for tennis buffs. There are eleven hard courts available for play and a tennis program run by a resident professional who has a number of years on the international tennis circuit.

An additional twenty-eight one-bedroom villas are located at the resort's marina on the mainland.

PALM ISLAND RESORT

Address:	**7092 Placida Road, Cape Haze 33946**
	www.palmisland.com
Phone:	**800/824-5412; 941/697-4800**
Fax:	**941/697-0696**
Rates:	**island rooms $285 – $515, Mainland rooms $90 – $135**
Units:	**160 units on the island; 28 units at the mainland marina**

CAPTIVA ISLAND

Bed tax 9 percent

There are several stories of how this island got its name. One goes back to the 1500s when a Spanish nobleman was held captive here by the local Calusa Indians. The other tale, which has even more Hollywood appeal, says it got its name because a famous local pirate, Juan Gaspar, held his female captives here.

Today this is a getaway island (accessible by car) known for its natural state—more than a third of the land on this and adjoining Sanibel Island are wildlife refuges—and extensive shell-covered beaches. Since there are no offshore reefs near Captiva to break up the shells, most make it to shore in one piece. The prime importance of shelling is evidenced by the presence of the only accredited seashell museum in the United States, the Bailey-Matthews Museum on adjoining Sanibel Island. Shelling is so popular on these two islands that the sheller's posture is often called the Captiva Crouch or the Sanibel Stoop. In addition to the lure of shelling, Captiva has several times earned the accolade of having one of the country's most romantic beaches.

South Seas Plantation

Unlike some other resorts that have adopted the word *plantation* for their name, this 330-acre resort occupying most of the northern tip of Captiva Island actually was a coconut palm and citrus plantation in the 1920s and '30s. Key limes were a main crop, and for a time the plantation was one of the largest key-lime distributors in the world.

Now the main crop—if we can stretch that term—is the guest who stays in one of the six hundred accommodations, uses one of the eighteen swimming pools or twenty-one tennis courts, strolls the two-and-a-half miles of beach, or takes part in a myriad of other resort activities.

Those hundreds of places to stay range from water view hotel rooms at the harbor to a variety of one-, two-, and three-bedroom cottages and villas. These are placed in clusters throughout the resort, offering you a choice of views of the beach, the bay, the marina, the tennis center, or the nine-hole golf course. Since the resort prides itself on living in harmony with nature, no building is taller than the tallest tree. And despite the fact that the resort can accommodate a couple thousand guests at one time, because it sprawls out in leisurely fashion among the trees in the tropical forest, you'll rarely feel crowded.

As for activities, this resort has it all, including swimming, canoeing, kayaking, bicycling, fishing, arts and crafts, crab races, bingo, and log rolling. Log rolling? They do it by substituting a twisting, turning foam-rubber device for a traditional log. You can go head over heels for that. Want to stop looking down for shells and get up there with the birds? Try parasailing. Want to learn how to sail? Steve Colgate's Offshore Sailing School offers lessons for both beginners and advanced sailors. The programs at the Tennis Center have repeatedly led *Tennis* magazine to list the plantation as one of the top fifty resorts in the United States every year for more that a dozen years. And if you prefer to relax and watch the world pass by, the *Lady Chadwick,* the resort's 150-passenger boat, offers a variety of daily cruises for everything from plain old sightseeing to visiting area islands to a Dolphin and Wildlife Adventure Cruise.

So, what do you do with the kids? Turn them over to the professional recreation specialists who run a full-time supervised Explorer Kids' Club activity program for ages three to eleven as well as a variety of programs for teens.

Your dining-out options range from full-service restaurants to a pizzeria and an ice cream emporium.

SOUTH SEAS PLANTATION

Address:	**P.O. Box 194, Captiva Island 33924**
	www.southseas.com
Phone:	**800/CAPTIVA (227-8482); 941/481-5600**
Fax:	**941/481-4947**
Rates:	**$180 – $820**
Units:	**over 600**

'Tween Waters Inn

You can walk the few hundred feet from a beach on the Gulf of Mexico to a beach on Pine Island Sound and, except for crossing Captiva Drive on the gulf side, never leave this inn's property. Located on the narrowest part of Captiva Island, it truly is 'tween waters. And its location means it's just a short walk to see a sunrise or a sunset over those waters.

What started as a small schoolhouse/cottage for a schoolteacher in 1925 is now a thirteen-acre resort offering you choices of accommodations that include motel rooms, efficiencies, suites, one- or two-bedroom cottages, and a three-bedroom suite, the majority with water views.

The motel rooms and some of the suites are in newer buildings with modern styling. So if you want the flavor of Old Florida, try the spacious cottages in the palm groves. They are nothing fancy. In fact, they are simply furnished—a few without water views—and some are about sixty years old. They have been well maintained, and we found their ambiance more in keeping with the leisurely island pace and beach life. All units get daily maid service, but if you're in a suite or a cottage with a kitchen, they don't do kitchens.

In addition to the white sand beaches that are like bookends to the property, the resort has an Olympic-size swimming pool, a locally popular restaurant and night club, three tennis courts, a fitness center, and a full-service marina. Small boats, canoes, and bicycles can be rented, and the staff can hook you up with fishing, shelling, sailing, and kayaking guides.

Even if you don't get a chance to eat there, check out the sketches and cartoons on the wall in the Ding Darling Room. "Ding" was a conservationist well before conservationism was "in." He was also a cartoonist and a regular at the inn for thirty years. The nearby wildlife refuge on Sanibel Island is named after him.

'TWEEN WATERS INN

Address:	**P.O. Box 249, Captiva Island 33924**
	www.tween-waters.com
Phone:	**800/223-5865; 941/472-5161**
Fax:	**941/472-0249**
Rates:	**$175 – $420**
Units:	**137**

CLEWISTON

Sales tax 7 percent

The two biggest things in this area are Lake Okeechobee and the sugarcane fields. The lake, the second largest freshwater lake entirely within the United States, covers an area nearly three-quarters the size of Rhode Island and is considered by many to be one of the world's best bass fishing lakes. Circling the lake, and keeping it in its place, is a 140-mile long, three-story grassy mound called the Herbert Hoover dike. Clewiston is the largest city on the lake and the unofficial capital of the Florida sugar industry. You can understand why it's called "America's Sweetest Town" as you drive into it from any direction and pass the miles and miles of sugarcane fields that extend down to the edge of the Everglades.

Clewiston Inn

When U.S. Sugar built a hotel here in 1926, it was designed to be a local showplace to house visiting company executives and dignitaries. Unfortunately, they built it on a wood frame with interiors and exteriors of one of their own by-products, Celotex, a fiber left over from the processing of sugar. Impressive in appearance, but not fire resistant, that inn burned down in 1936. Learning from their mistake, they rebuilt it in 1938. This time they built it solidly of brick on a steel frame with walls so thick they could withstand the occasional hurricane. But they still wanted it to be a local showplace, so they made it a two-story white building with pillared southern plantation-style portico entrance.

Now on the National Register of Historic Places, the inn is still owned by U.S. Sugar and occasionally houses sugar executives. Today, however, this attractive southern-style inn is better known as a bed-and-breakfast offering thirty-two rooms and thirteen suites to guests. There are also two one-bedroom and one two-bedroom efficiencies off the courtyard in the rear of the hotel that are the best buys for longer stays. All rooms have a simple colonial décor with cherry and pine furniture and thick walls that keep out traffic noise. The inn's popular restaurant is known for serving regional specialties southern style.

Even if you don't drink, make sure to visit the Everglades Lounge to see the original four-wall oil-on-canvas mural depicting Everglades scenery and wildlife. Painted in 1945, it is still a conversation piece.

CLEWISTON INN

Address:	**108 Royal Palm Avenue, Clewiston 33440**
	www.clewistoninn.com
Phone:	**800/749-4466; 941/983-8151**
Rates:	**$99 – $159**
Units:	**48**

ENGELWOOD

Bed tax 10 percent

Two special parks are among the places of interest in this small mainland town. The five-acre Indian Mound Park includes a prehistoric Indian mound site, dating from 1000 B.C., and the 195-acre Lemon Bay Park has a butterfly garden, an environmental center, and a canoe trail.

Manasota Beach Club

It's hard to be more guest friendly than this place. For example, if you are a guest here, they will take a photo of you and send you a copy of it enclosed in their family Christmas card. And if you come back, as many, many guests do, you'll find your photo and other photos of you and other guests in the club's collection of photo albums. Maybe that's one of the reasons this beach club has been successfully run by the same family since 1960.

There's nothing swank here. It's set up to encourage couples and families to enjoy Old Florida at an unspoiled getaway beach. Not that you'll be going primitive.   Accommodations include a number of one-, two-, and three-bedroom beach cottages and homes the family has accumulated over the years in an area that now covers twenty-six acres. Some are truly Old Florida, others are '50s style and there's even a bayside Polynesian-themed three-bedroom cottage with a private pool. All are nestled in a grove of palm trees, palmettos, and live oaks spotted with gopher tortoise nests. Located on Manasota Key, the property extends across the narrow key so you can enjoy a sandy beach on the Gulf of Mexico on one side and the mangrove-lined bay shore on the other.

It's set up for leisurely living, but if you want to do more than just sunbathe—perhaps with a book from the club's large library—there's plenty to do. There is fishing, swimming, kayaking, shelling, tennis, croquet, bocce, shuffleboard, or bird watching, and special activities for the kids.

This beach club offers American Plan rates—all meals included—in what it calls its social season from January to early April.

MANASOTA BEACH CLUB

Address:	**7660 Manasota Road, Englewood 34223**
	www.manasotabeachclub.com
Phone:	**941/474-2614**
Fax:	**941/473-1512**
Rates:	**$355 – $400 (includes meals)**
Units:	**29**

FORT MYERS

Bed tax 9 percent

When doctors told a seriously ill Thomas Edison he needed to winter in a warmer climate, he picked Fort Myers. That was in 1886 when he was in his late thirties. The prescription worked. He lived to the age of eighty-four. You can visit his home and lab here, as well as the winter estate of his friend Henry Ford, who lived next door.

Another popular site is the Shell Factory, where you can see, and buy from, one of the world's largest collections of shells and coral.

Sanibel Harbour Resort & Spa

This is a well-rounded resort offering something for everyone. *Family Circle* rated it one of the top ten family beach resorts, *Condé Nast Traveler* readers rated it one of the top ten spa resorts in the country, *Travel & Leisure* listed it as one of the "Five Best Values in the United States and Canada," and *Racquet* magazine rated it as one of the "Ultimate Tennis Resorts in America."

Nestled on a private eighty-acre peninsula, right before the causeway to Sanibel Island, there are 193 rooms and forty-seven suites in the hotel building, and sixty-eight two-bedroom, two-bath condos that are great for families. The hotel is built to carry on the pattern of the old Tarpon House Inn that burned down on this site in 1913. That inn had a rounded Victorian pavilion topped with a cupola and all the rooms overlooked the water. These traditional features survive in the resort's octagonal pavilion with cupola that houses the reception area and restaurants. All the rooms have balconies that overlook the harbor, and the Victorian ambiance is maintained in fabric patterns and tapestries throughout.

There's also a tennis complex that was home of two Davis Cup tournaments, four pools, a thousand-foot private beach, a marina with all types of watercraft rentals, a fishing pier, a large fitness center with classes, an assortment of cruises ranging from sunset dinner cruises aboard the resort's private yacht to a wildlife/dolphin sightseeing cruise. And, as the resort's name states, there is also a splendid spa offering sixty different "pampering" services. Although there's no golf course on the property, there are five courses less than fifteen minutes away.

So what do you with the kids while you're luxuriating in all this? Sign them up for the Kids' Klub, which features counselor-supervised activities every day for the crowd of five to twelve year olds.

SANIBEL HARBOUR RESORT & SPA

Address:	**17260 Harbour Pointe Drive, Fort Myers 33908**
	www.sanibel-resort.com
Phone:	**800/767-7777; 941/466-4000**
Rates:	**$145 – $700**
Units:	**308**

MATLACHA

Bed tax 9 percent

This town sits on Matlacha (mat-LĀ-CHEE) Pass Aquatic Preserve, which is known as an abundant feeding ground for fish. For a town of only about eight hundred, it has a dozen restaurants. If you catch your own dinner, several of them will cook it for you for a small fee.

The Bridge Water Inn

Their slogan is "Stay INN the water," and they aren't kidding. Built on 130 pilings, this inn extends 125 feet over the water. That means you can dock your boat right outside your room, and fish from your porch. Even if you don't fish, watching the dolphins at play in your front yard and the sunsets over the bay make it worthwhile.

The fish seem to love to hide among the inn's pilings, which are like a reef home to many of them. For more evidence, watch the fishermen elbow to elbow on the nearby "Fishingest Bridge in the World."

The inn started out as a bait-and-boat rental shack owned by a minister. And according to Steve and Osi McCarney, the present owners (it's their retirement dream), "he built with whatever the Lord provided and sometimes the Lord didn't give him the right nail." They've built on and improved it a great deal, but it's still a little rustic looking. Relatively small, it offers only two regular rooms and five efficiencies. All are clean and simply decorated with plenty of room for fishing gear. Room 3, a corner efficiency with a great view, is large enough for a small family. If you don't catch your own, fresh seafood is available from several shrimpers that dock nearby, and right across the bridge they sell blue crabs.

THE BRIDGE WATER INN

Address:	**P.O. Box 457, Matlacha 33993**
	www.bridgewaterinn.com
Phone:	**800/378-7666; 941/283-2423**
Fax:	**941/282-8440**
Rates:	**$39 to $139**
Units:	**7**

NAPLES

Bed tax 9 percent

In 1890 when the first developers of Naples went bust, the land was put up for auction. There was only one bidder, Walter Haldemann, the publisher of the *Louisville Courier-Journal.* He got all the town lots, eighty-six hundred acres outside the town plat, the only hotel, the pier, and the steamer *Fearless* (a boat was the only way to get to town at the time), all for fifty thousand dollars. But not much money changed hands because Haldemann already owned a huge mortgage on the property.

After Haldemann put the development on a good financial footing, in the 1920s Barron Collier, also a publisher, came in and was responsible for gathering Naples and its environs into a separate county, which, not surprisingly, was named after him. Today, Collier County, with 3,119 square miles, is the largest of Florida's sixty-seven counties. Barron Collier was also the man behind the completion of the Tamiami Trail in 1928. Tamiami Trail sounds like a Native American word when actually it is short for the <u>Tam</u>pa to <u>Miami</u> highway. Built in the 1920s, it was southwest Florida's only major highway for years.

Two area beaches, Clam Pass and Delnor-Wiggins, have been consistently rated in the top twenty in the National Best Beaches Survey compiled by Dr. Stephen Leatherman (a.k.a. Dr. Beach) of the University of Maryland. While the gulf beaches sit at its front door, the majestic wilderness of the Everglades is at its back. In addition to having one of the few Mobil Five-Star and AAA Five-Diamond hotels in the country, Naples also boasts the world's only teddy bear museum.

Registry Resort

As you look out from the tower-room balcony you can see the surf and miles of white sand beach. Exactly what you would expect at a gulffront resort. But what you might not expect to see is that the resort's beach is deliberately separated from the tower by a lush two-hundred-acre mangrove preserve, known locally as "The Registry's Back Yard." This might sound inconvenient, but actually it adds to the pleasure of going to the beach. The half-mile walk along the boardwalk through the preserve is like entering a calming, natural transition zone between the man-made tower and the secluded beach. As you stroll along the winding boardwalk, you'll find yourself unwinding. For those who don't want to walk, you can bike or take a tram. If you are into fitness, however, watch out for the Ice Cream Parlor and Patisserie that lies in wait for you among the shops at the beginning of the boardwalk.

The pleasant coolness of the lobby's Italian marble floors and handwoven rugs is enhanced by the sounds of gently flowing water from a manmade stream. There are 395 guest rooms and twenty-nine suites in the

eighteen-story tower, all with private balconies for gulf and sunset views. In addition, surrounding the fifteen Har-Tru tennis courts, are forty-nine garden suites. All are handsomely furnished with an obvious attention to detail. The resort's facilities include three swimming pools, a health spa, the tennis center, and seven restaurants and lounges. Golf can be arranged at three nearby courses.

For the kids, Camp Registry is a daylong supervised activity program for ages five to twelve years old.

REGISTRY RESORT

Address:	**475 Seagate Drive, Naples 34103**
	www.registryhotels.com
Phone:	**800/247-9810; 941/597-3232**
Fax:	**941/597-9151**
Rates:	**$395 – $695**
Units:	**473**

Ritz-Carlton Naples

When it opened in 1985, this was the first resort conceived by the worldwide Ritz-Carlton Company, and no expense was spared to create it. Located on twenty gulffront acres, the fourteen-story hotel has 431 guest rooms and thirty-two suites, all with a view of the gulf, all but eleven with balconies, and all decorated with understated grandeur.

Of course it's not the reason this Ritz-Carlton is a Mobil Five-Star and an AAA Five-Diamond hotel (the highest ratings given), but the hotel's wine list offers 550 selections, and they routinely have an in-house total of about fifteen thousand bottles. Another little item that didn't hurt is its staff of twenty concierges, who can handle virtually every guest request.

If you're an art lover, the concierge will give you a self-guided tour brochure so you can see for yourself the more than 250 pieces of museum-quality art and antiques scattered throughout the hotel. This includes a large collection of pieces from the eighteenth and the nineteenth centuries sporting art featuring horses and hounds, the status symbol of those periods.

The resort has six restaurants, including the Grill, where there's a fire in the fireplace all year. And when you can break away and get out of your lovely room, the resort offers a beach, a swimming pool, tennis courts, a fitness center, massage and body treatments, and all kinds of fun small watercraft for rent. They will also arrange a tee time for you at a twenty-seven-hole course designed by Greg Norman that is just five minutes away.

As befits one of the best hotels in the world, the service is speedy and quietly unobtrusive. And although the hotel's reputation alone can be impressive to the point of intimidation, at least on your first visit, you'll soon find yourself relishing the casual elegance.

While not usually thought of as a family resort, the hotel features a playground and the Ritz Kids Club, which offers supervised daily activity programs for kids three to twelve.

RITZ-CARLTON NAPLES

Address:	**280 Vanderbilt Beach Road, Naples 34108-2300**
	www.ritzcarlton.com
Phone:	**941/598-3300 (Reservations 800/241-3333)**
Fax:	**941/598-6667**
Rates:	**$425–$4,000**
Units:	**463**

PINELAND

Bed tax 9 percent

This is a small fishing town where you can catch a boat to Cabbage Key and other islands.

Cabbage Key Inn

An old travelers' cliché says that if you want a good restaurant, stop where the truckers stop. In this case, it's stop where the fishermen, the boaters, and the tour boats stop, and that's here at the Cabbage Key Inn.

This is a true rustic getaway island. No pool, no tennis courts, no television or room phones, no pretense, and—except for when the tour boats bring the day visitors for lunch or on weekends when the bar is busy—lots of privacy. It's a one-hundred-acre island accessible only by private boat or ferry that is truly Old Florida. While some guests spend their time just sitting on an isolated beach enjoying the blissful peace and privacy, others go shelling, or rent a skiff from the dockmaster to visit nearby uninhabited islands or go fishing.

Built in the 1930s as a getaway for popular mystery writer Mary Roberts Reinhart, it soon became a getaway for other celebrities of the time, including Ernest Hemingway. And it's still a celebrity hideout at times, welcoming visitors like Ted Koppel and Sean Connery. Singer Jimmy Buffett also visited and, as the story goes, wrote a song about the island restaurant called "Cheeseburger in Paradise."

For overnights you have a choice of staying in one of the six rooms in the old house that is now the inn or in one of six one- and two-bedroom cottages, some with kitchens.

The restaurant is famous not only for its food—like the island, simple and basic and always good—but also for the décor in the bar, where every inch of the walls and ceiling is covered with thousands and thousands of dollar bills, each autographed by a visitor. Even the piano is covered with dollar bills. The house policy is that any that drop off are donated to charity—a fact that is good for the charities since the dollar bills are only taped up, and the tape eventually loses its grip.

CABBAGE KEY INN

Address:	**P.O. Box 200, Pineland 33945**
	www.cabbage-key.com
Phone:	**941/283-2278**
Fax:	**941/283-1384**
Rates:	**under $100 to $300**
Units:	**12**

For Additional Information
on the Southwest Region:

CHARLOTTE HARBOR AND
GULF ISLANDS CVB
1600 Tamiami Trail, Suite 100,
Port Charlotte, 33948
800/4-PUR-FLA (478-7352);
941/743-1900
www.pureflorida.com

ENGLEWOOD AREA COC
601 S. Indiana Avenue,
Englewood 34223
800/603-7198; 941/474-9511
www.englewoodchamber.com

LEE ISLAND COAST CVB
2180 West First Street,
Suite 100, Fort Myers 33901
800/237-6444; 941/338-3500
Fax: 941/334-1106
www.leeislandcoast.com

SANIBEL AND CAPTIVA
ISLANDS COC
1159 Causeway Road, Sanibel 33957
941/472-1080
Fax: 941/472-1070
www.sanibel-captiva.org

GREATER FORT MYERS COC
6900 Daniels Parkway,
Fort Myers 33919
800/366-3622; 941/332-3624
www.fortmyers.org

NAPLES AREA COC
895 Fifth Avenue S., Naples 34102
941/262-6141
Fax: 941/435-9910
www.naples-online.com

MARTIN COUNTY

(Port Salerno, Stuart)

Sales Tax 7 percent

This is the subtropics, and at one time pineapple plantations flourished here before the great frost of 1895. Instead of pineapple, the county now boasts of an egg farm that produces more than 110 million eggs annually, and tens of thousands of acres of citrus, vegetables, sugar cane, and ornamental plants.

Stuart, the county seat, was originally named Potsdam. But in 1895 the residents decided to change the name to honor Homer Stuart, one of their own. They also might have been goaded into a name change because the conductors on the passenger trains took delight in announcing the station as "Pots. Dam Pots!"

Stuart claims to be the Sailfish Capital of the World. In 1941, when over a thousand sailfish were caught in one week, local fisherman adopted the "catch and release" policy to stop the depletion of the numbers of this prized sports fish. Another denizen of the sea that makes an annual impact here is the sea turtle. Every June and July, thousands of the females come up on the local beaches to nest and lay their eggs before going back to the sea.

Pirate's Cove Resort and Marina

You don't have to be a fisherman or a boating enthusiast to enjoy overnights at this resort, but if you are either, you may feel like you're in heaven. For boaters, there's a full-service marina with transient dockage and a large warehouse that provides indoor storage for 180 small boats. If you want to learn to be a mariner, or improve your powerboat or sailing skills, you can take courses at the Chapman School of Seamanship.

Just sixty-eight miles to the east is Grand Bahama Island. To help

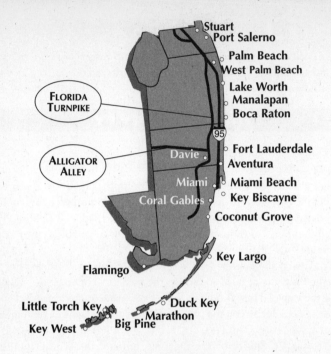

FLORIDA TURNPIKE

ALLIGATOR ALLEY

Stuart
Port Salerno
Palm Beach
West Palm Beach
Lake Worth
Manalapan
Boca Raton
95
Fort Lauderdale
Davie
Aventura
Miami
Miami Beach
Coral Gables
Key Biscayne
Coconut Grove
Key Largo
Flamingo
Little Torch Key
Duck Key
Marathon
Key West
Big Pine

High Season: Winter

(Note: All lodging rates are for high season. Off-season rates can be significantly lower.)

boaters with all the aspects of that trip, the Bahamas Tourist Office has set up the first Bahamas Marine Tourism Center in this resort.

If you don't bring your own boat, offshore charter boats, river and back-country guided boats, and deep sea party boats, all operate out of the marina, and bait and tackle are available. For divers, there's also always at least one dive boat at the marina.

The fifty rooms in the waterfront hotel are comfortably furnished in a tropical décor. All the rooms have television and balconies with views of either the harbor or the hotel's heated swimming pool. The Pirate's Loft Restaurant and Lounge has been locally popular since it opened in 1980.

PIRATE'S COVE RESORT AND MARINA

Address:	4307 S.E. Bayview Street, Port Salerno 34992
Phone:	800/332-1414; 561/287-2500
Fax:	561/220-2704
Rates:	$150-$225
Units:	50

HarborFront Inn

It looks like a Nantucket shingled cottage on the gentle St. Lucie River. Built in 1908 the house was once accessible only by water, but today, although it is a hideaway on a narrow road running along the river, it is in the heart of Stuart's historic district, surrounded by other grand homes.

Boats are still an important part of life at this inn. Dockage is available for overnight guests, and you can arrange with John Elbert, one of your hosts, to go fishing or sailing on the Silver Lady, a thirty-three-foot sailboat that holds up to four adults. That includes sunset sails and overnights. John also holds occasional learn-to-sail weekends. If you want to explore the river on your own, a two-person kayak is available for rent. Or, you can just relax and watch the river roll slowly by from a hammock slung between two trees in the backyard that slopes down to the water.

John's wife, JoAyne, who has a background in the hospitality industry, is the principal innkeeper. She offers guests a choice of eclectic lodgings that include rooms, suites, an apartment, and a cottage. All are cozily furnished in pleasant beach-house fashion, have private baths, a television, a VCR, a phone, and a private entrance.

Our favorite is the Courtyard Suite with a bedroom, a sitting room, a whirlpool tub, and a private deck with a view of the river. The riverfront apartment and the cottage both include a living room and kitchen and are best if you want to spread out for a longer stay. Both have a three-day minimum.

HARBORFRONT INN

Address:	310 Atlantic Avenue, Stuart 34994
	www.harborfront.com
Phone:	800/266-1127; 561/288-7289
Fax:	561/221-0474
Rates:	$85-$175
Units:	7

Hutchinson Island Marriott Beach Resort & Marina

This two hundred-acre resort is at the southern end of the sixteen-mile long Hutchinson Island, a lush barrier island between the Indian River and the Atlantic Ocean. The resort offers a well-rounded variety of land and sea facilities and activities. For sun and surf enthusiasts, there's the shell-covered beach on the Atlantic, with waverunners, kayaks, surfboards, and other fun watercraft available for rent at the marina. Inland are two outdoor Jacuzzis, and three heated swimming pools where beginners can take lessons in scuba diving or snorkeling.

Water comes into play on seventeen of the resort's two eighteen-hole golf courses. You can also knock balls out on the Aqua Driving Range.

For fishermen and boaters, there's a seventy-seven slip marina with a marine store, and deep-sea and river charter boats are available. If you don't have a boat but like to cruise, the eighty-four-foot *Island Princess* has regularly scheduled luncheon and dinner cruises, sunset cruises, and nature cruises. Other facilities include thirteen tennis courts, five lighted for night play, fitness facilities, four restaurants, three lounges, and a large conference center. For the family that may not want to play together all the time, there's the Tree Top Jungle Bunch Kids Camp to let you get away while your kids have supervised fun.

Since Hutchinson Island is a natural playground that has been preserved by strict zoning laws, the resort offers year-round guided eco-tours. Nearby, at Jensen Park Beach, is the third largest Loggerhead and Leatherback Sea Turtle nesting beach in the western hemisphere, and the resort is involved in the Sea Turtle Watch program each summer when the turtles come ashore to lay their eggs.

You have a choice of a variety of oceanfront and river view lodging that includes hotel rooms and one-and two-bedroom oceanfront suites with fully equipped kitchens, many with private balconies.

HUTCHINSON ISLAND MARRIOTT BEACH RESORT & MARINA

Address:	**555 N.E. Ocean Boulevard, Stuart 34996**
	www.marriott.com
Phone:	**800/775-5936; 561/225-3700**
Fax:	**561/225-0003**
Rates:	**$189-$399**
Units:	**298**

PALM BEACH COUNTY

(Boca Raton, Lake Worth, Manalapan, Palm Beach, West Palm Beach)

Palm Beach County is a mixed bag. It has the greatest agricultural sales in the state and because of the its billion-dollar sugar industry is eighth in sales in the country. With forty-seven miles of Atlantic beaches, more golf courses than any other county in the nation, and over forty museums, tourism plays a major role here. There are more than seventy-eight thousand people employed in the hospitality industry in over two hundred lodgings and two thousand restaurants.

Among the museums is the International Museum of Cartoon Art in Boca Raton. The Montreal Expos and St. Louis Cardinals hold spring training in Jupiter, and some of the best polo players in the world play at the Palm Beach Polo Club in Wellington. The United States Croquet Association and the National Croquet Championship are also located here. One of the unusual attractions in the country is Lion Country Safari, a drive-through wild animal preserve in Loxahatchee.

BOCA RATON

Bed tax 10 percent

Boca Raton Resort & Club

The slogan of this internationally known 356-acre resort is "The Elegant Place to Play." And indeed it is. As for the "play" part, there are two eighteen-hole golf courses and two golf schools, a tennis center with thirty-four courts, three fitness centers, an indoor basketball court, four indoor racquetball courts, five swimming pools, a half mile stretch of private Atlantic beach with a variety of water sports facilities, and a twenty-five slip marina with full fishing and boating facilities.

The "elegance" part is in the accommodations and the service.

It all started in 1926 when famous architect Addison Mizner designed and built the one hundred-room Cloister Inn, modeled after a Spanish castle with Moorish and Gothic influences. Mizner's dream was to

make it the greatest resort in the world, and for a time he almost succeeded. The Cloister's luxury and ambiance attracted royalty, Wall Street tycoons, and movie stars. But when Florida's land boom went bust, bankruptcy forced Mizner out. The resort was saved when it was turned into an exclusive, and expensive, "gentlemen's club."

Since then the property has changed hands a number of times, and fortunately, each new owner worked to preserve and expand the atmosphere of quiet luxury. The present owner is Boca Resorts, Inc., an H. Wayne Huizenga corporation. They have continued the tradition of elegance and excellence by putting around sixty million dollars into renovations since its purchase in 1997. They spend ten million dollars annually just on upkeep and maintenance.

Today, after many additions, renovations, and refurbishments, the resort buildings include the original Cloisters, the Tower, Boca Beach Club, Golf Villas, Boca Country Club, and a convention center. All the additions and developments have consistently adhered to Mizner's original Spanish-Mediterranean design with barrel tile roofs, archways, ornate columns, mosaics, ornate pecky cypress-beamed ceilings, and beautiful grounds with hidden gardens and fountains.

As for service, the resort has more than two thousand employees representing more than sixty nations. It also has a team of multilingual concierges for its overseas guests. For families, the resort offers an excellent and extensive selection of family events and children's programs covering all ages from Boca Baby, for ages two and under, up to Boca Teen for twelve to seventeen. The 963 guest accommodations include suites, junior suites, one-bedroom golf villas, and a concierge floor. And of course, there are several lounges and award-winning restaurants. If you want to visit without being a guest, the Boca Raton Historical Society holds tours twice a week. And if you really want to experience the pinnacle of luxury, the six-thousand-square-foot, two-level Presidential Suite is available for only fifty-five hundred dollars a night.

BOCA RATON RESORT & CLUB

Address:	P.O. Box 5025, Boca Raton 33431
	www.bocaresort.com
Phone:	888/495-BOCA (495-2622); 561/447-3000
Fax:	561/447-3183
Rates:	$240-$5,500
Units:	963

PALM BEACH AREA

Bed tax 10 percent

The Breakers

The Breakers is Palm Beach. The resort still exudes the lavish elegance of its historic past when the Rockefellers, Hearsts, and other notables came regularly to the "Palace by the Sea." Built in 1896 by Standard Oil tycoon and Florida railroad and land developer, Henry Flagler, it has been owned by the descendants of Mary Lily Kenan, his third wife, ever since. It was destroyed by fire twice in the early 1900s and was rebuilt both times, the last time in 1926. Listed in the National Register of Historic Places, it is one of the few remaining hotels in the nation that still has its original public rooms.

In addition to being a historic Florida landmark, the hotel is one of less than two dozen lodgings in the nation to receive the AAA Five Diamond and Mobil Five Star ratings. To maintain its quality of service and amenities for its guests, the resort has a ratio of approximately two employees for every guest room.

Located on 140 oceanfront acres on the island of Palm Beach, it offers 524 guest rooms and forty-five suites in Italian Renaissance-style buildings inspired by the magnificent Italian villas of the 1500s. The inspiration for the main lobby, for example, was the Great Hall of the Palazzo Carega in Genoa. It features majestic hand-painted vaulted ceilings, gigantic fifteenth century Flemish tapestries, and dozens of bronze and crystal chandeliers throughout. Furnishings and décor in all the rooms are comfortably elegant in keeping with the grand ambiance set by the lobby. We are particularly partial to the few oceanfront corner suites.

The Breakers features two eighteen-hole golf courses (one at another Breakers' property), a golf academy, a twenty thousand-square foot spa, a beach club overlooking a half a mile of private beach, two oceanfront swimming pools, an ocean view fitness center, twenty-one tennis courts, an outstanding selection of restaurants, and boutique shops.

In spite of all the architectural elegance, the resort is far from adults only. It is family-friendly with year-round recreational programs for every age. The Coconut Crew Camp has supervised programs for ages six to twelve and the Teen Scene for ages thirteen to seventeen. To make sure the children's programs meet the needs of younger guests, it has its own Kids' Advisory Board that "certifies" each program. (Make sure your children check out the Children's Secret Garden tucked away in the northwest corner of the resort property.)

THE BREAKERS

Address:	**One South Country Road, Palm Beach 33460**
	www.thebreakers.com
Phone:	**888/BREAKERS (273-2537); 561/655-6611**
Fax:	**561/659-8403**
Rates:	**$380-$2,700**
Units:	**569**

The Chesterfield Hotel

This charmingly elegant hotel is patterned after its sister hotel, The Chesterfield Mayfair in London, and certainly transplants more than a little "bit of England" to Palm Beach. For example, there's the intimate lobby that brings to mind a luxurious English country house with its

plush oriental rugs, antiques, a regular desk with chairs for registering guests, orchids in bowls, and fresh flowers everywhere. Then there's the dark paneled library with floor-to-ceiling shelves filled with books that guests can borrow, a fireplace, rich leather couches, comfortable chairs, and an abundance of current national and international newspapers. This is also the setting for traditional afternoon tea prepared as if you were royalty and served from cozied pots accompanied by—the also traditional—petite sandwiches, oven-warmed scones topped with homemade preserves, clotted cream, and an assortment of delicious pastries.

The Leopard Lounge and Restaurant is a popular Palm Beach luncheon gathering place that changes its spots at night when it offers both dining and dancing. (Be sure to look up at the hand-painted lounge ceiling filled with cherubs, satyrs, sexy women, and leering goats.) You can also dine in the delightful courtyard.

There are forty-three guest rooms and eleven suites here, all decorated with specially chosen fabrics, elegant furnishings, marble bathrooms, and brass knockers on the doors. Other facilities include a heated outdoor pool and Jacuzzi, and Churchill's Cigar Club, which has a circulation system insuring that all other areas of the hotel remain smoke free.

One of the serendipitous benefits of staying here is its great location, just two blocks from Worth Avenue, one of the most famous, and expensive, shopping streets anywhere.

THE CHESTERFIELD HOTEL

Address:	**363 Coconut Row, Palm Beach 33480**
	www.redcarnationhotels.com
Phone:	**800/243-7871; 561/659-5800**
Fax:	**561/659-6707**
Rates:	**$229-$1,099**
Units:	**54**

The Colony Palm Beach

The Colony's history is as glamorous as its present. For more than half a century it has been one of the places to see and be seen in the Palm Beach social realm of celebrities, royalty, and top corporate executives. For example, in 1961 a Palm Beach periodical wrote: "For what promises to be a particularly brilliant season, the Duke and Duchess of Windsor will arrive the end of March when they will take the Vice-Regal penthouse at The Colony Hotel as their residence through the month of April." Time has not faded this aura of glamour and elegance. During our visit, we saw a well-known movie and stage star in the lobby.

Accommodations in this intimate hotel include sixty-six guest rooms, fourteen suites, three penthouse suites—ah, memories of the Duke and Duchess!—and seven two-bedroom villas located adjacent to the hotel in the restored greathouse of a 1928 mansion. All the rooms, public and private, are beautifully furnished in combinations of Old Florida and British Colonial décor with polished brass, polished hardwoods, marble, and architectural detailing. The guest room décor includes tropical designer draperies and bed linens. For a family, or anyone planning on an extended stay, the villas offer fully equipped kitchens, a Jacuzzi tub, a private pool, and patios or balconies.

Facilities include a pool shaped like the state of Florida, a health spa, exercise room, restaurant and lounge. It is also located a short block from the ocean and just a few steps from the shops and sights of Worth Avenue, one of the most famous, and expensive, shopping streets anywhere.

THE COLONY PALM BEACH

Address:	155 Hammon Avenue, Palm Beach 33480
	www.thecolonypalmbeach.com
Phone:	800/521-5525; 561/655-5430
Fax:	561/659-8104
Rates:	$255-$695
Units:	90

Four Seasons Resort Palm Beach

Accolades, accolades, accolades!

If the fact that this resort has earned the coveted Mobil Five Star and AAA Five Diamond ratings doesn't impress you, there's more. The Zagat Hotel Guide consistently lists this Four Seasons as one of Florida's top five resorts, and its formal dining room, called simply The Restaurant, holds the AAA Five Diamond rating, a distinction only one other restaurant in Florida and twenty-nine others in the whole nation share. (It's only open for dinner and reservations are required.) There are still more ratings and awards, but you get the idea. This is top of the line in every aspect.

The luxury starts right at the resort's sweeping, arched porte cochére entrance with its cut coral columns flanked by palms and tropical flowers. Elegance is the word that comes to mind when you enter the marble lobby that continues into The Living Room with its hand-carved furnishings, dramatic tapestries, oil paintings, and large floral arrangements. The two-level Living Room offers a number of intimate sitting areas where you can enjoy live music every evening.

The resort, which sits on six acres of tropical landscaped ocean beachfront at the southern end of the island of Palm Beach, offers just about any recreational activity you might want. In addition to the beach, with its wide range of water sports equipment, the facilities include a heated pool and whirlpool overlooking the ocean, an excellent full-service fitness center and beauty spa, and three tennis courts (with a resident pro). You have a choice of 198 guest rooms or twelve suites all with a sitting area, full marble bathroom, and a private balcony. Furnished with light woods accented in soft pastels, many of the rooms offer an ocean view. If you think all this might be too stuffy, you should know that the resort is family friendly with an award-winning (another award!) complimentary year-round Kids for All Seasons program for ages three to twelve.

As if the executive chef doesn't have enough to do managing his top-rated restaurant, he and his culinary team also offer a cooking class each Wednesday morning that's open to both guests and visitors. Appropriately called Perfect Seasonings, the classes feature culinary themes that change each month. Kitchen novices and more seasoned cooks are all welcome.

FOUR SEASONS RESORT PALM BEACH

Address:	**2800 South Ocean Boulevard, Palm Beach 33480**
	www.fourseasons.com
Phone:	**800/432-2335; 561/582-2800**
Fax:	**561/547-1557**
Rates:	**$365-$2,500**
Units:	**210**

Hibiscus House Bed & Breakfast

Oh, what a combination of creativity, talent, and perseverance can do! This charming bed-and-breakfast is an outstanding example of a partnership that fully utilizes the talents of two gifted people, Raleigh Hill and Colin Rayner. Raleigh is an interior designer and antique collector, and Colin has a special skill in preserving and restoring historic homes and neighborhoods.

In 1986, when these two bought this 1920s house in the old Norwood section of West Palm Beach, it was a dilapidated crack house. Crime was so rampant in the area that they found it hard to talk to neighbors because they wouldn't open their doors. Today the two-story, fourteen-room house is an elegant bed-and-breakfast that is the pride of the neighborhood, and the neighborhood itself is now the city's first district listed in the National Register of Historic Places.

The restored house provides an elegant background for the antiques that Raleigh has collected over many years. In the living room, for example, you'll see a Scottish grandfather clock from 1830, a four-square piano more than one hundred sixty years old, chandeliers from Egypt and Spain, Waterford decanters and goblets, Chinese temple jars, and a lovely oriental rug.

Hibiscus House offers eight rooms and suites including two in a cottage. Each is named for its particular color and décor. All the upstairs rooms have a private terrace. Our favorite is the Burgundy Suite, which has a four-poster bed and a fireplace in the bedroom, a lovely sitting room, French doors to a private terrace overlooking the tropical pool area, and a small balcony off the bathroom that overlooks the gazebo and fish pond. The house has a swimming pool, landscaped tropical courtyard, rose garden, and of course, a multitude of hibiscus trees.

HIBISCUS HOUSE BED & BREAKFAST

Address:	501 30th Street, West Palm Beach 33407
	www.hibiscushouse.com
Phone:	800/203-4927; 561/863-5633
Fax:	561/863-5633
Rates:	$120-$240
Units:	8

Mango Inn Bed & Breakfast

One of the major attractions of this charming inn is its location just a short walk to the beach and two blocks from historic downtown Lake Worth.

Lake Worth had its beginnings in the early 1900s. It's said that things were so quiet here at that time that the first town marshall didn't ever use his shotgun to catch criminals, he used it to catch fish. Today, Lake Worth is one of the few coastal communities in Palm Beach County that has an extensive and attractive core downtown area where everything is within walking distance. That includes art galleries, museums, boutiques, restaurants, and an abundance of antique shops.

Both Erin and Bo Allen liked Lake Worth, and after settling in, Erin started the successful Lake Worth Street Painting Festival and Bo won a seat on the City Council. When they decided to pursue Erin's dream of having a bed-and-breakfast, they found this 1915 home, took a year and a half to restore it, and opened it in 1996 as Lake Worth's first bed-and-breakfast. They named it the Mango Inn because the field across the street was once a mango farm.

Guests have a choice of six guest rooms in the main house, a poolside cottage with kitchenette, and the Little House. The guest rooms are named after flowers, and each room is individually decorated to match the flower it is named after. All of the rooms have a private bath, a private entrance, and most have a television, phone, and refrigerator. For a family or two couples, the Little House is a good choice since it is a complete two-bedroom, two-bath house with family room, living room, dining, room, and full kitchen. Guests have use of the heated pool or may stroll or bike to the nearby beach.

MANGO INN BED & BREAKFAST

Address:	128 N. Lakeside Drive, Lake Worth 33460
	www.mangoinn.com
Phone:	888/MANGO-19 (626-4619); 561/533-6900
Fax:	561/533-6992
Rates:	$90-$225
Units:	8

PGA National Resort & Spa

One indication of how golf is king here is that there are around twenty-five golf pros on the staff. Then again, that's not a great number considering they offer ninety holes of golf on five tournament golf courses, and it is the home of both the Professional Golfers Association of America (PGA) and that association's famed National Academy of Golf.

The Champion Course, originally designed by Tom and George Fazio and later redesigned by Jack Nicklaus, hosts some of golf's most prestigious tournaments. The Fazios also designed the Haig Course, which they made so golfers of all skills can have enjoyable play. The General Course is named for Arnold Palmer who designed it to be reminiscent of Scottish links. The Squire Course is named after Gene Sarazen and known as a "thinking man's course" because it truly tests a golfer's skills. And finally, there's the Estate Course, designed by Karl Litten, that the PGA uses as the primary site for the Club Professional Winter Tournament.

And that's not all there is on this 2,340-acre resort. For tennis buffs, there are nineteen Har-Tru clay courts (twelve lighted). Swim, sun, and sail enthusiasts will be pleased with the nine swimming pools, including a tropical pool next to the hotel with Jacuzzi tubs, and a private white sand beach on a twenty-six acre lake with small craft available for rent. The 32,500-square-foot Health and Racquet Club includes all types of fitness equipment as well as racquetball and handball courts. To round out the facilities there are seven restaurants and lounges, including a Shula's Steakhouse. There's even a world class five court croquet complex.

Another major feature here is The Spa. Since it opened, The Spa has attracted so much clientele that it was expanded three times in its first seven years. A beautiful facility, The Spa offers more than one hundred health, fitness, and beauty services for both women and men, guests and day visitors, as well as its relaxing "Waters of the World," a collection of mineral pools with salts imported from the world's most renowned water sources.

So where do you stay when you're not using all these wonderful facilities? You have a choice of 279 guest rooms and sixty one-and two-bedroom suites in the main hotel, and eighty cottage suites. The guest rooms and suites in the main hotel all have light, bright, and comfortable furnishings and décor and either a private terrace or a balcony with a view of the lake, the pool, or a golf course. The equally well-decorated cottage suites all overlook the golf course and come with two bedrooms, two full baths, living room, and full kitchen.

PGA NATIONAL RESORT & SPA

Address:	400 Avenue of the Champions, Palm Beach Gardens 33418
	www.pga-resorts.com
Phone:	800/633-9150; 561/627-2000
Fax:	561/622-0261
Rates:	$369-$1,300
Units:	419

The Ritz-Carlton Palm Beach

"Luxurious" is an overused word, so we won't use it here. Instead we'll say "superluxurious." Don't just take our word for it. The readers of *Conde*

Nast Traveler magazine recently chose this Ritz-Carlton as the one of the best resorts in North America in their annual Readers' Choice Awards poll, AAA gave it the highest rating of Five Diamonds, and Mobil gave it Four Stars, its next to the top rating.

Situated on seven oceanfront acres with a beautiful beach in the tiny town of Manalapan on the southern end of the island of Palm Beach, the resort's architecture leans toward the Mediterranean style with Spanish mission bell towers, bisque-colored stucco exterior, and Italianate terra cotta tile roof. The elegant entrance is dramatically framed by royal palms that line the curved driveway leading to the porte cochére that carries the hotel chain's lion and crown emblem. The lobby is equally dramatic with its large, two-sided marble fireplace, Persian carpets, antique furnishings, and original art. (If you ask, they'll give you a tour of the outstanding art collection.)

The aura of comfortable posh continues in the 270 guest rooms that include fifty-six ocean view suites, and twenty-six guest rooms and nine suites on the hotel's extra-amenities club level. All are handsomely furnished and have a private balcony. Most rooms have an ocean view. The resort features a stunning sandy white beach, oceanfront heated pool with Jacuzzi, fitness center, seven tennis courts, restaurants and lounges. The service is as close to flawless as you can get because the outstanding multi-lingual staff lives by the Ritz-Carlton creed of "ladies and gentlemen serving ladies and gentlemen."

Two programs that deserve special note, because they show the resort can be luxurious and still relaxed, are its summer time "Behind the Scenes" cooking classes and its Ritz Kids Camp. The culinary classes provide the opportunity to learn from some of the best culinary talents in the area while witnessing the inner workings of a professional kitchen. Ritz Kids Camp is part of the resort's expanded program of family recreational programs. Open year round, it offers supervised fun activities for children ages five to twelve.

THE RITZ-CARLTON PALM BEACH

Address:	100 South Ocean Boulevard, Manalapan 33462
	www.ritzcarlton.com
Phone:	800/241-3333; 561/533-6000
Fax:	561/588-4702
Rates:	$375-$3,150
Units:	270

Sabal Palm House

If your favorite artist is Chagall, Dali, Degas, Lutrec, Michelangelo, or Rockwell, you can enjoy that artist's work in your room at this bed-and-breakfast inn. The six rooms and one suite here are not just named for those famous artists, but the décor of each is themed around that artist's time and work, highlighted by excellent reproductions. The Rockwell Room, for example, is designed with all the cozy warmth of a Norman Rockwell painting, and decorations include signed Rockwell prints. It's like living in a small exhibition gallery.

It all started while Michael and Lori Breece were enjoying their twentieth anniversary in a château in France. They decided that when Michael retired from the Florida Department of Law Enforcement they were going to open an upscale bed-and-breakfast. Their dream was to have a small bed-and-breakfast that was distinguished not only for its décor but also its comfort, concierge-like service, and attention to detail. Evidence of their accomplishment is that the Sabal Palm House is rated Four Diamonds by the AAA, a rating achieved by relatively few bed-and-breakfasts.

The Breeces like to say that the architecture of this two-story wood frame house, built in 1936, is a combination of Key West and New Orleans. The main house has three guest rooms and a two-room suite. A building in the rear, across a lovely courtyard, offers three more guest rooms. All rooms have a private bath (two with Jacuzzis), covered balconies, and antique furnishings. Our favorite is the Renoir Suite with its old world elegance, double French doors that separate the living/dining area from a bedroom, a canopy bed, oakwood floors, and a Jacuzzi for two. Another set of French doors lead to a private covered terrace that overlooks the tropical courtyard. And of course, there are excellent reproductions of Renoir paintings.

SABAL PALM HOUSE

Address:	109 N. Golfview Road, Lake Worth 33460
	www.sabalpalmhouse.com
Phone:	888/SABAL PALM (722-2572); 561/582-1090
Fax:	561/582-0933
Rates:	$100-$160
Units:	7

BROWARD COUNTY

(Greater Fort Lauderdale)

Bed tax 11 percent

With three hundred miles of navigable waterways, Fort Lauderdale and Broward County can both boast of being the "Venice of America." There are a number of other interesting water-related facts about this county.

- There are more than forty-four thousand registered boats, putting it in contention for the title of the "Yachting Capital of the World."

- On the eastern shoreline, it has twenty-tree miles of wide sandy beaches on the Atlantic, while much of the western two thirds of the county (more than five hundred thousand acres) lies in the Everglades, also known as the "River of Grass."

- More than two and a quarter million passengers a year take a cruise ship out of Fort Lauderdale's Port Everglades, making it the second largest cruise port in the world.

- Among its many attractions are: the International Swimming Hall of Fame, and world-famous anglers are honored in the Hall of Fame at the International Game Fish Association's World Fishing Center and Museum.

Among the area's other interesting and out of the ordinary attractions is Butterfly World, a three-acre park with a screened habitat you walk through to join thousands of butterflies and hummingbirds from five continents that are so close some of the butterflies may land on you. The Seminole Okalee Indian Village and Museum showcase the fascinating cultures and history of Florida's first residents. The Goodyear Blimp Base is one of only four active blimp bases in the world. And Davie, one of the thirty municipalities in the county, is a "western" town by mandate. Every structure must be built to a western theme and every week there's a rodeo here. Sawgrass Mills is reputed to be the world's largest designer outlet mall, and Antique Row in Dania is a two-square block area of two hundred fifty dealers.

For avid sports fans there are the professional Florida Marlins, Florida Panthers, Miami Dolphins, Miami Heat, Fusion Soccer, plus jai alai in Dania, thoroughbred racing at Gulfstream Park, harness racing in Pompano Beach, and greyhound racing in Hallandale. And the Baltimore Orioles hold their spring training here.

> ## WATER TAXI:
>
> One way to get around the Venice of America is by water taxi. These operate on demand, like a shared land taxi, seven days a week from 10 A.M. to the wee hours of the morning (what "wee hour" depends on business), making stops along the Intracoastal Waterway and New River and to the beach. You can use them to get to a number of major attractions, restaurants, lodgings, and shopping areas. Not cheap, one-way pass is about $8; so if you think you'll take the water route more than once in a day, an All Day Pass costs only twice that. That's also a great way to make your own sightseeing tour. (www.watertaxi.com)

Hyatt Regency Pier Sixty-Six

This resort's seventeen-story cylindrical building is a Fort Lauderdale landmark you can't and shouldn't miss. At the top is its famous Pier Top Lounge that makes a 360-degree revolution every sixty-six minutes, offering a complete and magnificent view of the Intracoastal Waterway, the Atlantic beaches, and much of the city of Fort Lauderdale. Have a seat, a drink, and enjoy the slow ride and the unforgettable view! They even give a preview of the view on the way up in an outside glass elevator.

The resort is located on its own twenty-two-acre island that extends to the Intracoastal Waterway, giving the feeling of an island retreat even though you are just minutes from the city's downtown. For boaters, the full-service marina has 142 slips that host everything from small craft to mega-yachts from all over the world.

For more views, the 380 rooms and eight suites in the Tower and Lanai building all have balconies or patios. (Tower rooms have the best views.) The rooms and suites are attractively furnished in a tailored sophisticated décor with light neutral colors of tone-on-tone cream and gold with green and russet accents. Some of the suites have whirlpool tubs.

Facilities and activities include three swimming pools with a forty-person hydrotherapy pool; an aquatic center where you can learn to sail, snorkel, or scuba dive; fitness rooms; six restaurants and lounges; two

tennis courts; guest privileges at a nearby private PGA golf course; and an elegant European-style health and beauty spa to pamper you.

A water taxi or private shuttle will take you to local beaches, restaurants, or shopping.

HYATT REGENCY PIER SIXTY-SIX

Address:	**2301 SE 17th Street Causeway, Fort Lauderdale 33316**
	www.hyatt.com
Phone:	**800/233-1234 (Hyatt Hotels); 954/525-6666**
Fax:	**954/728-3595**
Rates:	**$249-$299**
Units:	**388**

Lago Mar Resort & Club

Location, setting, and ambiance make Lago Mar delightful and irresistible.
The resort is located on ten acres with a private ocean beach in the

quiet, secluded upscale residential Harbor Beach area between Lake Mayan, which feeds the Intracoastal Waterway and the ocean. This setting creates an island-like atmosphere.

As always with ambiance, there are a number of factors that come together to create its charming casual elegance. First, the resort's tropical sea life theme is a fine blending of Old Florida, Key West, and Mediterranean influences. The décor and furnishings feature vibrant colors and bold patterns highlighted by many original works of art. An excellent example of this art is in the reception area where you are greeted by a stunningly dramatic and beautiful floor mosaic with a colorful coral reef motif, a huge verdigris wrought-iron chandelier in a pineapple motif, and towering natural coral fireplace. The tropical sea life theme is carried out throughout the resort in a number of ways such as custom designed carpeting.

Facilities include a private sandy beach with beach cabana rentals, a nine thousand-square-foot swimming lagoon and an Olympic-size heated pool, two tennis courts, mini-golf, shuffleboard, and beach volleyball, children's playground, fitness center, four restaurants (jackets required for dinner in its fine dining restaurant in season) and two bar areas. The resort also has regular daily water taxi service from the dock on Lake Mayan.

Your choices for lodging include fifty-two rooms and a hundred sixty suites. All the suites and most of the rooms have balconies. While all the accommodations are family size, even though they are the most expensive, the two-bedroom and penthouse suites are a great choice for a family or two couples. The resort is especially family-friendly, perhaps because it has been owned and operated for three generations by the Banks family. During Easter and Christmas holidays, for example, there are extensive complimentary children's activities, and at Christmas Santa Claus arrives by water taxi. Lago Mar is the only Broward County hotel ever to make *Conde Nast Travelers'* magazine prestigious annual Gold List of the "best of the best."

LAGO MAR RESORT & CLUB

Address:	**1700 South Ocean Lane, Fort Lauderdale 33316**
	www.lagomar.com
Phone:	**888/LagoMar(524-6627); 954/523-6511**
Fax:	**954/524-6627**
Rates:	**$195-$675**
Units:	**212**

A Little Inn by the Sea

The sea in the inn's name, is the Atlantic Ocean. And it is located on one of the widest Atlantic beaches in the area. It is also located in the little community of Lauderdale-by-the-Sea, a resort enclave in the larger city of Fort Lauderdale. While high rise condos and other buildings dominate much of Fort Lauderdale's oceanfront, they are not permitted here. Lauderdale by the Sea retains its Old Florida charm because years ago a three-story height restriction was put on buildings. The result is about six blocks of pleasant boutique hotels and inns along the beachfront.

This inn is operated much like a small European hotel, which is understandable when you learn that Uli Brandt came from Switzerland, and his wife, Brigitte, came from Morocco. They both were in the fashion industry and met in Hong Kong when both were on a business trip. For several years they came on vacation for two weeks to Florida to lie on the beach. Finally, they decided this was where they wanted to live, and the best way to do that was to buy a bed-and-breakfast on the beach and be innkeepers. Having spent a number of years as international travelers, they felt they knew what guests expected in a small inn and were fully prepared to meet those expectations.

Brigitte's sister and her husband soon joined them. So now the staff has a deep resource of linguists in French, German, and Scandinavian, which attracts a large number of Europeans as regular guests.

The twenty-nine rooms and suites in two buildings give you a choice of a hotel room, efficiency/studio, a one-bedroom suite, or a two-bedroom apartment. Fourteen of the units have a direct ocean view, all the others have a good view with at least a slice of the ocean. The efficiencies have a full kitchen, the suites and apartments have that plus a living/dining room. A number have balconies and each has a Florida theme built around shells, boats, birds, and fish. Being family oriented, two children can stay free in a room with their parents.

The heated pool in the courtyard has a fountain set among palm trees and flowers.

A LITTLE INN BY THE SEA

Address:	**4546 El Mar Drive, Lauderdale by the Sea 33308**
	www.alittleinn.com
Phone:	**800/492-0311; 954/772-2450**
Fax:	**954/938-9354**
Rates:	**$109-$298**
Units:	**29**

Riverside Hotel

This hotel is a superb example of classic Old Florida kept right up to date. When it opened in 1936, it immediately generated a lot of attention because of its location on Las Olas Boulevard, Fort Lauderdale's first road to the beach. Although it's actually a couple of miles from that beach, this was before beach hotels became popular, a time when women carried parasols and everyone wore big hats to protect themselves from the sun. Since then, the beach hotels have come, but tree-shaded Las Olas Boulevard is still a draw because it developed into the city's most fashionable thoroughfare for strollers. Here you'll find chic fashion shops, distinctive antique and art galleries, elegant jewelry stores, and a number of popular restaurants, pubs, and sidewalk cafes. All of this is just outside the doors of the Riverside.

Unlike other older hotels, this one has been steadily maintained and continuously upgraded to stay in harmony with its upscale surroundings.

The exterior of the hotel looks like a combination of New Orleans and the Wild West with its second floor wrought-iron balcony, hooked-back shutters, and French doors, all made more distinctive by the large French Quarter-style mural on the façade. While fashionable Las Olas Boulevard is at its front door, the New River is in its backyard. For boaters, there's five hundred feet of dockage on the river, and it's a water taxi stop.

Your choice of lodgings include 102 guest rooms and seven suites. All are stylishly decorated with antique oak furnishings and French prints and include a television, phone, and refrigerator. Some have a balcony with a Boulevard view and others with a river view. While the suites offer the most space and private balconies, we were fascinated by the twelve small, but cozy, rooms with canopy-king beds and mirrored ceilings. They are romantic and sexy at the same time.

The hotel has an outdoor heated pool, a secluded tropical garden, and several restaurants and lounges, including The Grill Room, which is rated Four Diamond by AAA (next to the top rating), and The Wine Room, designed to showcase the hotel's cellar of approximately three thousand bottles of wine. Classic English afternoon tea is served daily in the lobby and patio area.

RIVERSIDE HOTEL

Address:	**620 E. Las Olas Boulevard, Fort Lauderdale 33301**
	www.riversidehotel.com
Phone:	**800/325-3280; 954/467-0671**
Fax:	**954/462-2148**
Rates:	**$179-$319**
Units:	**109**

Sheraton Suites Plantation

If you were born to shop, have we got a hotel for you! Located in Plantation, one of the suburban communities west of Fort Lauderdale in Broward County, this Sheraton is actually situated between Lord and Taylor and Macy's. An all-suites hotel, it is directly connected to the shops of the Fashion Mall, so you can stroll there without going outdoors. And if that doesn't satisfy your shopping urges, the hotel has shuttle service (for a fee) to nearby Sawgrass Mills, the world's largest designer outlet mall with more than three hundred stores. Still not satisfied? It's not far to Plantation's Fountain Shops of Distinction and another 125 stores at Broward Mall.

Then when you come back to the hotel, you can rest your weary body in your attractively decorated suite that features a master bedroom, comfortable living room, an oversized bathroom, separate dressing area, two televisions, and a stocked refrigerator. And if you really want to relax, get one of the twenty-eight suites (out of 263) that have a whirlpool tub.

The neoclassic architecture is eye-catching. One of the features of this hotel we really liked was the rooftop heated swimming pool offering a panoramic view. Other facilities include a fitness center with sauna and whirlpool, and a restaurant and bar.

This area of western Broward County is often referred to as "Shop and Golf." We've told you a little about the shopping (there is more!), and if golf is your game, the staff at this hotel can arrange for you to play at the nearby semiprivate thirty-six-hole Jacaranda Gulf Club.

SHERATON SUITES PLANTATION

Address:	**311 N. University Drive, Plantation 33324**
	www.sheratonsutiesfl.com
Phone:	**800/325-3535; 954/424-3300**
Fax:	**954/452-3031**
Rates:	**$119-$356**
Units:	**263**

Wyndham Resort & Spa

The Wyndham motto is "Where there's a Wyndham, there's a way." We believe they've fulfilled that motto in this twenty-three-acre resort and spa that is located in the western suburbs of Fort Lauderdale.

Take the spa, for example. In its thirty-one-thousand-square-foot building you have a choice of ways to focus on health, rejuvenation, relaxation, and regeneration. There are nutrition and aerobics programs, saunas, whirlpools, massage, aromatherapy, wraps and other body treatments, state-of-the art fitness equipment, and a full-service salon. The spa pools—separate for men and women—are clothing optional. Horizons, the spa dining room, serves tasty dishes tailor-made for you.

If golf is your game, the resort has two eighteen-hole courses right next door. If tennis is your thing, there are fifteen professional clay courts. If you like swimming, try out the five free-form swimming pools. Other facilities include restaurants and lounges.

Parents Magazine has rated this one of America's best family-friendly hotels. To start with, you are greeted by two large aquariums in the lobby that will fascinate the kids. Then there's the tropical rainforest area outside. You can take in the overall beauty and the banyan trees, but what the kids will probably enjoy more is seeing the waterfall and the koi in the ponds. Want some time off to enjoy the adult facilities while knowing that your child is safe and happy? From nine to three daily, the Wyndham Kids Klub offers supervised fun activities for ages five to twelve.

Your choices among the accommodations include four hundred guest rooms and ninety-six suites that have balconies or patios. These are in ten low-rise buildings among the lush landscaping. The décor in all the rooms is in vivid tropical hues and patterns designed to be in harmony with the natural beauty of the grounds. Although we didn't pick a favorite room here, our choice for the best value overall is an extended King.

WYNDHAM RESORT & SPA

Address:	250 Racquet Club Road, Fort Lauderdale 33326
	www.wyndham.com
Phone:	800/Wyndham (996-3426); 954/389-3300
Rates:	$188-$426
Units:	496

MIAMI-DADE COUNTY/ GREATER MIAMI

(Coconut Grove, Coral Gables, Key Biscayne,
Miami, Miami Beach)

In the early 1880s, Coconut Grove became the first real community in the area, attracting northern intellectuals, European nobility, and displaced southerners. A few years later, the city of Miami came into its own. Railroad magnate Henry Flagler extended his railroad to Miami in April 1896, then he opened his Royal Palm Hotel in January 1897; Miami's first tourist season began. Through a number of ups and down, the city has continued to grow and attract visitors ever since.

Today, Miami-Dade County's tourism statistics are impressive. There are more than forty-seven thousand hotel/motel rooms available for the approximately ten million annual overnight visitors (more than half from abroad). Miami International Airport is second in international passenger traffic in the U.S., and the Port of Miami is the largest cruise ship port in the world, handling about three million passengers annually. There are museums, theaters, and other attractions you would expect to find in Miami-Dade. There is also an Art Deco District on Miami Beach, where the famed South Beach offers more than eight hundred structures with architecture than goes back to the 1930s and 1940s when Art Deco was the rage. The whole district is on the National Register of Historic Places. For something different that's also on the National Register, take a swim in the Venetian Pool in Coral Gables, a lagoon curved out of rock with caves, stone bridges, and waterfalls. This is also the home of the Florida Marlins, Maimi Dolphins, Miami Heat, and Florida Panthers.

COCONUT GROVE

Bed tax 12.5 percent

The Mayfair House

Two members of the staff do nothing but maintain the 180 Jacuzzis and Japanese hot tubs in this all-suite hotel. There is one for each of the 179 suites plus one at the rooftop pool, where you can also enjoy a first-rate view of Coconut Grove and the ocean.

The Mayfair House, nestled in the heart of trendy Coconut Grove, a Miami enclave famed for upscale shopping, restaurants, and entertainment centers, has greenery everywhere. The suites are all built around an open atrium with waterfalls, fountains, palms, ferns, and the largest orchid garden in any hotel in South Florida. All this is background to the stained glass and Art Nouveau items throughout.

The feeling of graceful luxury begins the moment you enter the cozy registration room off the small lobby. As you sit and register, the mood is set with a welcoming glass of champagne or a mimosa. Each of the well-appointed suites is different in size and décor. What they have in common is a comfortable bedroom and living room, hand-carved furniture, an oversized marble bathroom, and mahogany doors, many hand-carved with intricate designs in character with the suite's name. Fifty of the suites are adorned with antique British pianos. Even the turn-down service is delightfully different here. It features a rose atop Japanese kimono robes folded like fine origami.

Other facilities include an excellent and elegant restaurant, a lounge, and meeting rooms. It's no wonder the hotel has earned a Mobil Four Star and AAA Four Diamond rating, just one step below the top of the line for each of those national rating systems.

THE MAYFAIR HOUSE

Address:	**3000 Florida Avenue, Coconut Grove 33133**
	www.mayfairhousehotel.com
Phone:	**800/443-4555; 305/441-0000**
Fax:	**305/443-9284**
Rates:	**$199-$599**
Units:	**179**

CORAL GABLES

Bed tax 12.5 percent

The Biltmore Hotel

After its gala opening in 1926, the hotel played host to royalty both from Europe and Hollywood. It also was a favorite of Chicago's Al Capone. President Clinton has even stayed in the suite that is unofficially known as the Al Capone Suite. Its grande dame reign ended at the on-set of World War II. After it closed in 1968, the City of Coral Gables took it over in 1973, but for ten years they couldn't decide what to do with it. Finally, the city fathers decided to restore it and open it as a hotel under a management contract with a hotel corporation. The first attempt failed. But a new management corporation reopened it in 1992 and still runs it today.

The centerpiece of the Biltmore's Mediterranean-revival architecture is a fifteen-story, three hundred foot copper clad tower modeled after the Giralda tower in Seville Spain. Some of the hotel's other architectural features include: a colonnaded lobby with two large aviaries populated with colorful finches and forty-five-foot high ceiling with hand-painted beams, an open air courtyard and fountain, balconies, terrazzo and tile floors, and splendid rooms furnished with period reproductions.

It also has what is reputedly the largest hotel pool in the Continental United States. In the 1930s, Olympic medalist, Johnny Weissmuller, who later played Tarzan, was a swimming instructor here, and Ester Williams starred in aquatic shows. Other facilities include a golf course, ten lighted tennis courts, a health club and spa, and two restaurants. One of the restaurants brings in Michelin-rated guest chefs from France for special programs each month. Other regular hotel programs include a weekly Opera Night, a night for cigar lovers, "Afternoon Tea" every weekday, and a magnificent (and expensive) Sunday Champagne Brunch that is so popular you best reserve a week in advance (two months for holiday brunches).

The hotel is extremely popular for weddings, but they do have a deal for what they call "the wedding of a lifetime." You can have the whole hotel exclusively for the wedding party and guests for four nights for just one million dollars. And they'll throw in a top-of-the line reception with entertainment.

THE BILTMORE HOTEL

Address:	**1200 Anastasia Avenue, Coral Gables, FL 33134**
	www.biltmorehotel.com
Phone:	**800/727-1926; 305/445-1926**
Rates:	**$339-$2,500**
Units:	**280**

Hotel Place St. Michel

It was built in 1926, but you might say this charming ivy-clad, boutique hotel of today truly began its new life in the 1970s, and it started with a *crepe*.

In keeping with its name, the hotel has a decided European flavor. This is understandable since Bornstein had gone to Europe a number of times and named it after Mount St. Michel in France. Both the public rooms and the twenty-seven guests rooms and junior suites are decorated with many of the lovely antiques he brought back from his travels. On the first floor are the lobby, the bright and airy Restaurant San Michel (a lounge popular with the locals), and a French deli. The guest rooms are on the two upper floors, which you get to by riding in the original brass Otis elevator. The comfortably furnished rooms are all different in size, shape, and character. Two common items in most rooms are a television that sits on the base of an old Singer foot-peddle sewing machine, and an antique armoire instead of a closet.

HOTEL PLACE ST. MICHEL

Address:	**162 Alcazar Avenue, Coral Gables 33134**
	www.hotelplacestmichel.com
Phone:	**800/848-HOTEL (848-4683); 305/444-1666**
Fax:	**305/529-0074**
Rates:	**$165-$200**
Units:	**27**

KEY BISCAYNE

Bed tax 12.5 percent

Sonesta Beach Resort Key Biscayne

A secluded urban island setting with sun, sand, beautiful facilities, and outstanding art—all just a short drive over the bridge to Miami—is just part of what this resort offers. The resort sits on ten acres of beachfront property, and as you drive up, the step-terraces on the ends of the main building might make you think of an Inca pyramid. The white coral-sand beach, by the way, has been named one of the ten best family beaches in the nation by Dr. Stephen P. Leatherman, also known as Dr. Beach, as well as by *Conde Nast Traveler Magazine*. Everything you might need to have fun at the beach is available. You can also take sailing lessons, catamaran rides, or go parasailing. If you prefer a pool, there's one overlooking the beach.

For the tennis enthusiast there are nine tennis courts, and lessons are available, plus the nationally known Crandon Park Tennis Center is nearby. The same Crandon Park has a golf course that has been rated the number one public course in Florida. Other facilities include a fitness center, bike and moped rental, restaurants and lounges. Supervised activities for ages three to seventeen are available.

Your lodging choices range from ocean view or island view rooms to one- and-two-bedroom suites, all with a balcony or terrace. Since this is a beach resort, it's appropriate that the color scheme is sand tones for the walls complemented by fabrics in emerald, gold, purple, and ruby. If you really want space, fully furnished three- and four-bedroom vacation homes, each with a private pool, are also available adjacent to the hotel.

SONESTA BEACH RESORT KEY BISCAYNE

Address:	**350 Ocean Drive, Key Biscayne 33149**
	www.sonesta.com
Phone:	**800/SONESTA (766-3782); 305/361-2021**
Fax:	**305/365-3096**
Rates:	**$285-$1,700**
Units:	**300**

MIAMI

Bed tax 12.5 percent

Doral Golf Resort & Spa

"Golf" and "spa" are definitely the highlights of this resort, but, as you'll see, they are just the beginning. There are ninety-nine holes of golf on this 650-acre resort, offering golf for players at every skill level. The best known of the five courses is The Blue Monster, on which the eighteenth hole is considered one of the most challenging finishing holes on the PGA circuit. The great White Course, named after Greg Norman, has the eighteenth green on an island. In fact, water plays an important role on all the courses. Sixteen holes play to water on the Jerry Pate Silver Course, fourteen holes wind around a lake on the Red Course, and the Gold Course has water surrounding sixteen holes. The final nine holes in the ninety-nine are in the par three Green Course. If you need instruction before or after playing any of those courses, the Jim McLean Golf School is here.

If you want to pamper your body, there is a 148,000 square-foot spa that is a self-contained oasis within the resort. It has forty-eight suites of its own. Frequently cited as one of the best spas in the country, its facilities include forty-five treatment rooms, hydrotherapy, Jacuzzis, hot and cold plunge pools, a hydromassage, saunas, a whirlpool, a sun deck, a beauty salon, a kitchen dedicated to health and nutrition, and the resort's fine restaurant. All are used to support an extensive range of fitness, nutrition, stress relief, and beauty programs for both men and women.

In addition to the forty-eight guest suites in the spa, the resort has 646 comfortably furnished guestrooms and one- and two-bedroom suites with private balconies or terraces situated in three- and four-story lodges close to the main clubhouse. Some of the things not in the name include the Arthur Ashe Tennis Center that has ten courts and instructors, a fitness center, a heated swimming pool, bike rentals, and a total of five restaurants and lounges.

The Doral also caters to families. For kids there is the Blue Lagoon, a water recreation area that includes five pools and a 125-foot water slide. And while you do your thing—like golf or being pampered at the Spa—you can feel secure that your kids will be happy in Camp Doral, the resort's supervised activity program for kids ages five to twelve.

DORAL GOLF RESORT & SPA

Address:	**4400 NW 87th Avenue, Miami 33178**
	www.doralgolf.com
Phone:	**800-71-DORAL (713-6725) Spa: 800/331-7768; 305/592-2000**
Fax:	**305/591-6630**
Rates:	**$325-$1,300**
Units:	**694**

The Inn at Fisher Island Club

If you have ever wanted to actually sit on the lap of luxury, this former Vanderbilt island estate is the place to do it. Once the southernmost tip of Miami Beach, the 216-acre Fisher Island was created in 1905 when the government sliced through the land to create a shipping channel. It's named after Carl Fisher, Miami Beach's prime developer, who bought the island in the 1920s. Fisher, however, wound up trading it to William K. Vanderbilt II, one of America's wealthiest men of the time, for his 220-foot yacht. Vanderbilt immediately turned the island into his winter retreat.

The island had a number of owners after Vanderbilt, including, in the early 1960s, an investment group that included Richard Nixon and Charles (BeBe) Rebozo. Vanderbilt's original complex still forms the core of the island, which has been developed to include spacious Mediterranean-style condos, many owned by celebrities. The Fisher Island Club is for members only, however, there are about sixty guest accommodations available in the Inn's luxurious junior suites, cottages, and seaside villas.

To preserve privacy, there are fifty full-time security officers, and you can only reach the island by boat or air. There are three ferry boats that service the island around the clock. Before you can get on the ferry, however, you have to be cleared by one of those security officers, which means you must have an invitation or a reservation. If you go by your own boat, there are two deep-water marinas on the island. If you go by air, there is a helipad and a seaplane ramp.

In addition to luxurious Vanderbilt-era quarters, facilities available to guests include a Bahamian sand beach almost a mile long, a nine-hole golf course, a tennis center with eighteen lighted courts, six restaurants, and the Spa Internazionale that *Town & Country* magazine called one of the world's premier spas. You can also visit Vanderbilt's Aviary featuring exotic birds from around the world.

THE INN AT FISHER ISLAND CLUB

Address:	**One Fisher Island Drive, Fisher Island 33109**
	www.fisherislandclub-florida.com
Phone:	**800/537-3708; 305/535-6020**
Fax:	**305/535-6000**
Rates:	**$425-$1,400**
Units:	**60**

Hotel Inter-Continental-Miami

Most high-rise hotels offer a good view from rooms on the upper floors. This majestic, thirty-four story triangular building offers a spectacular view of Biscayne Bay, the Port of Miami, or the downtown Miami skyline from every room.

The view inside is almost as impressive. If you enjoy the cool elegance of marble, as we do, the artistic combinations in the interior will be a joy to see. The stunning setting was created by infusing Travertine marble with antique Florentine marble, Brazilian green granite, Roseate marble from Portugal, black granite from South America, burnt cedar from forests in Asia, and black teak from the Orient. The focal point of all this in the five-story atrium lobby is "The Spindle," an eighteen-foot, seventy ton, marble sculpture created by the late Sir Henry Moore.

The 602 posh rooms and thirty-seven suites have oversized bathrooms (in marble, of course) with separate dressing areas, and large granite windowsills for sitting and enjoying the view. Forty-three rooms on two club floors include extra amenities. Facilities include a rooftop terrace with heated swimming pool, a sun deck, and a jogging track, a well staffed fitness center, lounges, and several restaurants ranging from fine dining to a deli.

The hotel is adjacent to two hundred fashionable shops and restaurants of Bayside Marketplace. It is also just a short walk from the Miami Metromover that will take you all over downtown and connects to Metrorail that covers much of Miami and even goes to attractions in the suburbs.

HOTEL INTER-CONTINENTAL-MIAMI

Address:	**100 Chopin Plaza, Miami 33131**
	www.miami.interconti.com
Phone:	**800/327-0200; 305/577-1000**
Fax:	**305/577-0384**
Rates:	**$259-$2,500**
Units:	**639**

Turnberry Isle Resort & Club

It's not really on an isle, but once you enter this three hundred-acre secluded retreat in an exclusive enclave in north Miami, you feel like you're on an island of luxury and comfort. And to ensure that feeling continues throughout your stay, the resort has a European-trained staff with a ratio of three very attentive, knowledgeable, and hospitable employees for every guest room.

The 395 large guest rooms and suites in the Mediterranean-style hotel are in four wings connected by covered marble walkways. As you walk the lush tropical grounds you can understand why the wings are named Hibiscus, Jasmine, Magnolia, and Orchid. Your choices of accommodations include a variety of room types from the junior suites and one-bedroom suites to the two grand presidential suites that are so large they look like they could almost be wings of the White House. Most rooms have terra-cotta floors, plush oriental area rugs, armoires, overstuffed couches, marble bathrooms with both a whirlpool tub and a glass walled shower, and French doors opening to a balcony with views of the manicured fairways of the golf courses or pool gardens.

The two golf courses were both originally designed by the famed Robert Trent Jones, Sr., and the pro staff offers a variety of clinics and individual instruction. With twenty courts and an outstanding pro staff, the

resort is rated one the "Top 50 Greatest U.S. Tennis Resorts" by *Tennis Magazine.* If you want to swim you have a choice of three heated pools or the private beach on the Atlantic. For boaters, there's a full-service 117-slip marina where you can also arrange fishing or cruising charters. There are six lounges and five restaurants including the award winning Veranda where, as a tiny example of the resort's "they think of everything service," they keep three types of reading glasses on hand for guests who have difficulty reading the menu.

The latest addition to this resort is the splendid three level, full-service Turnberry Spa and Fitness Center. The resort is rated Four Diamonds by AAA and Four Stars by Mobil, the next to the top rating for both. As for shopping, the resort is across the street from the 250-store Aventura Mall.

TURNBERRY ISLE RESORT & CLUB

Address:	19999 W. Country Club Drive, Aventura 33180
	www.turnberryisle.com
Phone:	800/327-7028; 305/932-6200
Fax:	305/933-3811
Rates:	$335-$3,500
Units:	395

MIAMI BEACH

The Alexander Hotel

This upscale all-suites beachfront hotel is located on Millionaire's Row in Miami Beach, a little north of the Art Deco district. Slightly off-the beaten track, its exclusivity and intimately low-key ambiance has made it a favorite of international dignitaries, movie stars, and business executives. Once you pass though the mahogany doors at the entrance you'll find the entire hotels is elegantly decorated with paintings, sculptures, tapestries, and antiques, many of which came from a Cornelius Vanderbilt mansion. While the lobby is lavish with marble, the overall décor is warm West Indian Caribbean. The 150 guest suites, all individually decorated, are equally lavish without being pretentious. Most suites are one or two bedroom with a full kitchen (they'll deliver groceries), living room, dining

room, two full bathrooms, and a terrace overlooking either the Intracoastal Waterway and the city of Miami or the ocean. If you need more space, they do have three- and four-bedroom suites.

The hotel's two lagoon-shaped pools are set in an acre of lush tropical gardens and grottos with two Jacuzzis and a cascading waterfall. If you prefer more active water sports, the Aqua Sports Center at the resort's own sandy beach offers both onshore and off-shore activities as well as all types of watercraft from paddleboats to hobie cats for rent. The Health Club has a variety of exercise machines and free weights. For boaters, there's a twelve slip marina across the street from the hotel. There is also tennis and golf nearby.

If you want to literally leave your mark on this hotel, join the "48 oz. Club" at Don Shula's Steak House. If you eat a forty-eight-ounce porterhouse steak, your name will be engraved on a gold plaque and displayed in the restaurant among its mementos of the 1972 Miami Dolphin's 17-0 perfect season.

THE ALEXANDER HOTEL

Address:	5225 Collins Avenue, Miami Beach 33140
	www.alexanderhotel.com
Phone:	800/327-6121; 305/865-6500
Fax:	305/864-8525
Rates:	$325-$825
Units:	150

Bay Harbor Inn & Suites

Have you ever wanted to turn in a report card on the staff at a hotel or restaurant? Well, you don't actually do it here, but your comments help the manager and key staff do just that because the majority of the staff are students from the Johnson and Wales University, and the senior staff are their teachers. The students are future managers and executive chefs from the university's College of Hospitality and College of Culinary Arts. They are evaluated daily, and according to Lior Dagan, the general manager, "The hotel is a live classroom where the guest is the judge of service and level of skill." Since it is a live classroom, the staff to guest room ratio is about six to one in high season.

There are forty-five units, half of which are guest rooms and the other half are suites. All are located in two buildings in this waterfront property on Bar Harbor Island in Biscayne Bay. One of the buildings is full of antiques and the rooms reflect this in a mixture of old and modern that combines Victorian furnishings with modern baths and upscale amenities. The waterfront building has more modern rooms with a view of Indian Creek.

The inn has an outdoor heated pool, two dining rooms, a bar that is a replica of a London bar, a waterside dining terrace, and a small anchored yacht, *Celeste,* that serves as the site for the complimentary continental breakfast buffet. There's also dockage for guest boaters. For shoppers, the inn is a short stroll from Bal Harbor Village known for its upscale designer shops.

BAY HARBOR INN & SUITES

Address:	**9660 E. Bay Harbor, Bay Harbor Islands 33154**
	www.bayharborinn.com
Phone:	**305/868-4141**
Fax:	**305/867-9094**
Rates:	**$139-$225**
Units:	**45**

Eden Roc Resort & Spa

If you want to talk about the history of Miami Beach, you have to include the Eden Roc and its next door neighbor, the Fontainebleau. Together they imparted the glitz and glamour in the 1950s and 60s that lured the stars who spread the word about this barrier island paradise. The glitz and glamour are still here, and this flamboyant hotel still lures entertainers and other celebrities as guests.

The hotel was designed and built in 1956 by famed architect Morris

Lapidus, who also designed the Fontainebleau. For inspiration, Lapidus visited Eden Roc in France. While in Europe he collected art, marble, Venetian glassware, and other objects he brought back to use in the hotel. Recently, under the guidance of Lapidus, who was ninety-six at the time, the hotel underwent extensive renovations that restored it to its original glory.

In this fourteen-story beachfront hotel, you have a choice of 350 rooms and suites, all with Italian marble baths and magnificent ocean or bay views. You can catch sun or waves on the beach, or rent a variety of watersports equipment ranging from aquabikes to hobie cats. Parasail rides and scuba instruction are available. The private marina will accommodate eighteen vessels up to 112 feet. For freshwater swimming, there are two pools. If you just want to watch the swimmers, you can do that through the porthole in one of the lounges.

The Eden Roc Spa includes the only rock climbing arena in a south Florida resort, plus regulation basketball, squash and racquetball courts, and a fitness center. There is also a wellness center offering programs to help you live your life to the fullest, and the Spa of Eden, a full-service spa and salon offering body and beauty pampering services from aromatherapy to Swedish massage. Other facilities include two restaurants and three lounges.

EDEN ROC RESORT & SPA

Address:	**4525 Collins Avenue, Miami Beach 33140**
	www.edenrocresort.com
Phone:	**888/EDENROC (333–6762); 305/531–0000**
Fax:	**305/674–5555**
Rates:	**$250 – $3,000**
Units:	**360**

Essex House

There's air-conditioning, of course, but still the windows in this three-story hotel can be opened to receive breezes from the nearby ocean. And when closed, they are built to absorb the sound, which can be even more important since the hotel is in the heart of South Beach (called SoBe) where the nightlife makes quiet a rare luxury.

Built in 1938, the hotel was once a favorite of Al Capone and his buddies who habitually played cards in a game room off the lobby. Now it exudes a real sense of that time and space. As one manager of the hotel said, "it's like traveling back to the 1930s and 40s."

This well-restored Art Deco gem is a classic example of Streamline Modern style with its rounded corner entrance, exterior eyebrows, and large circular portholes at the roofline. Guides on the official tour of the Art Deco District say this is "the most authentic Art Deco lobby on the Beach."

Your lodging choices include sixty-one rooms in the main building and nineteen suites, some with Jacuzzi tubs, in the garden courtyard buuilding. All feature custom built mahogany furniture with Art Deco design elements throughout. Our favorites were the suites farthest from the street with lots of space, extra amenities, and quiet. The hotel has a small pool and whirlpool, a day spa/salon, and a restaurant.

ESSEX HOUSE

Address:	1001 Collins Avenue, Miami beach 33139
	www.essexhotel.com
Phone:	800/553-7739; 305/534-2700
Fax:	305/532-3827
Rate:	$149–$385
Units:	79

Fontainebleau Hilton Resort & Towers

If you're driving north on Collins Avenue toward the Fontainebleau, don't try to drive under the hotel's arch that leads to the tropical lagoon-shaped swimming pool. It's a 106-foot by 120-foot *trompe l'oeil* (illusionary painting) on the hotel's southern wall that reveals what the hotel would look like if the wall wasn't there. This grandiose picture is a perfect symbol of this hotel that has been a Miami Beach landmark since it opened in 1954. It was designed by Morris Lapidus who wanted to make sure it was no ordinary

hotel. What he built is just about as far from the ordinary as you can get. In the lobby, for example, the three giant chandeliers have eighteen hundred pieces of crystal in each. (Even the laundry statistics are impressive: ten million pounds of laundry a year.)

Every president since Eisenhower has stayed here, as well as top name entertainers and other notables. With close to twelve hundred rooms and sixty suites, most with water views, in three buildings on twenty beachfront acres and more than twelve hundred employees, it is almost a city in itself. It has been a favorite location for a number of movies including *The Bodyguard* and *Analyze This*. In addition to the white sandy ocean beach, there are two swimming pools (one with a half-acre rock grotto lagoon-style pool with a cascading waterfall) three whirlpools, and water sports equipment rentals. Other facilities include a fitness center, seven lighted tennis courts, volleyball, and basketball courts, and even a bocceball court. For body and beauty pamperings, there's a full-service spa and beauty salon. The hotel's club puts on Las Vegas-style floor shows.

You might get lost figuring out what to do in this vast resort, but your kids won't if you enroll them in the Kid's Korner's supervised fun programs for ages five to twelve. There's also a teen program for thirteen to seventeen year olds.

FONTAINEBLEAU HILTON RESORT & TOWERS

Address:	**4441 Collins Avenue, Miami Beach 33140**
	www.fontainebleau.Hilton.com
Phone:	**800/548-8886; 305/538-2000**
Fax:	**305/535-3263**
Rates:	**$269-$850**
Units	**1,206**

The Hotel

The Tiffany and Company people may have made a mistake. For fifty-nine years after its 1939 opening, this hotel was known as the Tiffany. Then, after years of neglect, Tony Goldman rescued it. Goldman Properties has an impressive record of restoring historic buildings in architecturally significant locations. Goldman himself is passionate about preserving the

exterior architecture to retain the building's heritage. This is what he did to the exterior, but he reinvented the interior with such brilliance that it attracted national attention. It was then that the other Tiffany sued for trademark infringement, forcing the hotel to adopt a new name. However, since the hotel is on the National Register of Historic Places and its twenty-four-foot rooftop spire with the Tiffany name on it is a landmark, the spire remains. But in every other way, since it reopened in 1998, it has been known simply as The Hotel.

What makes The Hotel irresistible is the uniqueness of its décor. It is the only hotel we know of that wasn't designed by an architect or interior designer, but by a well-known fashion designer, Todd Oldham. He custom designed almost everything—the bed linens, the dishes, the gem-shaped lighting fixtures, the Persian-inspired lanterns, even the Do Not Disturb signs.

The Hotel's public rooms and fifty-two guest rooms and suites reflect Oldham's vision of the lush colors of South Beach's sun, sand, sea, and sky, all done with his elegant signature style. All the bathrooms have two-person tubs and shower handles on a blank wall so you won't get wet trying to adjust the water before getting in.

Two other parts of this boutique hotel worth special mention are its rooftop emerald shaped pool that overlooks the ocean and Wish, the excellent restaurant with a health-conscious gourmet menu.

THE HOTEL

Address:	801 Collins Avenue, Miami Beach 33139
	www.thehotelofsouthbeach.com
Phone:	877/THE HOTEL (843-4683); 305/531-2222
Fax:	305/531-3222
Rates:	$185-$375
Units:	52

The Marlin

Funky. Hi-tech. Wired. Striking. Those are words that come to mind here. And since it has played host to music giants like Mick Jagger, Aerosmith, and U2, it is also dubbed the "rock 'n' roll hotel" of South Beach

To understand the Marlin you have to understand its owner, Chris Blackwell. Raised in Jamaica, Blackwell has built his life and career around music. First he founded Island Records to produce the kind of music he liked with a wide variety of artists. Then he carried that same idea to hotels. His Island Outpost Properties gathered a group of different hotels—"each a theater where a different play is performed"—under one umbrella.

The Marlin was the first of six hotels he acquired in Miami Beach. The others are the Casa Grande, Cavalier, Kent, Leslie, and The Tides. In each case, the hotel interior was redesigned to give it a distinctive character that is appealing to what Blackwell calls "a certain kind of person." At the same time all the hotels are near each other and function as "a village" where the guests at each can enjoy the facilities of all the others.

The building is Art Deco, but once you walk into the Marlin's lobby, you know it's not typical. Everywhere you look there's brushed stainless steel, and the furniture is on caster wheels. Techno-Deco!

Just as striking are each of the thirteen spacious one- and two-bed-room suites. All have an entertainment technocenter with Internet access, a television, a VCR, and a CD player. There are several specialty suites, like one with exercise facilities (206), another with a private recording booth (305), and an exotic honeymoon suite (205).

THE MARLIN

Address:	1200 Collins Avenue, Miami Beach 33139
	www.islandoutpost.com
Phone:	800-OUTPOST (688-7678); 305/640-5063
Fax:	305/673-9609
Rates:	$195-$450
Units:	13

Ocean Surf Hotel

It may be hard to believe, but there are quiet, uncrowded sections of Miami Beach, and this hotel is in one of them. Located on an oceanfront road that's only two blocks long, this small hotel has been family owned and operated since 1951.

The four-story beachfront hotel, built in 1940, was completely renovated and revitalized in 1997. An Art Deco jewel, its architecture cre-ates the appearance of an ocean liner with large porthole windows that look directly to the ocean and balconies with railings that resemble the bridge of a ship.

Nothing fancy here. All forty-nine rooms, attractively furnished in Florida décor, private baths, cable television, phones, and compact refrig-erators. You can almost feel the family pride in the sparkling cleanliness and attention to detail. The beach is just across the road, but there's so little traffic here, you may not even realize it is a road.

OCEAN SURF HOTEL

Address:	7436 Ocean Terrace, Miami Beach 33141
	www.oceansurf.com
Phone:	800/555-0411; 305/866-1648
Fax:	305/866-1649
Rates:	$89-$129
Units:	49

The Park Central Hotel

In 1987 when Tony Goldman restored and reopened this fifty-year old Art Deco hotel, the *New York Times* called it the "Blue Jewel," and one of the finest Deco hotels on Miami Beach." *Conde Nast Traveler* said "The gorgeous monolithic Park Central Hotel is a Deco Palace."

When the Blue Jewel was first opened in 1937, it was an immediate favorite of such Hollywood stars as Clark Gable and Rita Hayworth. Then after World War II, like most of Miami Beach, it started a downhill slide. Just how far downhill it went is visible today on a poster in the original elevator (also restored) advertising rooms for a dollar a night. Today it continues to be a celebrity favorite, attracting many of the "beautiful people." The hotel's original "Deco Palace" splendor starts with the hotel's pastel-colored Art Deco façade. In tribute to its glorious past, there are antique black and white photos throughout the hallways and guest rooms, many of 1930s bathing beauties. This charming ambiance of casual sophistication carries into the rooms, which are furnished with period furniture.

Your choice of lodging includes rooms, one-bedroom suites and one-bedroom apartments in the main hotel and two other buildings. Located across from the beach, some rooms are oceanfront and all have large windows that can be opened to let in the ocean breezes, cable TV, and all the usual hotel amenities. Facilities include a swimming pool, fitness studio, rooftop sundeck, an open-air sculpture garden, a restaurant on the oceanfront terrace and another indoors, and two bars.

THE PARK CENTRAL HOTEL

Address:	**640 Ocean Drive, Miami Beach 33139**
	www.theparkcentral.com
Phone:	**800/678-8946; 305/538-1611**
Fax:	**305/534-7520**
Rates:	**$165-$305**
Units	**127**

Pelican Hotel

"Where do you want to be tonight? The thirties, the forties, Las Vegas?"

This is the first hotel created by the international clothing company

Diesel Jeans, famed for its hip and fashionable collections and eccentric and irreverent advertising. Diesel had Swedish Designer Magnus Ehrland keep the Art Deco façade of this 1950s hotel, but transformed the interior from routine lodgings to a unique and eccentric space updated with modern comforts. All twenty-five theme rooms have been furnished to carry out the theme name, each fleshed out with details you might expect in a mini movie set. The "Psychedelic Ate Girl Room," for example, has plastic furniture, a psychedelic striped wall, and posters from the 70s, while the "Best Whorehouse Room" has bordello-like red walls. Rooms are furnished with one-of-a-kind Art Deco vintage furniture and state-of-the-art video and stereo equipment.

And then there are the two James Bond penthouses. For only $2,000 a night you get such goodies as a rooftop deck with hot tub, a living room with a nine-screen video wall, a six-foot round tropical fish tank embedded in a copper wall, three bedrooms, three baths, and two terraces, one with an oversized Jacuzzi tub overlooking the ocean.

The hotel has a bar and inside restaurant with a sidewalk café. In addition to the wonderful view from the oceanfront rooms, you might also get a great view of fashion models since the Ford Model Agency, one of the top agencies in the world, has an office here.

PELICAN HOTEL

Address:	**826 Ocean Drive, Miami Beach 33139**
	www.pelicanhotel.com
Phone:	**800/7-PELICAN (773-5422); 305/673-3373**
Fax:	**305/673-3255**
Rates:	**$180-$2,000**
Units:	**30**

Ritz Plaza Hotel

The two-story-high lobby introduces guests to the cool, airy trends of the original 1940s construction essential in pre-air-conditioning days. Its elegant original genuine terrazzo floor has been brought to light after being accidentally discovered under an overlay of more recent flooring. The original keystone front desk has also been brought back to life. The restaurant's eighteen-foot high ceiling, circular design, and floor-to-ceiling windows offer panoramic views of the gardens and the ocean. There is also an outdoor dining area. Naturally, there is beach access, or if you prefer fresh water swimming, an Olympic-size pool.

None of the 128 guest rooms and four penthouse suites are alike in size or shape because of the original placement of the columns in the building. All are furnished to reflect tropical Florida ambiance. Our favorites are the eight corner rooms on each floor that offer wide views. The hotel has also become a favorite South Beach location of the film and fashion industry.

Lincoln Road, a trendy walking street of outdoor cafes, boutique shopping, art galleries, and entertainment, is an easy stroll away.

RITZ PLAZA HOTEL

Address:	1701 Collins Avenue, Miami Beach 33139
	www.ritzplaza.com
Phone:	800/522-6400; 305/534-3500
Fax:	305/604-8605
Rates:	$109-$699
Units:	132

The Tides

The Tides is the tallest Art Deco hotel (twelve stories) on South Beach's Ocean Drive. It offers forty-five rooms and suites all with spectacular ocean views. And if you want a close-up of something on the ocean—or someone on the beach—there's a telescope in every room. Another little extra touch is a chalkboard in each room where you can leave a note for your companion or the maid.

This is one of Chris Blackwell's six Miami Beach Island

Outpost hotels (see The Marlin on page 234). It is a part of what he calls his "village" since the facilities of all the hotels are available to the guest at any one.

Originally opened in 1936 with 115 rooms, it was extensively and artfully restored in 1997. They tore out walls to create just forty-two spacious rooms and suites and three extra-spacious and ultra-luxurious penthouse suites. The hotel's three restuarants include one on the front terrace that's perfect for people-watching.

THE TIDES

Address:	**1220 Ocean Drive, Miami Beach 33139**
	www.islandoutpost.com
Phone:	**800/OUTPOST (688-7678); 305/604-5000**
Fax:	**305/604-5180**
Rates:	**$375-$2,000**
Units:	**45**

MONROE COUNTY/THE FLORIDA KEYS

(Flamingo, Big Pine Key, Duck Key, Key Largo,
Key West, Little Torch Key, Marathon)

The Florida Keys consist of 822 islands, all within Monroe County, making it a county of islands. An elongated chain that stretches more than 220 miles, the Keys extend the southernmost tip of the Florida peninsula out between the Atlantic and the Gulf of Mexico to the Dry Tortugas. These islands were built by nature on top of the submerged foothills of the very old Appalachian Mountains. But nature didn't build them very high. Windley Key, the highest point in the Keys, is only eighteen feet above sea level. The entire chain has been designated the Florida Keys National Marine Sanctuary. The only living coral reef in the continental U.S. is here, and Key Largo's John Pennekamp Coral Reef State Park is the first underwater preserve in the nation.

With water, water everywhere (even on the largest island, no point in the Keys is more than four miles from water), and the International Game Fish Association has declared that the Keys hold more sportsfishing world records than any other fishing destination in the world.

The world-renowned Overseas Highway (U.S. Highway 1) connects the major islands—only about thirty are actually inhabited—covering the 115 miles from Key Largo to Key West. It was built in 1935 when a hurricane wiped out Henry Flagler's Florida East Coast Railroad, which reached Key West in 1912. The highway has forty-three new bridges, including one at Marathon that's seven miles long.

As one might guess, tourism is a major source of employment for local residents throughout the Keys. Key West, the southernmost city in the continental United States, is the final stop on the Overseas Highway. Although Hemingway is probably the best-known writer who lived here, the locals (called "Conchs," pronounced konks) claim the laid-back ambiance of this two-by-four mile island has nurtured more writers per capita than any other city in the country. The artistic community on the island is also noted for most of the other arts.

One final point, parking spaces in Old Town Key West are about as hard to find as a mountain peak in Florida. Note that any space marked RP is for resident parking only. The police pay attention to these and other tow-away zones, so you'd best, too. Rent a bike or walk. You might also check on the parking at your lodging when you make your reservation.

FLAMINGO

Bed tax 11.5 percent

Flamingo Lodge in Everglades National Park

Located on Florida Bay, the Flamingo is the only lodging in the one and a half million-acre Everglades National Park. (The park, by the way is only one-seventh of the area of the entire Everglades.) The Everglades is an area unique in the world made up of vast sawgrass prairies, deep mangrove swamps, subtropical jungle, and warm waters. It is often aptly called "The River of Grass."

The park is a delight for nature lovers and an experience worth trying for all. You will find peace and quiet here, along with more than two hundred species of birds, sixty-five kinds of reptiles, and fourteen endangered species including the Florida panther and the manatee. One species that's not endangered, unfortunately, is the mosquito. They're always around so you'll need insect repellent. They are usually the least trouble-some from December to March.

The Everglades are wild and primitive, but the Flamingo Lodge, Marina and Outpost Resort is not. The complex offers 103 basic but comfortable rooms and twenty-four family-size cottages with kitchenettes. Facilities include a swimming pool, restaurant, lounge, convenience store, visitors center, and full-service marina for fifty boats. If you want home-like comforts while exploring the more remote regions of the park, they have houseboats for rent from October through May. For closer-in explo-rations, they rent canoes, kayaks, and skiffs with outboard motors. You can also book guided fishing charters.

Guided boat tours of the backcountry and Florida Bay are offered, and in the winter months, sunset cruises.

FLAMINGO LODGE IN EVERGLADES NATIONAL PARK

Address:	#1 Flamingo Lodge Highway, Flamingo 33034
	www.flamingolodge.com
Phone:	800/600-3813; 941/695-3101
Fax:	941/695-3921
Rates:	$95-$135
Units:	127

BIG PINE KEY

Bed tax 11.5 percent

Bahia Honda State Park

If you are a nature lover, this park is a must. Bahia Honda State Park is not only Florida's most southern state park, it also has a natural environment found nowhere else in the continental U.S. and unlike most of the Keys, two excellent white sand beaches that have been rated among the best in the nation.

Much of the 524-acre park's vegetation was brought here from the Caribbean islands by hurricanes. Take the Silver Palm Trail through the tropical forest and you'll see unusual West Indian plants such as sea laven-der, thatch palm, key spider, Jamaican morning glory, yellow satinwood, the endangered small-flowered lily thorn. The bird life includes white-crowned pigeons, great white herons, roseate spoonbills, reddish egrets, ospreys, brown pelicans, and least terns.

There are six cabins on the bay and one efficiency apartment over the administrative office. The cabins, two each in three buildings on stilts, are not fancy, but they are comfortable, with two bedrooms, one bath, living room, a kitchen/dining room in each, and a bayview deck with rocking chairs.

Other facilities include a small marina, two boat ramps, a fishing pier, watersports and a dive shop and convenience store. Kayaks and bikes are available for rent. The park is a popular spot for fishing, snorkeling, and swimming. For divers, the Looe Key National Marine Sanctuary is nearby. Park rangers give interpretive and campfire programs in the winter months.

Bahia Honda Key is part of the National Key Deer Refuge. The main refuge is on Big Pine Key, where the tiny deer, no larger than a mid-size dog, roam freely.

Cabin reservations may be made up to eleven months in advance. Unfortunately, cabins are so few and so popular, the reservation line is often busy and all the available reservations go quickly. Be flexible on dates and don't give up. It's worth the time and trouble.

BAHIA HONDA STATE PARK

Address:	P.O. Box 782, Big Pine Key 33043
	www.fl-keys.com/stateparks
Phone:	305/872-2353
Fax:	305/292-6857
Rates:	$126
Units:	7

Barnacle Bed & Breakfast

This bed-and-breakfast is a star, literally. It's built in the form of a six-pointed star, with not a square corner in any of the rooms. It was this unique design that attracted Tim and Jane Marquis to come here from Louisiana.

The setting also has star quality. As you rest in a hammock in a shady spot between two coconut palms on its beautiful and secluded private white sandy beach, you may feel like you're on a Caribbean island. Adding to this sense of the islands is the Caribbean-style house that offers you a choice of four guest rooms, plus a small cottage outside the main house.

The attractive décor comes from a blending of Caribbean, antique, and nautical. The interiors of the house and cottage are stone and dark-stained woods that reflect the island influence. All have private baths, television, and phone. Our favorite is the first floor Ocean Room with its small kitchen, sitting area, beach patio, private entrance, and an ocean view from your bed. The second floor rooms open onto the Mexican-tiled atrium where you can soak in a hot tub. The Blue Heron Cottage has a full kitchen and is the most private of the accommodations. Among its romantic points are the stained glass windows.

Four miles off the beach is Looe Key where you can scuba dive among the magnificent reefs. Tim and Jane previously owned a dive shop and Tim is a scuba instructor offering complete dive packages.

The National Key Deer Refuge is centered on Big Pine Key. It is estimated that about three hundred of these tiny Key deer are making a last stand against man (drive carefully) and nature in this refuge.

BARNACLE BED & BREAKFAST

Address:	**P.O. Box 780, Big Pine Key 33043**
Phone:	**305/872-3298**
Fax:	**305/872-3863**
Rates:	**$95-$140**
Units:	**5**

DUCK KEY

Bed tax 11.5 percent

Hawk's Cay Resort & Marina

This is one of only a handful of places in Florida where you can get in the water with dolphins. The Dolphin Discovery Program lets you enjoy contact with these delightful mammals in a saltwater lagoon under the guidance of professional trainers. And if you don't want to actually get in the water with them, there are dockside programs for both adults and children. Note, however, these programs are extremely popular, so make reservations well in advance. Ninety days isn't too soon. (888/814-9154, www.dolphinconnection.com)

Interacting with the dolphins is just one of the many fun things to do at this sixty-acre island resort. Take your pick of glass-bottom boat tours, sunset cruises, fishing, scuba diving and snorkeling, parasailing, bicycling, guided kayak tours, ecology tours, and boat rentals. In addition to saltwater lagoon swimming, there are adult and family swimming pools, whirlpools, eight tennis courts, putting green, fitness and exercise room, and four restaurants. For boaters, there's a full-service 110-slip marina.

Want to learn a fun skill on your vacation? They have lessons on wakeboard and waterskiing, sailing, and fly-fishing. For kids there's a special pool outfitted with a pirate ship and water cannon, and a tree house. They also have special supervised programs for ages three to twelve.

Your choices in lodgings are almost as varied as your choices in activities. There are 160 guest rooms, sixteen suites, and 129 two-bedroom villas. Rooms are spacious and have a balcony or porch. Villas are like small homes with living/dining rooms, kitchen, two bedrooms and baths. The villas have their own pool and restaurant, but you are located a long walk or a short drive from most of the rest of the facilities.

HAWK'S CAY RESORT & MARINA

Address:	61 Hawk's Cay Boulevard, Duck Key 33050 (At Mile Marker 61) www.hawkscay.com
Phone:	800/432-2242; 305/743-7000
Fax:	305/743-5215
Rates:	$220-$950
Units:	305

KEY LARGO

Bed tax 11.5 percent

Holiday Inn Sunspree Resort & Marina

One of the things that sets this Holiday Inn apart is that it is the home berth of the original *African Queen*, the small boat made famous by Katherine Hepburn and Humphrey Bogart in the movie of the same name. The antique *Queen* is sometimes available for short cruises. Coincidentally, in 1947 Bogart gave this Key one of its first tastes of notoriety when he and Lauren Bacall stared in the hit movie *Key Largo*.

Water sports are the big attraction at this resort located on the ocean side of Key Largo, the first and longest island in the Keys. It has its own small harbor that includes a full-service marina with docks where you can take a two-hour glass-bottom boat trip to view the underwater world of the nearby coral reefs, sunset catamaran cruises, and snorkel and diving trips. Charter boats for deep-sea and back country fishing are available, as well as motorboat and water sport equipment rentals. There are two large freshwater swimming pools set among lush tropical gardens. Other facilities include a Jacuzzi and exercise room, a video game room and an outdoor playground for the kids, restaurant, and bar.

A perk for guests is unlimited boarding passes to the SunCruz Casino that offer daily Las Vegas-style gambling cruises offshore in international waters. Water taxis run from the hotel to the casino ship on a regular schedule.

The 132 guest rooms are in several buildings. All feature colorful and attractive tropical décor with the usual Holiday Inn amenities. Our favorites are the second floor rooms in the building overlooking the harbor docks.

HOLIDAY INN SUNSPREE RESORT & MARINA

Address:	99701 Overseas Highway, Key Largo 33037 (At Mile Marker 100)
	www.fla-keys.com/keylargo/holidayinn.com
Phone:	800/THE KEYS (843-5397) ext 2; 305/451-2121
Fax:	305/451-5592
Rates:	$139-$309
Units:	132

Jules' Undersea Lodge

When you look out your room window here, you'll see fish looking back at you. The name says it all. This is the world's first underwater hotel, thirty feet down in a tropical Lagoon. You have to scuba dive to get into it. But, don't worry, even if you've never put on scuba gear before, they'll give you a three hour class ($75) to make certain you know all you need to know to comfortably dive accompanied by a dive instructor. According to Ron Peters, the manager, about 30 percent of the guests are first time divers. The only other thing you need is a spirit of adventure.

Entrance is up through the bottom into a moonpool in the ten- by twenty-foot wetroom. Off the wetroom are two living chambers. One is divided into two private bedrooms, each with a forty-two-inch round view-port window. The other chamber is the common room with dining and entertainment facilities including a VCR and stereo, and another viewport window. The real entertainment and underwater experience, at least for beginners, is through those windows where you can watch the undersea world. The mangrove lagoon in which it's located is a natural nursery area for many reef fish.

If you are a certified scuba diver, you can make unlimited dives to explore outside the lodge with limitless air supplied by one-hundred-foot-long "hookah" lines, instead of heavy scuba tanks. This is no amusement park gimmick. These hookah lines are a remnant from the lodge's original role as an underwater lab used for deep sea ocean exploration, where high pressures required more air than a normal scuba tank could supply. As the La Chalupa research laboratory, in the 1970s it was used as an undersea habitat to explore the continental shelf off the coast of Puerto Rico. When its lab life was over, it was sold, moved here in 1986, and converted into this unique hotel that sleeps up to six.

Fresh air, water, and power are supplied from a land-based command center that also monitors everything and provides services twenty-four hours a day. That includes a "Mer-Chef" who dives down to prepare your meals.

If you really want a wedding that's out of the ordinary, you can have one under the sea. For about a thousand dollars, the two of you can have the whole lodge to yourself for a honeymoon you'll never forget.

JULES' UNDERSEA LODGE

Address:	**P.O. Box 3330, Key Largo 33037**
	www.jul.com
Phone:	**305/451-2353**
Fax:	**305/451-4789**
Rates:	**$225-$325 per person all year**
Units:	**2**

Kona Kai Resort

Joe and Ronnie Harris gave up the fast lane of the media in New York to come to Florida to "get away from it all." They bought what was then a typically tacky Mom and Pop resort, rebuilt it almost from scratch, and established a truly charming get-away-from-it-all retreat.

It is indeed an ideal retreat, a quiet adults-only resort set in a tropical garden with fruits and rare native plants creating an ambiance of tranquillity and beauty. The garden is a delight. The day we were there, Ronnie and Joe were excited because their gardener had brought them a rare and ripe Jackfruit from their garden, which they would serve to their guests. Other fruits include eight types of bananas, including one called the ice cream banana, key limes, mangos, pineapples, and an *onstera deliciouso*, which is so accommodating that it peels itself when ripe.

You can just laze away the days here in one of their swaying hammocks by the white sandy beach, or go swimming in their heated pool. And then there are the colorful sunsets over Florida Bay. Or there's fishing, snorkeling, diving, tennis, Ping-Pong, volleyball, or you can take out a kayak or pedalboat. For boaters, there's a boat ramp and dockage. Several restaurants are within walking distance, and Joe and Ronnie only recommend ones they eat in themselves.

Appropriately, all eleven guest rooms and one- and two-bedroom suites are named after fruits. Some have small kitchens, some have bay views, and all have private baths and private entrances. Comfortably and attractively furnished in a tropical décor, each room has a CD player and television, but to retain the retreat concept there are no phones. Also to keep from disturbing guests, fresh linens and towels are provided but no maid service.

Nestled in the heart of this resort is the Gallery at Kona Kai that has as its theme "Interpretations of South Florida by artists of South Florida."

The resort is closed for a month from early September to early October. (Perhaps so Joe and Ronnie can have their own retreat from running this remarkable retreat.)

KONA KAI RESORT

Address:	97802 S. Overseas Highway, Key Largo 33037 (At Mile Marker 97.8)
	www.konakairesort.com
Phone:	800/365-STAY (365-7829); 352/852-7200
Fax:	305/852-4629
Rates:	$212-$654
Units:	11

Marriott's Key Largo Bay Beach Resort

Located on seventeen acres on Florida Bay, this Marriott is spread out in four-story low-rise buildings so that many of the rooms have balconies with direct water views.

A complete water sports resort, it has a dive shop and marina offering snorkel and dive trips, deep-sea and back country fishing, windsurfing, sunset cruises, parasailing, and rentals of a variety of fun watercraft from waverunners to Hobie cats.

Other facilities include a heated pool, a Jacuzzi, the beach, a fitness center, a tennis court, a recreation room with a variety of game courts, a full-service open air day spa in a tiki hut, a nine-hole miniature golf course, restaurants and bars, and a nightclub with dancing and entertainment on weekends. The Marriott Kids Club is available Wednesday through Sunday to provide supervised fun activity programs for kids five to thirteen.

A bonus for guests is a complimentary water shuttle to the SunCruz Casino ship, that is anchored in international waters three miles offshore, offering Las Vegas-style gambling.

Your lodging choices here include 132 guest rooms, with Floribbean décor, twenty two-bedroom suites, big enough for a family of five, with waterfront balconies, and a spacious one-bedroom penthouse suite.

MARRIOTT'S KEY LARGO BAY BEACH RESORT

Address:	**103800 Overseas Highway, Key Largo 33037 (At Mile Marker 103.8)**
	www.fla-keys.com/keylargo/marriott.htm
	www.marriott.com
Phone:	**800/932-9332; 305/453-0582**
Fax:	**305/451-6054**
Rates:	**$225-$625**
Units:	**153**

KEY WEST

Bed tax 11.5 percent

The Artist House

The architect who built this house in the late 1890s was a former ship-wright. Today the house has been restored to its original grandeur and the beautiful carpentry throughout shows he was skilled at that job.

The two-story Queen Anne-style Victorian mansion, with a touch of Bahamian influence, is an architectural gem made even more attractively authentic by the antiques and excellent reproductions furnishing its seven rooms. All have a private bath, television, phone, refrigerator, and CD player.

Our favorite is Anne's room. The former master bedroom has a four-poster bed, leather couch, fireplace, and an expansive master bath with Victorian tiles and a clawfoot tub (with shower added). The room is named after Anne Otto, a concert pianist and the wife of artist Robert Otto. This was originally the Otto's family home, and Robert grew up here, married Anne while studying art in France, and brought her back to live in Key West. After he died, she sold the house and moved out before she died, but it's said her spirit is still here.

An interesting choice for lodging here is the two-level Turret Suite. This consists of a large bedroom, sitting room, bath, and private porch on the second floor, and a circular wooden staircase that ascends to a second bedroom in the turret with windows on seven of its eight sides. The small tropical garden has a whirlpool, sundeck, and an antique fish pond. For guests wanting more space, the Artist House Guest Villas are just a block away. The six private suites here all have a kitchen, bedroom, sitting area, and private porch, all set around a large pool. Five are one-bedroom and one is a three-bedroom suite. Both the house and the villas are located just a short walk from Key West's famous Duval Street.

THE ARTIST HOUSE

Address:	524 Eaton Street, Key West 33040
	www.artisthousekeywest.com
Phone:	800/582-7882; 305/296-3977
Fax:	305/296-3210
Rates:	$129-$299
Units:	13

Banyan Resort

The gigantic banyan trees here can most easily be described by just saying "Wow!" The centuries-old banyans not only give the place its name but also a great deal of its timeless character. The huge trees provide a lovely canopy over acres of lush botanical gardens containing two hundred varieties of tropical flora, making the whole compound feel more secluded and tranquil than you'd expect from its central Old Town location. A luxury adults-only time-share development, the Banyan Resort takes up half a city block and features thirty-eight individually designed lodgings in eight renovated white Victorian mansions, five of which are on the National Register of Historic Places.

Your choices here include studios for two, one-bedroom one-bath suites, and two-bedroom, one- and two-bath suites. All the suites have a kitchen and many have French doors that open onto either a private patio or verandah overlooking the lavish gardens. One of our favorite rooms is 702 in the Town House because it's located between one of the great banyan trees and the swimming pool. Other facilities include a second pool, whirlpool, and a bar.

BANYAN RESORT

Address:	323 Whitehead Street, Key West 33040
	www.banyanresort.com
Phone:	800/225-0639; 305/296-7786
Fax:	305/294-1107
Rates:	$200-$350
Units:	38

Curry Mansion Inn

What a wonderful blend of elegant rooms at a historic mansion in the heart of Key West's Old Town that's also a home museum.

The original house was built in 1869 by William Curry, Key West's first millionaire. It's said that he served dinner guests on solid gold dinner plates from Tiffany's. Part of his fortune came from salvaging shipwrecks, and he used some of the fine items he salvaged in the construction of his home. William's original house is now the rear section of the house that was expanded into a mansion by his son Milton in 1899. Milton wanted to have the most modern house in Key West, so among his additions were three baths and an inside kitchen. The final result is this grandiose twenty-two room, three-story mansion topped by a New England-style widow's walk.

Edith and Al Anderson bought the mansion as their home in 1974. Soon after they had restored it and furnished it with family antiques, they decided to share the history and beauty and opened their home to visitors as the Curry Mansion Museum. Next they opened some of their rooms to guests, a practice that became so popular that they eventually added a total of sixteen rooms in a guest wing and eight suites in the historic James House across the street. There are four guest rooms (now seldom used) in the main house.

Rooms in the guest wing surround a tropical courtyard with heated pool and hot tub, while the James House accommodations are all balcony suites. Each room and suite has a private bath, a television, a phone, a refrigerator, and all are beautifully furnished with fine wicker and antiques.

As a guest, you are welcome to join the paying visitors to take a self-guided tour of the mansion that is listed in the National Register of Historic Places. There you can view its high ceiling rooms, spacious verandahs, Tiffany sliding glass doors, and other grand and elegant adornments that make it an unparalleled example of Victorian and Old Key West luxury. You can also come away with a copy of the original recipe for key lime pie, reportedly created by Curry's cook.

As you might expect, the mansion is a favorite for weddings, and Al is licensed to perform the ceremony.

CURRY MANSION INN

Address:	**511 Caroline Street, Key West 33040**
	www.currymansion.com
Phone:	**800/253-3466; 305/294-5349; 305/294-4093**
Rates:	**$180-$325**
Units:	**28**

Gardens Hotel

The splendid botanical garden at this hotel in the midst of the city was developed over more than thirty years by Peggy Mills, known in Key West as "The Lady of the Orchids." Starting in the 1930s, she collected plants from all over the world to create her dream garden that she opened to the public in 1968 and kept open until her death in 1979.

By the time Bill and Corinna Hettinger bought the property in 1992, it had changed hands several times, and the garden was overgrown. Bill and Corinna came from families in the restaurant and hotel business in Europe, so they saw the potential of turning this garden and the property into a small luxury hotel.

Today, their eye-catching hotel consists of seventeen guest rooms and suites in the main house, dating from the 1870s and listed on the National Register of Historic Places, and four other buildings. All are simply but elegantly furnished with items such as brass and iron beds, china lamps, beveled glass accent mirrors, and original paintings. Some have a Jacuzzi and, of course, all have the lush and colorful garden at their doorstep. Guests also have the use of a large free-form pool and outdoor heated spa.

Among the breadfruit, umbrella, palm, and other exotic trees, and the thousands of plants in the hotel's garden, there are four non-growing things that show Mrs. Mill's zeal and patience. These are the four one-ton earthenware jars, called *tinajones*, which were used by Spanish settlers in Cuba to collect rainwater. Around 1950, she bought the tinajones in Cuba. It took seven trips to that island to obtain Cuban government permission to ship them to Key West, and the story of the shipping is almost as interesting as their history. First they were moved by oxcart three hundred miles to the port at Havana. There they had to be recrated with rubber bumpers before a ship would accept them as cargo to Port Everglades, where they sat until another ship company agreed to take them to Miami. Ashore at last, she couldn't find a trucking company that would move them until a sod hauler agreed to take them on his flatbed truck cradled in a load of sod and sand. Finally, to get them into the garden, a section of the wall had to be torn down. Mission accomplished.

GARDENS HOTEL

Address:	**526 Angela Street, Key West 33040**
	www.gardenshotel.com
Phone:	**800/526-2664; 305/294-2661**
Fax:	**305/292-1007**
Rates:	**$245-$675**
Units:	**17**

Island City House Hotel

What kid could resist jumping into a pool with an eighteen-foot tile alligator on the bottom? (Parents, please note the word "tile.")

This whimsical decoration is an example of how Janet and Stan Corneal, who have children of their own, were determined to go against the grain of most Key West lodgings and create a small hotel with an "all welcome" policy that would include families as well as couples. Both are architects, and when they renovated the old hotel in 1992, they made sure to provide accommodations large enough for families.

Located in Old Town, within easy walking or biking distance of the attractions of Duval Street, the hotel consists of three buildings connected by meandering brick walkways through a flourishing tropical garden. There's also a large pool with a tile alligator, a Jacuzzi, and a sundeck.

The main building is the historic Island City House, a three-story Victorian mansion built as a private home in the 1880s and converted into

a hotel in 1912. There are ten one-bedroom parlor suites and two two-bedroom suites in this house. The Arch House, also built in the late 1880s, is Key West's oldest standing carriage house. Here your choices are four one-bedroom studio suites and two two-bedroom parlor suites. The third building is the Cigar House, built in 1980 to replicate the Alfonso Cigar Factory that occupied the site more than a hundred years ago. The red cypress wood house has six parlor suites. All the suites are spacious, tropically decorated, and have a full kitchen, living/dining room, and a private bath.

Janet offers her guests another display of whimsy in *The Island House Cats Book*, a children's book she wrote about the several cats who live on the premises and are the "real" owners of the hotel.

ISLAND CITY HOUSE HOTEL

Address:	**411 William Street, Key West 33040**
	www.islandcityhouse.com
Phone:	**800/634-8230; 305/294-5702**
Fax:	**305/294-1289**
Rates:	**$175-$315**
Units:	**24**

Key Lime Inn

In the late 1930s, the Maloney House (built in 1854 and once the home of the town's mayor) was the centerpiece of the Cactus Terrace Motor Court, the first motel in Key West. Today, this British-Caribbean-style house, on the National Register of Historic Places as one of the oldest residences on the island, is still a centerpiece, but this time it is in a completely reconstructed and refurbished series of buildings that make up the Key Lime Inn.

This is the product of the vision and careful planning of owner Julie Fondrist. Julie was a CPA in Ohio when she decided she wanted to move someplace where she could sail all year long. She gave up her accounting career to manage the Flamingo Lodge in the Everglades National Park. There she gained the hotel experience that led her to go out on her own, move to Key West (where she could sail), and buy and rehab the Merlin Bed-and-Breakfast. As soon as she had that up and running, she bought the nearby run-down Key Lime Village, which consisted of the Maloney House and the cabins and other remnants of the old motel. After she reconstructed that, she christened it the Key Lime Inn.

The inn offers nine rooms in the historic Maloney House, sixteen one-bedroom cottages, and twelve poolside cabanas. All the rooms are comfortably but simply furnished, have a television, a phone, and a private bath. The Maloney House has wraparound porches, and all its rooms have a refrigerator, a VCR, and either a private porch or a patio area. All of the cottages have a refrigerator and some have a VCR and private patio area. Even some of the poolside cabanas, which are the budget accommodations here, have a private patio.

While it may not rank with some of the more fancifully furnished lodgings on the island, one of the unheralded attractions of this inn is that it offers something that's scarce in Old Town Key West: ample free parking.

KEY LIME INN

Address:	**725 Truman Avenue, Key West 33040**
	www.keylimeinn.com
Phone:	**800/549-4430; 305/294-5229**
Fax:	**305/294-9623**
Rates:	**$149-$255**
Units:	**37**

Key West Bed & Breakfast

If you like to be surrounded by art, this bed-and-breakfast fills the bill. Owner Jody Carlson, herself an artist, has filled the walls of her house with an art collection she brought with her from the West Indies as well as the works of many Key West artists, including her own. She's also a weaver and keeps her loom in the living room where the shelves are

lined with skeins of colorful yarn. All this creates the
dual impression of staying
in a home that's part art
gallery.

Each of the eight
guest rooms is individually
decorated in bright colors
with much of the furniture
painted in yellows and reds.
There is art from either
local or Caribbean artists
on the walls.

The 1898 house is
on the National Register of
Historic Places. In 1987 it
was a health spa. At that
time Jody was working in
management at the Pier
House. There were only a handful of guest houses in Key West then,
(there are more than fifty now) but Jody saw the trend, bought this
house, and with the help of eight friends from the Pier House, worked
over Christmas (she says she let them go home for Christmas dinner) in
order to open on December 27 to a full house. And the house continues
to be popular to this day.

While the four rooms on the second floor share two bathrooms,
the other four rooms each have a private bath. House doors stay open all
the time, so only the guest rooms are air-conditioned, and none have television or phones. There is a Jacuzzi, a sauna, a piano in the common area
waiting for anyone who wants to play, a library, a Jacuzzi, a sauna and
great porches.

KEY WEST BED & BREAKFAST

Address:	**415 William Street, Key West 33040**
Phone:	**800/438-6155; 305/296-7274**
Fax:	**305/293-0306**
Rates:	**$79-$250**
Units:	**8**

Key West Hilton Resort & Marina

Whether you want to be right in the center of Key West's downtown activity or in a more secluded lodging, you have your choice here.

The Hilton Resort and Marina is on the water at Sunset Pier, just off Old Town's famous Mallory Square, where locals and visitors alike gather daily for the almost ceremonial setting of the sun. Its several rambling, low-rise, Caribbean-style Victorian buildings give you a choice of 178 rooms and one- to three-bedroom suites. All upstairs rooms have a private balcony, many with almost picture-perfect harbor views. The rooms are decorated in Key West tropical décor with all the amenities.

Resort facilities include a fitness center and spa, a swimming pool, restaurants and lounges, and a four-hundred-car parking garage—a real perk in downtown Key West. You can rent all types of fun water sports equipment and boats as well as arrange for fishing charters, parasailing, snorkeling and scuba diving, catamaran sunset and casino cruises at the full-service thirty-six slip marina. From October to May, you can take a sunset cruise on a tall ship. There's also a shuttle boat to the resort's beach facilities on Sunset Key.

If you prefer, there is a twenty-four hour launch service at the marina for a ten-minute ride to stay at one of the thirty-seven guest cottages on Sunset Key, about five hundred yards away from the resort and what seems like miles away from the hubbub of the touristy downtown. Here, the one- two- and three-bedroom cottages all have kitchens, living and dining areas, and views of either the gardens and pool area or the ocean. If you want, a grocery shopping service will prestock the cottage. If you really want to splurge and luxuriate, the concierge can arrange for a private chef and server to cook meals in your cottage.

There is a café and bar on the Key, two tennis courts, a white sandy beach, zero-degree entry pool, and two whirlpools. And, of course, all the attractions of Key West are just a ten-minute launch ride away.

KEY WEST HILTON RESORT & MARINA

Address: **245 Front Street, Key West 33040**
www.keywesthilton.com
www.sunsetkeycottages.hilton.com
Phone: **800/HILTONS (445-8667); 305/294-4000**
Fax: **305/294-4086**
Rates: **$500-$1,295**
Units: **178 in hotel**
Cottages: **37 on Sunset Key**

La Mer & Dewey House

These two upscale Victorian mansions are the only bed-and-breakfasts on a beach in Key West. And not just any beach, this is a shady and usually uncrowded beach.

Located in Old Town, just steps from the popular Duval Street, the side-by-side adults-only homes offer a total of nineteen guest rooms, many with ocean views—eleven in La Mer and eight in The Dewey House.

La Mer, built in 1903, has the turret and wraparound porch typical of the period. The Dewey House, which dates from the late 1890s, is named after John Dewey, famed philosopher and educator who stayed here often. A gazebo gateway leads to the entrance to both houses as well as a charming garden fountain.

The rooms all have high ceilings and are beautifully furnished with cool wicker and antiques and fine reproductions, including armoires. All have a private bath with Italian tile and marble, a television, a phone, and either an ocean or garden view. Some of the rooms feature sitting areas, private balconies or verandahs, and all the rooms in the Dewey House include Jacuzzi tubs. Our favorites were the second floor rooms 418 and 419 in the Dewey House, both of which have French doors opening onto large private balconies with the best ocean views in the house.

There is a small pool at the Dewey House, however these two houses are part of the properties that make up Old Town Resorts, and guests are welcome to use the three pools and other facilities at the South Beach Ocean Motel and the Southernmost Motel (which is truly the southernmost hotel in the Continental U.S.—you can't stay any further south than here.)

LA MER & DEWEY HOUSE

Address:	506 & 504 South Street, Key West 33040 or Old Town Resorts, 1319 Duval Street, Key West 33040 www.oldtownresorts.com
Phone:	800/354-4455; 305/296-5611
Fax:	305/294-8272
Rates:	$205-$315
Units:	19

Marquesa Hotel

If we were asked to pick models for an intimate, elegant, luxury hotel, the Marquesa would be near the top of our list.

Your lodging choices here are twenty-seven rooms and junior suites in four classic Conch-style buildings attractively set around two swimming pools, a three-tiered waterfall, and a flourishing tropical garden of colorful exotic plants that includes a flowering wall covered with orchids from around the world.

The Greek-Revival-style main building, built in 1884, is on the National Register of Historic Places. It had been operated as a boarding house for eighty years and by 1987 had twenty-one sleeping spaces and two barely functioning bathrooms. Two Key West couples bought it that year and spent nine months and well over a million dollars restoring it. The twenty-one rooms were reduced to nine spacious guest rooms. They also added a wing, and opened it as the Marquesa Hotel in 1988. The hotel was so well received that a few years later they bought two neighboring historic buildings, also built in the 1880s, and transformed them with another multi-million-dollar attention-to-detail restoration.

The airy guest rooms are all different. Each has the characteristic high ceilings and décor that can best be described as a charmingly eclectic mixture of West Indies style with modern fabrics and furnishings, including four-hundred pound sleigh beds from Indonesia, four-poster iron beds, custom-made teak tables from the Philippines, and yew wood armoires from England. All have a marble bath, a television, and a phone, and each junior suite features a sitting area and private outdoor porch.

The hotel's forty-eight-seat restaurant, Café Marquesa, has been lauded by a number of gourmet and travel magazines including *Bon Appetit, Gourmet,* and *Food Arts.*

MARQUESA HOTEL

Address:	**600 Fleming Street, Key West 33040**
	www.marquesa.com
Phone:	**800/869-4631; 305/292-1919**
Fax:	**305/294-2121**
Rates:	**$245-$380**
Units:	**27**

Paradise Inn

It takes nerve to call your inn "Paradise" and even more hospitality smarts to live up to your name. But we're happy to say this inn comes as close as any to living up to that name. Of course paradise should have a spectacular Garden of Eden, and they come close because Shel Segal, the managing partner, is a former florist. The one-acre compound reflects his floral knowledge enhanced by the skill of an award-winning landscape architect. According to Segal, the garden and grounds have more exotic plants then any other place in Key West. Each is nicely labeled with its name and what country it's from, so you can identify such floral exotica as night blooming jasmine, pink tabebuias, gumbo limbo, red ginger, and the ylang-ylang, the tree from which Chanel captured the famous scent of her Number 5. The garden is designed so it is the most colorful during high season.

Guest lodgings are in several meticulously renovated one- and two-bedroom "cigar makers" cottages and two authentically reproduced Bahamian-style tin-roofed houses with vine-covered porches. All are well-appointed mini-suites or full-size suites. Mini-suites have one large room with a sitting area and a marble bathroom. Suites have one or two bedrooms a living room, and one or two baths. All the suites have a television and a phone. Our favorite is the top-of-the-line Royal Poinciana Suite with two bedrooms and two baths, both with Jacuzzi tubs, and a wraparound porch. This and the other two- bedroom suite, the Sapodilla, have loads of space and amenities for a family or two couples to share.

There is a pool, a lotus pond with koi, and a hot tub. The inn has on-site parking and is located in Old Town.

PARADISE INN

Address:	819 Simonton Street, Key West 33040
	www.paradiseinn.com
Phone:	800/888-9648; 305/293-0807
Fax:	305/293-0807
Rates:	$210-$545
Units:	18

Pier House Resort & Caribbean Spa

It's not called the Pier House for nothing. While most of the resort sprawls contentedly along the waterfront, a major section, including its superb and highly rated Pier House Restaurant and the Havana Docks Sunset Deck, sticks its nose, like a pier, right out into the Gulf of Mexico. And look at its location! An entire city block with an address at the first number on the action end of the most famous street in Key West.

When the Pier House first opened as a motel and restaurant in 1968, it included what was then a cubbyhole of a bar called The Chart Room (still there, but enlarged) where Jimmy Buffett is said to have begun his career. At that time Key West was hardly a tourist destination. The Pier House Restaurant was a strong contributor to the town's rise in popularity, drawing celebrities like Truman Capote and Tennessee Williams to enjoy its fresh seafood dishes.

Over the years the Pier House has grown, been continually

upgraded, and developed along with the town until today the resort as a whole is as well known as the restaurant.

One thing for sure, it has made the most of its five-acre prime location. Some of its buildings are Old Florida-style with peaked tin roofs and railed porches, while others, the Caribbean Spa building, for example, are more contemporary. Your choices here include 126 guest rooms and sixteen suites with balconies or terraces. All are well-appointed with wicker furniture, Key West art, and tropical décor. Most have views of either the ocean or the tropical garden/pool area. Our favorites were the Beach Building's rooms that overlook the gulf, but if you can give up that view, most of the Caribbean Spa rooms include such additional niceties as an extra-large bathroom with whirlpool tub, a CD player, and VCR.

The Caribbean is a full-service spa and salon offering a wide range of body and beauty services including therapeutic massage, aromatherapy, facials, reflexology, as well as fitness classes and a spa cuisine lunch.

There is a small beach—a private section for topless sunbathing—an expansive swimming pool with whirlpool, a couple of restaurants, and bars with live entertainment, and of course, the sunsets.

PIER HOUSE RESORT & CARIBBEAN SPA

Address:	**One Duval Street, Key West 33040**
	www.pierhouse.com
Phone:	**800/327-8340; 305/296-4600**
Fax:	**305/296-7568**
Rates:	**$290-$1,600**
Units:	**142**

Weatherstation Inn

This inn may be one of the few relatively undiscovered jewels in Old Town Key West, and the only one with the security of a gated community. If you walk one direction from this inn, located in the quiet Truman Annex that is now a residential community, you can visit the Truman White House. Walk the other way, and you come out in midst of all the pizzazz and flash of Duval Street and Mallory Square.

Listed in the National Register of Historic Places, this solidly handsome two-story building, typical of the military architecture of the period, was once the U.S. Weather Bureau Station. Built in 1912, it is located on what was, at that time, part of the large U.S. Naval Station on the island. This Navy base played a major role in the nineteenth and early twentieth centuries, from fighting Caribbean pirates to operations during the Cuban Missile Crisis of 1962. It also provided security for President Truman during his lengthy visits. Starting about 1951 the building was used as Navy housing until the base closed in 1974.

In the early 1990s it was bought as a private home by Tim and Kelly Koenig. It was the Koenigs who turned it into this inn, opening it in 1997. As solid as it looks on the outside, inside the inn maintains the integrity of pure Key West style with Bahama shutters, hardwood floors, and comfortable furnishings that bring to mind the West Indies. There are eight guest rooms, all distinctly different and all with private baths. A couple of the rooms have balconies. The landscaping is also typical Key West with lush tropical plants and stately Washingtonian Palms secluding a private heated pool.

Now, instead of Naval vessels, the big cruise ships tie up at what were the nearby Navy docks, just a long stone's throw from the inn. In fact, you are so close you almost have to look up at those colorful ships which tower over the building. Fortunately, the dock regulations require that all ships have to be gone by 5 P.M., so you can enjoy watching these behemoths sail from the rooftop sundeck and then watch the sunset.

WEATHERSTATION INN

Address:	**57 Front Street, Key West 33040**
	www.weatherstationinn.com
Phone:	**800/815–2707; 305/294-7277**
Fax:	**305/294-0544**
Rates:	**$195-$315**
Units:	**8**

Wyndham Casa Marina Resort & Beach House

This is the last grand hotel built by railroad and oil tycoon Henry Flagler. One could say this was a fitting ending of his love affair with Florida that had led to building his railroad from Jacksonville to Key West, studding this ribbon of steel with other grand hotels along the way so his affluent friends would have elegant places to stay.

Although Flagler financed it, he did not live to see the opening of the Casa Marina (The House by the Sea) in December 1920. It was designed by Thomas Hastings and John Carrere, whose reputation was built by the projects Flagler assigned them. They later were commissioned to do buildings like the Metropolitan Opera House and the New York Public Library. The Casa Marina represents the culmination of more than a decade of refining their architectural knowledge and design that produced grand structures suitable to the South Florida environment. This was to be the grandest of the grand, a final tribute to the man who had given them success. And they succeeded. It soon became the playground of aristocrats, artists, actors, socialites, and literary lions.

Like all older grande dames, it had its down times. For a while it was Navy quarters and, during the Cuban Missile Crisis, headquarters for an Army missile battalion. But it survived and flourished until today. Now it is the oldest resort in the Keys. Listed in the National Register of Historic Places, its Spanish architecture, gracious verandahs, billowing archways, palladian windows, and palm-studded lawns, still all spell grandeur. But its grandeur brought up-to-date with all the modern conveniences, while keeping true to the eccentric and laid-back character of Key West.

Your choices here include 242 guest rooms and sixty-nine one- and two-bedroom loft suites. A little less than half are in the original historic building and the rest are in two wings. About half the rooms have ocean views, and most have balconies overlooking either the ocean or Old Town.

Facilities include three lighted tennis courts, two swimming pools, a health and fitness club, a restaurant (where they lay claim to the best Sunday brunch in Key West) and bar, facilities for water sports, a fishing pier, and the largest private beach in Key West.

WYNDHAM CASA MARINA RESORT & BEACH HOUSE

Address:	**1500 Reynolds Street, Key West 33040**
	www.casamarinakeywest.com
Phone:	**800/626-0777; 305/296-3535**
Fax:	**305/296-9960**
Rates:	**$245-$766**
Units:	**311**

LITTLE TORCH KEY

Bed tax 11.5 percent

Little Palm Island

When we were researching this resort, we kept running across descriptions that ranged from "the most wonderful romantic getaway" to "a true tropical paradise." Since it is our business as travel writers to be skeptical, we wondered if it could live up to all this high praise. Then we spent the night and found out it did. And after a gourmet dinner at the island's restaurant, Loys, who is a key lime pie aficionado, added another accolade: "This is the best key lime pie I've ever tasted."

Of course, it also lived up to its reputation of being one of the most exclusive and expensive resorts in the state. But you definitely get what you pay for. As the 800-3-GET LOST number indicates, this is a place to get lost from all the cares of the world. No phones, no television, no radio, just a chance to relax and detach yourself from the pressures of everyday life.

First, there's the setting, a five-acre tropical island three miles offshore, accessible only by boat or seaplane. Once a fishing camp and secluded haven for VIPS, including Presidents Roosevelt, Truman, Kennedy, and Nixon, it brings to mind a South Seas island with palm trees, tropical foliage, white sandy beaches, and warm seas. In fact, it looks so much like the South Seas that it was chosen as the location for the film *PT 109*, the story of JFK's World War II exploits in the South Pacific.

Then there are the palm-thatched bungalows scattered gracefully among the palms, enhancing the romantic ambiance. Furnished in simple elegance, all have a bedroom, a living room, a bath with a whirlpool made for two, and a private sundeck with a hammock and ocean view.

The award-winning restaurant also deserves the praise heaped upon it. The goal here is to make dining an affair to remember. The cuisine is Floribbean with a touch of French and Asian.

What can you do on this island paradise? From the minute the private launch brings you here until you return to the shore station, you have a wide variety of activities available. Facilities include a beach, a lagoon-style freshwater pool, a full-service marina, complimentary use of watercraft ranging from kayaks to sailboats with larger boats available for rent, a fitness room, a dive center with certification courses, everything you need for fishing including charters, a Zen garden, and the full-service Island Spa and Salon.

To ensure the romantic exclusivity, no children under sixteen are permitted.

LITTLE PALM ISLAND

Address:	28500 Overseas Highway, Little Torch Key 33042 (Shore station at Mile Marker 28.5)
	www.littlepalmisland.com
Phone:	800/3-GET LOST (343-8567); 305/872-2524
Fax:	305/872-4843
Rates:	$850-$1,600
Units:	30

MARATHON

Bed tax 11.5 percent

Conch Key Cottages

After you pass Mile Marker 62 going south, look carefully or you're liable to miss the small sign and the causeway entrance to this pleasant group of cottages on its own secluded microisland. The ambiance created by its semi-isolated location makes this a true hideaway.

Each Conch (pronounced konk) Key cottage has its own hammock and barbecue grill, some have a screened porch, and some are on sturdy twelve-foot high pilings that push them up so they have a better view of the water. Your choices here range from what they call a "hotel efficiency" up to a two-bedroom cottage. All are simply but well furnished in rustic tropical décor with mostly reed, rattan, and wicker furniture. Owners Ron Wilson and Wayne Byrnes are both into cooking, so the kitchens are set up for the gourmet cook.

Before they found this place, Ron and Wayne had been rehabbing and then selling properties in Winter Park. Both were getting burned out, but when they first saw these cottages, which were a mess, they knew this was an ideal situation for their rehab expertise. They also quickly decided this would be their last rehab project. With this one, they would stay put. They bought the place in 1990, fixed it up so they could open, and have been steadily improving it ever since.

With a small beach on the ocean, a freshwater pool, a quiet location away from traffic, and a no-fuss atmosphere, this is a great, inexpensive (for the Keys) getaway place for both couples and families. Ron used to be a landscape architect, and the bountiful and colorful plants and greenery on the little island are evidence of his skill.

CONCH KEY COTTAGES

Address:	P.O. Box 424, Marathon 33050
	www.florida-keys.fl/:us/ckc.htm
Phone:	800/330-1577; 305/289-1377
Fax:	305/743-8207
Rates:	$105-$249
Units:	13

For Additional Information
on the Southeast Region:

STUART/MARTIN COUNTY COC
1650 S. Kanner Highway
Stuart, FL 34994
561/287-1088
Fax: 561/220-3437
www.goodnature.org

PALM BEACH COUNTY CVB
1555 Palm Beach Lakes Blvd. Suite 204
West Palm Beach, FL 33401
561/471-3995
Fax: 561/471-3990
www.palmbeachfl.com

MONROE COUNTY TDC
FLORIDA KEYS & KEY WEST
1201 White Street, Suite 102
Key West, FL 33040
800/648-5510
305/296-1552
Fax: 305/296-0788
www.fla-keys.com

GREATER MIAMI CVB
701 Brickell Ave., Suite 2700
Miami, FL 33131
800/933-8448
305/539-3000
Fax: 305/539-3113
www.tropicoolmiami.com

GREATER FORT LAUDERDALE CVB
1850 Eller Drive, Suite 303
Fort Lauderdale, FL 33316
800/22-SUNNY (227-8669)
954/765-4466
Fax: 954/765-4467
www.sunny.org

EVERGLADES NATIONAL PARK
HEADQUARTERS
40001 State Road 9336
Homestead, FL 33034
305/242-7700

CATAGORY INDEX

(NW=Northwest, NC=North Central, NE=Northeast
CW=Central West, C=Central, CE=Central East
SW=Southwest, SE=Southeast & The Keys)

To help you narrow down your search for the type lodging that you're looking for, we've come up with a list of categories that highlight why each one is irresistible. Many irresistible overnights can easily be listed under a number of different categories, so here is just a sampling for each category.

Animal Lover's Delight

Continental Acres Equine
   Resort (C) 128
Hawks Cay Resort (SE) 244
River Ranch (C) 123
Wildlife on Easy Street (CW) 108

Antique Lover's Delight

(These places have a large number of *genuine* antiques.)

Amelia Island Williams House (NE) 46
Bailey House Bed &
   Breakfast (NE) 47
Bayboro House (CW) 98
Behind the Fence (CW) 92
Casablanca (NE) 70
Casa de Solana (NE) 67
Cedar Key Bed & Breakfast (NC) 25
Collier Inn (SW) 173
Coombs House Inn (NW) 4
Coquina Inn (CE) 161
Courtyard at Lake Lucerne (C) 141
Cypress Inn (CW) 89
Herlong Mansion (NC) 30
Hibiscus House Bed &
   Breakfast (SE) 203

Hotel Place St. Michel (SE) 221
Hoyt House (NE) 52
Kenwood Inn (NE) 71
Night Swan (CE) 164
Palmer Place (NC) 33
Pensacola Victorian (NW) 14
Ritz-Carlton Naples (SW) 187
Sabal Palm House (SE) 208
Stanford Inn (C) 119
The Villa (CE) 161
Westcott House Inn (NE) 74

Architectural/Design Gem

Artist's House (SE) 249
Barnacle Bed & Breakfasr (SE) 243
The Breakers (SE) 198
Biltmore Hotel (SE) 220
Casa Monica (NE) 68
Don Cesar Beach Resort
   & Spa (CW) 103
Eden Roc Resort & Spa (SE) 229
Essex House (SE) 230
Fontainebleau Hilton Resort (SE) 231
The Hotel (SE) 233
Hotel Inter-Continental-
   Miami (SE) 225

The Marlin (SE) 234
Park Central Hotel (SE) 236
The Tides (SE) 238

Art Lover's Delight

Alexander Hotel (SE) 227
Henderson Park Inn (NW) 8
Key West Bed & Breakfast (SE) 256
Kona Kai Resort (SE) 247
Lago Mar Resort and Club (SE) 211
Ritz-Carlton Amelia Island (NE) 53
Ritz-Carlton Naples (SW) 187
Ritz-Carlton Palm Beach (SE) 206
Sabal Palm House (SE) 208
Shady Oaks (NC) 31
Sonesta Beach Resort
  Key Biscayne (SE) 222

Beach Lover's Delight

(These are properties where you'll find some
of the best beaches.)
Alexander Hotel (SE) 227
Amelia Island Plantation (NE) 45
Bahia Honda State Park (SE) 242
Barnacle Bed & Breakfast (SE) 243
Boca Raton Resort & Club (SE) 196
The Breakers (SE) 198
Cabbage Key Inn (SW) 189
Collier Inn (SW) 173
Colony Beach & Tennis
  Resort (CW) 86
Disney's Vero Beach Resort (CE) 169
Don Cesar Beach Resort
  & Spa (CW) 103
Eden Roc Resort & Spa (SE) 229
Elizabeth Pointe Lodge (NE) 49
Fontainebleau Hilton Resort (SE) 231

Four Seasons Resort Palm
  Beach (SE) 202
Henderson Park Inn (NW) 8
Holiday Inn Hotel and Suites Longboat
  Key (CW) 87
Hutchinson Island Marriott Beach
  Resort & Marina (SE) 194
Inn at Cocoa Beach (CE) 157
Inn at Fisher Island Club (SE) 224
Lago Mar Resort & Club (SE) 211
La Mer & Dewey House (SE) 259
Little Inn by the Sea (SE) 213
Little Palm Island (SE) 266
Manasota Beach Club (SW) 181
Marriott's Key Largo Bay Beach
  Resort (SE) 248
Ocean Surf Hotel (SE) 235
Old Salty's Inn (CE) 162
Palm Island Resort (SW) 175
Park Central Hotel (SE) 236
Pelican Hotel (SE) 237
Ponte Vedra Beach Resorts (NE) 62
Registry Resort (SW) 186
Resort at Longboat Key (CW) 87
Ritz-Carlton Amelia Island (NE) 53
Ritz-Carlton Naples (SW) 187
Ritz-Carlton Palm Beach (SE) 206
Ritz Plaza Hotel (SE) 238
Sandestin Golf & Beach
  Resort (NW) 9
Sanibel Harbour Resort &
  Spa (SW) 183
Sawgrass Marriott Resort (NE) 63
Seaside Cottages (NW) 22
Sonesta Beach Resort
  Key Biscayne (SE) 222
South Seas Plantation (SW) 178
The Tides (SE) 238
Topaz Motel/Hotel (NE) 56
Tradewinds Island Resorts (CW) 106

Turnberry Isle Resort
and Club (SE) 226

'Tween Waters Inn (SW) 179

Windemere Inn by the Sea (CE) 159

Birder's Delight

Amelia Island Plantation (NE) 45

Bahia Honda State Park (SE) 242

Flamingo Lodge (SE) 241

Hyatt Regency Westshore (CW) 107

Old Saltworks Cabins (NW) 17

Perri House (C) 137

Refuge at Ocklawaha (C) 127

Registry Resort (SW) 186

Boater's Delight

(These all have marinas either on the property or close by.)

Alexander Hotel (SE) 227

Best Western Crystal River
Resort (CW) 81

Boca Raton Resort & Club (SE) 196

Collier Inn (SW) 173

Eden Roc Resort & Spa (SE) 229

Flamingo Lodge (SE) 241

Hawk's Cay Resort & Marina (SE) 244

Holiday Inn Sunspree Resort &
Marina (SE) 245

Hontoon Landing Resort &
Marina (CE) 155

Hutchinson Island Marriott Beach
Resort & Marina (SE) 194

Hyatt Regency Pier Sixty-six (SE) 210

Inn at Fisher Island Club (SE) 224

Key West Hilton Resort &
Marina (SE) 257

Little Palm Island (SE) 266

Marriott's Key Largo Bay Beach
Resort (SE) 248

Mission Inn Golf & Tennis
Resort (C) 117

Pirate's Cove Resort & Marina (SE) 199

Renaissance Vinoy Resort (CW) 100

Sandestin Golf & Beach
Resort (NW) 9

Sanibel Harbour Resort &
Spa (SW) 183

South Seas Plantation (SW) 178

Turnberry Isle Resort & Club (SE) 226

Wyndham Harbour Island
Hotel (CW) 110

Croquet Courts

(These places are an example of the wide
variety of facilities.)

Chalet Suzanne Country Inn (C) 122

Collier Inn (SW) 173

Disney's Vero Beach Resort (CE) 169

Manasota Beach Club (SW) 181

PGA National Resort & Spa (SE) 205

Renaissance Vinoy Resort (CW) 100

Tradewinds Island Resorts (CW) 106

Definitely Different

Adventures Unlimited (NW) 11

Bay Harbor Inn & Suites (SE) 228

Behind the Fence (CW) 92

Bridge Water Inn (SW) 185

Cabbage Key Inn (SW) 189

Cassadaga Hotel & Psychic
Center (CE) 154

Celebration Hotel (C) 131

Chalet Suzanne Country Inn (C) 122

Club Continental (NE) 61

Continental Acres Equine
Resort (C) 128

Courtyard at Lake Lucerne (C) 141

Curry Mansion Inn (SE) 251

Darst Victorian Manor (C) 118
Doubletree Castle Hotel (C) 142
Driftwood Resort (CE) 171
Fontainebleau Hilton Resort (SE) 231
Herlong Mansion (NC) 30
Holiday Inn Family Suites Resort Lake Buena Vista (C) 133
The Hotel (SE) 233
Hyatt Regency Pier Sixty-six (SE) 210
Hyatt Regency Westshore (CW) 107
Inn at Fisher Island Club (SE) 224
Jules' Undersea Lodge (SE) 246
Little Palm Island (SE) 266
The Marlin (SE) 234
Paradise Lakes Resort (CW) 110
Portofino Bay Hotel (C) 144
Refuge at Ocklawaha (C) 127
River Ranch (C) 123
Sheraton Studio City (C) 148
Wildlife on Easy Street (CW) 108
World Golf Village Renaissance Resort (NE) 75

Eco-Tours
Amelia Island Plantation (NE) 45
Flamingo Lodge (SE) 241
Hawk's Cay Resort & Marina (SE) 244
Hutchinson Island Marriott Beach Resort & Marina (SE) 194
Refuge at Ocklawaha (C) 127
Turtle Beach Inn (NW) 18

Elegant Luxury
Alexander Hotel (SE) 227
Biltmore Hotel (SE) 220
Boca Raton Resort & Club (SE) 196

The Breakers (SE) 198
Casa Monica (NE) 68
Chesterfield Hotel (SE) 199
Collier Inn (SW) 170
Colony Palm Beach (SE) 201
Disney's Vero Beach Resort (CE) 169
Don Cesar Beach Resort & Spa (CW) 103
Doral Golf Resort & Spa (SE) 223
Four Seasons Resort Palm Beach (SE) 202
Hotel Inter-Continental-Miami (SE) 225
Hyatt Regency Grand Cypress (C) 143
Inn at Fisher Island Club (SE) 224
Key West Hilton Resort & Marina (SE) 257
Little Palm Island (SE) 266
Mayfair House (SE) 218
Peabody Orlando (C) 144
PGA National Resort & Spa (SE) 205
Portofino Bay Hotel (C) 145
Registry Resort (SW) 185
Renaissance Orlando Resort (C) 147
Renaissance Vinoy Resort (CW) 100
Resort at Longboat Key (CW) 87
Ritz-Carlton Amelia Island (NE) 53
Ritz-Carlton Naples (SW) 97
Ritz-Carlton Palm Beach (SE) 206
Sonesta Beach Resort Key Biscayne (SE) 222
Turnberry Isle Resort & Club (SE) 226
The Villa (CE) 161
Wyndham Casa Marina Resort & Beach House (SE) 264
Wyndham Harbour Island Hotel (CW) 110
Wyndham Palace Resort & Spa (C) 139

Fisherman's Delight

(These are properties where fishing is a major sport.)

Amelia Island Plantation (NE) 45

Angler Inn (CE) 167

Bahia Honda State Park (SE) 242

Bridge Water Inn (SW) 185

Collier Inn (SW) 173

Davis House Inn (CE) 168

Flamingo Lodge (SE) 241

Floridian Sports Club (NE) 78

Grenelefe Golf & Tennis Resort (C) 120

Hontoon Landing Resort & Marina (CE) 155

Mission Inn Golf & Tennis Resort (C) 117

Pirate's Cove Resort & Marina (SE) 193

Sandestin Golf & Beach Resort (NW) 9

Sanibel Harbour Resort & Spa (SW) 183

South Seas Plantation (SW) 178

Ghosts

Artists House (SE) 249

The Biltmore (SE) 220

Casablanca Inn (NE) 70

Cassadaga Hotel & Psychic Center (CE) 154

Don Cesar Beach Resort & Spa (CW) 103

Gibson Inn (NW) 5

Herlong Mansion (NC) 30

Gardeners Delight

Amelia Island Plantation (NE) 45

Bahia Honda State Park (SE) 242

Banyan Resort (SE) 250

Boca Raton Resort & Club (SE) 196

Gardens Hotel (SE) 252

Hyatt Regency Grand Cypress (C) 143

Hyatt Regency Westshore (CW) 107

Island City House Hotel (SE) 254

Kona Kai Resort (SE) 247

Marquesa Hotel (SE) 260

Mayfair House (SE) 218

Old Mansion Inn (NE) 72

Paradise Inn (SE) 261

Registry Resort (SW) 186

Renaissance Orlando Resort (C) 147

Thurston House (C) 140

Golfer's Delight

(Some of the best hotel golf courses in Florida.)

Amelia Island Plantation (NE) 45

Belleview Biltmore Resort & Spa (CW) 94

Biltmore Hotel (SE) 220

Boca Raton Resort & Club (SE) 196

The Breakers (SE) 198

Doral Golf Resort & Spa (SE) 223

Grenelefe Golf & Tennis Resort (C) 120

Hutchinson Island Marriott Beach Resort & Marina (SE) 194

Hyatt Regency Grand Cypress (C) 144

Mission Inn Golf & Tennis Resort (C) 117

PGA National Resort & Spa (SE) 205

Plantation Inn & Golf Resort (CW) 82

Ponte Vedra Beach Resorts (NE) 62

Resort at Longboat Key (CW) 87

Ritz-Carlton Amelia Island (NE) 53

River Ranch (C) 123

Saddlebrook Resort-Tampa (CW) 112

Sandestin Golf & Beach
Resort (NW) 9

Sawgrass Marriott Resort (NE) 63

Turnberry Isle Resort & Club (SE) 220

Westin Innisbrook Resort (CW) 95

World Golf Village Renaissance
Resort (NE) 75

Wyndham Resort & Spa (SE) 217

Historic Lodgings

(These places are on the National Register of
Historic Places)

Amelia Island Williams House (NE) 46

Bailey House (NE) 47

Banyan Resort (SE) 215

Belleview Biltmore Resort &
Spa (CW) 94

The Biltmore (SE) 220

The Breakers (SE) 198

Casa de Solana (NE) 67

Casa Marina Resort & Beach
House (SE) 263

Casa Monica (NE) 68

Casablanca Inn (NE) 70

Chalet Suzanne (C) 122

Château Nemours Seaport
Inn (NW) 16

Clauser's Inn (CE) 154

Clewiston Inn (SW) 180

Club Continental (NE) 61

Collier Inn (SW) 173

The Consulate (NW) 3

Coquina Inn (CE) 161

Courtyard at Lake Lucerne (C) 141

Crowne Plaza, Pensacola Grand
Hotel (NW) 12

Curry Mansion Inn (SE) 251

Don Cesar Beach
Resort & Spa (CW) 103

Driftwood Resort (CE) 171

Fairbanks House (NE) 50

Florida House Inn (NE) 51

Gardens Hotel (SE) 252

Gibson Inn (NW) 5

Herlong Mansion (NC) 30

The Hotel (SE) 233

Key Lime Inn (SE) 255

Key West Bed & Breakfast (SE) 256

Marquesa Hotel (SE) 260

McFarlin House (NC) 34

Palmer Place (NC) 33

Renaissance Vinoy Resort (CW) 100

Ritz Plaza Hotel (SE) 238

St. Francis Inn (NE) 73

Seven Sisters Inn (C) 127

Sweetwater Branch Inn (NC) 28

The Villa (CE) 161

Wakulla Springs State Park and
Lodge (NC) 39

Weatherstation Inn (SE) 263

Wyndham Casa Marina Resort &
Beach House (SE) 264

Houseboats

Flamingo Lodge (SE) 241

Hontoon Landing Resort &
Marina (CE) 155

Island Retreats

Cabbage Key Inn (SW) 189

Collier Inn (SW) 173

Hawks Cay Resort (SE) 244

Inn at Fisher Island Club (SE) 224

Key West Hilton Resort & Marina (SE) 257

Little Palm Island (SE) 266

Palm Island Resort (SW) 175

Kid's Delight

Amelia Island Plantation (NE) 45

Boca Raton Resort & Club (SE) 196

The Breakers (SE) 198

Colony Beach & Tennis Resort (CW) 86

Disney Vero Beach Resort (CE) 169

Don Cesar Beach Resort & Spa (CW) 103

Doral Golf Resort & Spa (SE) 223

Fontainebleau Hilton Resort & Towers (SE) 231

Four Seasons Resort Palm Beach (SE) 202

Hawks Cay Resort (SE) 244

Holiday Inn Family Suites Resort Lake Buena Vista (C) 133

Holiday Inn Hotel and Suites Longboat Key (CW) 87

Holiday Inn Hotel & Suites Main Gate East (C) 132

Holiday Inn Sunspree Marina Cove (CW) 99

Holiday Inn Sunspree Resort Lake Buena Vista (C) 135

Hutchinson Island Marriott Beach Resort (SE) 194

Hyatt Regency Grand Cypress Resort (C) 144

Marriott's Key Largo Bay Beach Resort (SE) 248

Pointe Vedra Beach Resorts (NE) 62

Registry Resort (SW) 186

Resort at Longboat Key Club (CW) 87

Ritz-Carlton Amelia Island (NE) 53

Ritz-Carlton Naples (SW) 187

Ritz-Carlton Palm Beach (SE) 206

Saddlebrook Resort-Tampa (CW) 112

Sandestin Golf & Beach Resort (NW) 9

Sanibel Harbour Resort & Spa (SW) 183

Sawgrass Marriott Resort (NE) 62

Sonesta Beach Resort Key Biscayne (SE) 222

South Seas Plantation (SW) 178

Tradewinds Island Resorts (CW) 106

Westin Innisbrook Resort (CW) 95

World Golf Village Renaissance Resort (NE) 75

Wyndham Palace Resort & Spa (C) 139

Wyndham Resort & Spa (SE) 217

Old Florida Ambiance

(These places are samples of how Floridians lived before tourism)

Addison House (NE) 43

Adventures Unlimited (NW) 11

Angler Inn (CE) 166

Bahia Honda State Park (SE) 242

Bungalow Beach Resort (CW) 84

Cabbage Key Inn (SW) 189

Carriage Way (NE) 66

Casa de Sueños (NE) 67

Château Nemours Seaport Inn (NW) 16

Club Continental (NE) 61

Colony Palm Beach (SE) 201

Conch Key Cottages (SE) 267

Cypress Inn (CW) 89

Essex House (SE) 230

Flamingo Lodge (SE) 241

Fontainebleau Hilton Resort (SE) 231

Gibson Inn (NW) 5

Harborfront Inn (SE) 193

Harrington House (CW) 84

Higgins House (C) 149

Hotel DeFuniak (NW) 7

Hotel Place St. Michel (SE) 221

Island City House (SE) 254

Island's End Resort (CW) 104

Kenwood Inn (NE) 71

La Mer & Dewey House (SE) 259

Lago Mar Resort & Club (SE) 211

Little Inn by the Sea (SE) 213

Little River Inn (CE) 169

Manasota Beach Club (SW) 181

Mango Inn (SE) 204

McFarlin House (NC) 34

Mission Inn Golf & Tennis Resort (C) 117

Night Swan (CE) 164

Ocean Surf (SE) 235

Old Salty's Inn (CE) 162

Palm Island Resort (SW) 175

Paradise Inn (SE) 261

Park Plaza Hotel (C) 150

Pier House Resort & Caribbean Spa (SE) 262

Plantation Manor Inn (NE) 59

Riverside Hotel (SE) 214

Riverview Hotel (CE) 165

Sabal Palm House (SE) 208

St. Francis Inn (NE) 73

Shamrock Thistle & Crown (C) 129

Sprague House Inn (NE) 55

Steinhatchee Landing Resort (NC) 35

Terrace Hotel (C) 121

Thurston House (C) 140

Topaz Motel/Hotel (NE) 56

'Tween Waters Inn (SW) 179

Wakulla Springs State Park Lodge (NC) 39

Romantic Favorites

Brigitte's Romantic Retreat (NW) 2

Boca Raton Resort & Club (SE) 196

Club Continental (NE) 61

Disney's Vero Beach Resort (CE) 169

Harborfront Inn (SE) 193

Harrington House (CW) 84

Henderson Park Inn (NW) 8

Josephine's French Country Inn (NW) 21

Little Palm Island (SE) 266

Little River Inn (CE) 163

Magnolia Plantation (NC) 27

Riverside Hotel (SE) 214

Rooms with Especially Good Water Views

Alexander Hotel (SE) 227

Amelia Island Plantation (NE) 45

Apalachicola River Inn ((NW) 1

Bayboro House (CW) 98

Bay Harbor Inn & Suites (SE) 228

Boca Raton Resort & Club (SE) 196

The Breakers (SE) 198

Bridge Water Inn (SW) 185

Casablanca (NE) 70

Celebration Hotel (C) 131

Club Continental (NE) 61

Colony Beach & Tennis Resort (CW) 86

The Consulate (NW) 3

Disney's Vero Beach Resort (CE) 169

Driftwood Resort (CE) 171

Eden Roc Resort & Spa (SE) 229

Elizabeth Pointe Lodge (NE) 49

Fontainebleau Hilton Resort (SE) 231

Four Seasons Resort Palm
Beach (SE) 202

Harrington House (CW) 84

Henderson Park Inn (NW) 8

Highlands House (NW) 20

Hilton Jacksonville Riverfront (NE) 57

Holiday Inn Hotel and Suites Longboat
Key (CW) 87

Hontoon Landing Resort &
Marina (CE) 155

Hotel Inter-Continental-
Miami (SE) 225

House on Cherry Street (NE) 58

Hutchinson Island Marriott Beach
Resort & Marina (SE) 194

Hyatt Regency Westshore (CW) 107

Inn at Cocoa Beach (CE) 157

Key West Hilton Resort &
Marina (SE) 257

La Mer & Dewey House (SE) 259

Little Inn by the Sea (SE) 213

Little River Inn (CE) 163

Marriott's Key Largo Bay Beach
Resort (SE) 248

Night Swan (CE) 164

Ocean Surf (SE) 235

Old Saltworks Cabins (NW) 17

Palm Island Resort (SW) 175

Park Central Hotel (SE) 236

Pelican Hotel (SE) 237

Pier House Resort & Caribbean
Spa (SE) 262

Pirate's Cove Resort & Marina (SE) 193

Ponte Vedra Beach Resorts (NE) 62

Registry Resort (SW) 186

Renaissance Vinoy Resort (CW) 147

Resort at Longboat Key (CW) 87

Ritz-Carlton Amelia Island (NE) 53

Ritz-Carlton Naples (SW) 187

Ritz-Carlton Palm Beach (SE) 206

Ritz Plaza Hotel (SE) 238

River view Hotel (CE) 165

Sandestin Golf & Beach
Resort (NW) 9

Sanibel Harbour Resort & Spa (SW) 183

Sonesta Beach Resort
Key Biscayne (SE) 222

The Tides (SE) 238

Tradewinds Island Resorts (CW) 106

Turtle Beach Inn (NW) 18

'Tween Waters Inn (SW) 179

Westcott House Inn (NE) 74

Windemere Inn by the Sea (CE) 159

Wyndham Casa Marina Resort &
Beach House (SE) 264

Sea Turtle Nesting Programs
Disney's Vero Beach Resort (CE) 169

Hutchinson Island Marriott Beach
Resort & Marina (SE) 194

Palm Island Resort (SW) 175

Ritz-Carlton Amelia Island (NE) 53

South Seas Plantation (SW) 178

Turtle Beach Inn (NW) 18

Shopper's Delight
(These places have at least one mall or shopping area at your doorstep.)
Bay Harbor Inn & Suites (SE) 228

Chesterfield Hotel (SE) 199

Colony Palm Beach (SE) 201

Hotel Inter-Continental-Miami (SE) 225
Mayfair House (SE) 218
Riverside Hotel (SE) 165
Sheraton Suites Plantation (SE) 216
Turnberry Isle Resort & Club (SE) 226

Splendid Spas

Doral Golf Resort & Spa (SE) 223
Eden Roc Resort & Spa (SE) 229
Fontainebleau Hilton Resort (SE) 231
PGA National Resort & Spa (SE) 205
Pier House Resort & Caribbean
   Spa (SE) 262
Ponte Vedra Beach Resorts (NE) 62
Portofino Bay Hotel (C) 145
Saddlebrook Resort-Tampa (CW) 112
Safety Harbor Resort and Spa (CW) 96
Sanibel Harbour Resort & Spa (SW) 183
Turnberry Isle Resort and Club (SE) 226
Wyndham Palace Resort & Spa (C) 139
Wyndham Resort & Spa (SE) 217

Terrific Tennis

Amelia Island Plantation (NE) 45
Biltmore Hotel (SE) 220
Boca Raton Resort & Club (SE) 196
The Breakers (SE) 198
Colony Beach & Tennis
   Resort (CW) 86
Doral Golf Resort & Spa (SE) 223
Fontainebleau Hilton Resort (SE) 231
Grenelefe Golf & Tennis
   Resort (C) 120
Hutchinson Island Marriott Beach
   Resort & Marina (SE) 194
Hyatt Regency Grand Cypress (C) 143
Inn at Fisher Island Club (SE) 224

Mission Inn Golf & Tennis
   Resort (C) 117
Palm Island Resort (SW) 175
PGA National Resort & Spa (SE) 205
Ponte Vedra Beach Resorts (NE) 62
Renaissance Vinoy Resort (CW) 100
Resort at Longboat Key (CW) 87
Saddlebrook Resort-Tampa (CW) 112
Safety Harbor Resort & Spa (CW) 96
Sandestin Golf & Beach
   Resort (NW) 9
Sanibel Harbour Resort &
   Spa (SW) 183
Sawgrass Marriott Resort (NE) 63
Sonesta Beach Resort Key
   Biscayne (SE) 222
South Seas Plantation (SW) 178
Westin Innisbrook Resort (CW) 95
Wyndham Resort & Spa (SE) 217

Theme Lodgings

Clauser's Inn (CE) 154
Club Continental (NE) 61
The Consulate (NW) 3
Doubletree Castle Hotel (C) 142
Governor's Inn (NC) 37
Heritage Country Inn (C) 125
Holiday Inn Family Suites Resort Lake
   Buena Vista (C) 133
Little River Inn (CE) 163
Magnolia Plantation NC) 27
The Marlin (SE) 234
New World Inn (NW) 13
Old Powderhouse Inn (NE) 73
Pelican (SE) 237
Portofino Bay Hotel (C) 144
Rustic Inn (NC) 29
Sabal Palm House (SE) 208

Sheraton Safari Hotel (C) 138
Sheraton Studio City (C) 148
Sunset Bay Inn (CW) 101
Sweetwater Branch Inn (NC) 28
Turtle Beach Resort (CW) 90
The Villa (CE) 261
Yacht House (NW) 15

Wedding Favorites

Biltmore Hotel (SE) 220
Brigitte's Romantic Retreat (NW) 2
Casa de Sueños (NE) 67
Club Continental (NE) 61
Courtyard at Lake Lucerne (C) 141
Curry Mansion Inn (SE) 251
Henderson Park Inn (NW) 8
Herlong Mansion (NC) 30
Jules' Undersea Lodge (SE) 246
Perri House (C) 137
Ponte Vedra Beach Resorts (NE) 62
Seven Sisters Inn (C) 126
The Villa (CE) 161
Windemere Inn by the Sea (CE) 159

INDEX

Addison House Bed &
  Breakfast 43

Adventures Unlimited 11

Alexander Hotel, The 227

Amelia Island and Fernandina
  Beach 43

Amelia Island Plantation 45

Amelia Island Williams
  House 46

Angler Inn, The 167

Apalachicola 1

Apalachicola River Inn 1

Artist House, The 249

Bahia Honda State Park 242

Bailey House Bed &
  Breakfast 47

Banyan Resort 250

Barnacle Bed & Breakfast 243

Bartow 119

Bayboro House 98

Bay Harbor Inn & Suites 228

Behind the Fence 92

Belleview Biltmore
  Resort & Spa 94

Best Western Crystal
  River Resort 81

Big Pine Key 241

Biltmore Hotel, The 220

Boca Raton 196

Boca Raton Resort & Club 196

Bokeelia 173

Brandon 92

Brandenton Beach 84

Breakers, The 198

Brevard County and the Space
  Coast 156

Bridge Water Inn, The 185

Brigitte's Romantic Retreat 2

Broward County 209

Bungalow Beach Resort 84

Cabbage Key Inn 189

Cape Haze 175

Captiva Island 177

Carriage Way Bed &
  Breakfast 66

Casa de Solana Bed &
  Breakfast 67

Casa de Sueños Bed &
  Breakfast 67

Casa Monica Hotel 68

Casablanca Inn Bed &
  Breakfast 70

Cassadaga and Lake Helen 154

Cassadaga Hotel & Psychic
  Center 154

Cedar Key 25

Cedar Key Bed & Breakfast 25

Celebration 131

Celebration Hotel 131

Chalet Suzanne
  Country Inn 122

Château Nemours
  Seaport Inn 16

Chesterfield Hotel, The 199

Clauser's Inn Bed &
  Breakfast 154

Clearwater 94

Clewiston 180

Clewiston Inn 180

Club Continental Bed &
  Breakfast 61

Cocoa Beach 157

Coconut Grove 218

Collier Inn at Useppa
  Island Club 173

Colony Beach & Tennis
  Resort 86

Colony Palm Beach, The 201

Conch Key Cottages 267

Consulate, The 3

Continental Acres Equine
  Resort 128

Coombs House Inn 4

Coquina Inn Bed &
  Breakfast, The 161

Coral Gables 220

Courtyard at Lake Lucerne 141

Crescent City 55

Crowne Plaza, Pensacola Grand
  Hotel 12

Crystal River 81

Curry Mansion Inn 251

Cypress, a Bed & Breakfast
  Inn, The 89

Darst Victorian Manor Bed
  & Breakfast 118

Davis House Inn, The 168

Daytona Beach 161

Daytona Beach Area 160

Daytona Beach Shores 162

Defuniak Springs 6

Deland 155

Deland/West Volusia Area 153

Destin 7

Disney's Vero Beach Resort 169

Don Cesar Beach Resort
  & Spa 103

Doral Golf Resort & Spa 223

Doubletree Castle Hotel 142

Driftwood Resort, The 171

Duck Key 243

Eden Roc Resort & Spa 229

Elizabeth Pointe Lodge 49

Engelwood 181

Essex House 230

Fairbanks House Bed &
  Breakfast 50

Flagler Beach 56

Flamingo 240

Flamingo Lodge in Everglades National Park 241

Florida House Inn Bed & Breakfast 51

Floridian Sports Club 78

Fontainbleau Hilton Resort & Towers 231

Fort Myers 183

Four Seasons Resort Palm Beach 202

Gainesville 27

Gainesville Area 26

Gardens Hotel 252

Gibson Inn, The 5

Governors Inn 37

Greater Orlando Area 130

Grenelefe Golf & Tennis Resort 120

Haines City 120

Harborfront Inn 193

Harrington House Bed & Breakfast 84

Hawk's Cay Resort & Marina 244

Henderson Park Inn 8

Heritage Country Inn 125

Herlong Mansion, The 30

Hibiscus House Bed & Breakfast 203

Higgins House Victorian Bed & Breakfast 149

Highlands House, A 20

High Springs 29

Hilton Jacksonville Riverfront 57

Holiday Inn Family Suites Resort Lake Buena Vista 133

Holiday Inn Hotel & Suites Longboat Key 87

Holiday Inn Hotel & Suites, Main Gate Eas 132

Holiday Inn Sunspree Marina Cove 99

Holiday Inn Sunspree Resort Lake Buena Vista 135

Holiday Inn Sunspree Resort & Marina 245

Holmes Beach 84

Hontoon Landing Resort & Marina 155

Hotel, The 233

Hotel Defuniak 7

Hotel Inter-Continental-Miami 225

Hotel Place St. Michel 221

House on Cherry Street 58

Houseboats 157

Howey-in-the Hills 117

Howey-in-the-Hills Mission Inn Golf & Tennis Resort 117

Hoyt House Bed & Breakfast 52

Hutchinson Island Marriott Beach Resort & Marina 194

Hyatt Regency Grand Cypress 143

Hyatt Regency Pier Sixty-six 210

Hyatt Regency Westshore   107

Indialantic   159

Inn at Cocoa Beach, The   157

Inn at Fisher Island
   Club, The   224

Island City House Hotel   254

Island's End Resort   104

Jacksonville Area/Jacksonville   57

Josephine's French
   Country Inn   21

Jules' Undersea Lodge   246

Kenwood Inn Bed &
   Breakfast   71

Key Biscayne   222

Key Largo   245

Key Lime Inn   255

Key West   249

Key West Bed & Breakfast   256

Key West Hilton Resort &
   Marina   257

Kidsuites   134

Kissimmee   132

Kona Kai Resort   247

La Mer & Dewey House   259

Lago Mar Resort & Club   211

Lake Buena Vista   133

Lake County   115

Lakeland   121

Lake Wales Area   122

Land o' Lakes   110

Little Inn by the Sea, A   213

Little Palm Island   266

Little River Inn Bed &
   Breakfast   163

Little Torch Key   266

Lodging at Walt Disney
   World   136

Longboat Key   86

Magnolia Plantation Bed &
   Breakfast Inn   27

Maifair House, The   218

Maitland   140

Mango Inn Bed & Breakfast   204

Manasota Beach Club   181

Marathon   267

Marlin, The   234

Marquesa Hotel   260

Marriott's Key Largo Bay Beach
   Resort   248

Martin County   191

Matlacha   184

McFarlin House Bed & Breakfast
   Inn, The   34

Miami   223

Miami Beach   227

Miami-Dade County/Greater
   Miami   218

Milton   11

Micanopy   30

Monroe County The Florida
   Keys   239

Monticello   32

Mount Dora   118

Naples 185

New Smyrna Beach 163

New World Inn 13

Night Swan Intracoastal Bed & Breakfast 164

Ocala 125

Ocean Surf Hotel 235

Ocklawaha 127

Old Mansion Inn 72

Old Powder House Inn 72

Old Saltworks Cabins 17

Old Salty's Inn 162

Orange Park 61

Orlando 141

PGA National Resort & Spa 205

Palm Beach Area 198

Palm Beach County 195

Palm Harbor 95

Palm Island Resort 175

Palmer Place 33

Paradise Lakes Resort 110

Paradise Inn 261

Park Central Hotel, The 236

Park Plaza Hotel 150

Peabody Orlando 144

Pelican Hotel 237

Pensacola 12

Pensacola Victorian Bed & Breakfast 14

Perri House Bed & Breakfast 137

Pier House Resort & Caribbean Spa 262

Pineland 188

Pirate's Cove Resort & Marina 193

Plantation Inn & Golf Resort 82

Plantation Manor Inn 59

Polk County 119

Ponte Vedra Beach 62

Ponte Vedra Inn & Club/ Ponte Vedra Lodge & Club 62

Port St. Joe 16

Portofino Bay Hotel at Universal Studios Escape 145

Quincy 33

Refuge at Ocklawaha, The 127

Registry Resort 186

Renaissance Orlando Resort at Seaworld 147

Renaissance Vinoy Resort 100

Resort at Longboat Key Club, The 87

Ritz-Carlton Amelia Island 53

Ritz-Carlton Naples 187

Ritz-Carlton Palm Beach, The 206

Ritz Plaza Hotel 238

River Ranch 123

Riverside Hotel 214

Riverview Hotel 165

Rustic Inn, The 29

Saddlebrook Resort-Tampa 112

Safety Harbor 96

Safety Harbor Resort & Spa 96

Sabal Palm House 208

Sandestin Golf & Beach Resort 9

Sanford 149

Sanibel Harbour Resort &
Spa 183

Santa Rosa Beach 20

Sarasota 89

Sarasota Area 83

Sawgrass Marriott Resort 63

Sea Turtles 19

Seaside 21

Seaside Cottages 22

Sebastian 167

Seven Sisters Inn Bed &
Breakfast 126

Shady Oak Bed & Breakfast 31

Shamrock Thistle and
Crown 129

Sheraton Safari Hotel 138

Sheraton Studio City Hotel 148

Sheraton Suites Plantation 216

Siesta Key 90

Sonesta Beach Resort Key
Biscayne 222

South Seas Plantation 178

Sprague House Inn 55

St. Augustine 65

St. Francis Inn 73

St. Pete Beach 103

St. Petersburg 98

Stanford Inn 119

Steinhatchee 35

Steinhatchee Landing Resort 35

Sunset Bay Inn 101

Sweetwater Branch Inn 28

Tallahassee 37

Tampa 107

Tampa Bay Area 91

Terrace Hotel 121

Thurston House 140

Tides, The 238

Topaz Motel/Hotel 56

Tradewinds Island Resorts 106

Turnberry Isle Resort &
Club 226

Turtle Beach Inn 18

Turtle Beach Resort 90

'Tween Waters Inn 179

Vero Beach 169

Vero Beach Area 167

Villa, The 161

Wakulla Springs 39

Water Taxi 210

Weatherstation Inn 263

Weirsdale 128

Wakulla Springs State Park
Lodge 39

Welaka 77

Westcott House Inn 74

Westin Innisbrook Resort 95

Wesley Chapel 112

Wildlife on Easy Street 108

Windemere Inn by the Sea 159

Winter Park 150

World Golf Village Renaissance
    Resort 75

Wyndham Casa Marina Resort &
    Beach House 264

Wyndham Harbour Island
    Hotel 110

Wyndham Palace Resort &
    Spa 139

Wyndham Resort & Spa 217

Yacht House Bed &
    Breakfast Inn 15

ABOUT THE AUTHORS

Irresistible Overnights co-author BOB RAFFERTY has written a number of travel guides including *Frommer's Guide to America's 100 Best-Loved State Parks*. He is also a humor writer for a number of magazine cartoonists and has written for children's television. He is a member of the American Society of Journalists and Authors, the Authors' Guild, and the Society of Children's Book Writers and Illustrators. *Irresistible Overnights* co-author LOYS REYNOLDS, Rafferty's wife, is a clinical psychologist who has been honored for Outstanding Contributions to Education by North West London University in England. This is her second travel guide co-authored with her husband. Today she does some consulting on personal growth and is a freelance writer with her husband. They both live in Wellington, Florida.